THE WAR OF 1948

T0341768

An Israel Studies Book

An Israel Studies Book is sponsored by the Ben-Gurion Research Institute for the Study of Israel and Zionism, Ben-Gurion University of the Negev and the Schusterman Center for Israel Studies, Brandeis University.

THE WAR OF 1948

Representations of Israeli and Palestinian
Memories and Narratives

Edited by Avraham Sela and
Alon Kadish

Indiana University Press

Bloomington and Indianapolis

This book is a publication of

Indiana University Press
Office of Scholarly Publishing
Herman B Wells Library 350
1320 East 10th Street
Bloomington, Indiana 47405 USA

iupress.indiana.edu

© 2016 by Indiana University Press

All rights reserved

No part of this book may be reproduced or utilized in any form or
by any means, electronic or mechanical, including photocopying
and recording, or by any information storage and retrieval
system, without permission in writing from the publisher. The
Association of American University Presses' Resolution on
Permissions constitutes the only exception to this prohibition.

The paper used in this publication meets the minimum requirements
of the American National Standard for Information Sciences—
Permanence of Paper for Printed Library Materials, ANSI Z39.48-1992.

Manufactured in the United States of America

Cataloging information is available from the Library of Congress.

ISBN 978-0-253-02242-4 (paperback)
ISBN 978-0-253-02341-4 (ebook)

1 2 3 4 5   20 19 18 17 16

Contents

Preface and Acknowledgments

THIS BOOK CONSISTS of studies of Israeli representations, both Jewish and Palestinian, of memory and historical narratives of the 1948 War. The chapters map and explain the ongoing evolution of Israeli-Jewish and Israeli-Palestinian perspectives of the 1948 War as represented in literature, museums, art, visual media and landscape, as well as in competing official and societal narratives.

Most chapters included in this book were originally presented and discussed in periodical meetings during 2009–2010, by a research group on "Myth, Memory and Historiography: The Case of the 1948 War," comprised of Israeli-Jewish and Palestinian scholars, sponsored by the Van Leer Institute in Jerusalem. Notwithstanding the tensions stemming from different national and disciplinary approaches, the presentations, including by outside guest speakers, and discussions that followed, the group developed into a vibrant and educative forum for exchanging views and insights based on fresh original studies of distinct aspects of memory and historiography of the war. The research group's work culminated in an international symposium which was held in Jerusalem in December 2010, co-sponsored by the Van Leer Institute and the Harry S. Truman Institute of the Hebrew University. We are especially grateful to the Van Leer Institute for its generous funding and congenial accommodation of the research group through-out its meetings, and to the Truman Institute for sharing the financial cost of the international symposium.

We wish to thank all those who were involved in the earlier stages in the development of this project: members of the research group, including Efrat Ben-Ze'ev, Tal Ben-Zvi, Ofer Bord, Hillel Cohen, Ami Elad-Buskila, Bosmat Garami, Dror Greenblum, Aziz Haidar, Mustafa Kabha, Noga Kadman, Yechiel Klar, Ziva Kolodny, and Adel Manna; guest speakers Hadas Baram, Sinai Peter, Boaz Gaon, Rafi Nets-Zehngut, and Rona Sela; and participants in the international symposium, including Larry Abramson, Meron Benvenisti, Neil Caplan, Alon Confino, Yifat Gutman, the late Yoram Kanyuk, Eman Nahhas, Sarah Ozacky-Lazar, Anita Shapira, Muhammad 'Ali Taha, Dan Tzahor, and Jay Winter. All contributed valuable insights and helped to clarify and hone our views. We are also indebted to Lior Lehrs, our research group's administration assistant, for his dedication and perceptive summaries of our discussions. Last but not least, we are especially thankful for the interest shown in our project by the editors of *Israel Studies*, Ilan Troen and Natan Aridan.

Avraham Sela and Alon Kadish

vii

THE WAR OF 1948

Israeli and Palestinian Memories and Historical Narratives of the 1948 War—An Overview

Avraham Sela and Alon Kadish

Preface

This volume consists of a collection of studies of Israeli representations, both Jewish and Palestinian, of memory and historical narratives of the 1948 War. The studies map and explain some Israeli-Jewish and Israeli-Palestinian perspectives of the 1948 War as represented in literature, historical museums, art, visual media, and landscape, as well as in competing official and societal narratives. They are examined especially against the backdrop of the Oslo process, which had strongly brought into relief tensions within and between both sides of the national divide concerning identity and legitimacy, justice, and righteousness of "self" and "other." Five chapters represent varied aspects of Israeli-Jewish memory and historical narratives of 1948, while two others offer representations of Israeli-Palestinian memory of that cataclysmic event and its consequences.

Each chapter represents a particular version or expression of a sectorial memory of the war and its consequences, not necessarily identical with the single national interpretation the national institutions (Israeli and Palestinian) provided. The collection as a whole demonstrates how the diversity of the historical experience (as well as cultural legacy, ideologies, etc.) of different components of society is reflected in the diversity of memory. Moreover, most of the chapters demonstrate how memory changes and evolves along with the historical changes within the various components of the national communities.

This collection is the first of its kind offering new perspectives of Israeli memory, both Jewish and Palestinian, based on in-depth empirical studies. Whether the case is myth construction by the religious Zionist movement, museum exhibitions by rival ideological groups, or drawings of the *Nakba* by an Israeli-Palestinian artist, they all represent diverse layers of memory and carry a particular contribution to their specific discipline or field of research. We hope that the diversity of substance and form of the groups' memories of a supposedly unifying national event within the national community, and the dynamics of

1

The War of 1948 (2016); 1–24, DOI: 10.2979/warof1948.0.0.02

change presented in this issue will contribute to the development of theory of the nexus of memory, narrative, and historiography.

We offer a brief discussion on the dialectics of memory, narratives, and historiography as well as the main trends and characteristics of Israeli and Palestinian memory and historiography of the 1948 War. While Israel's Palestinian citizens are historically part of the Arab world, including the Palestinian people at large, their post-1948 separation from other Palestinian and Arab communities coupled by their particular social, administrative, and political experience as an ethnic and religious minority in the Jewish state, shaped their consciousness and cultural world as a distinct Arab-Israeli identity group and memory community.[1] The introduction explains these distinct characteristics of Israel's Palestinian citizens within the broader Palestinian national context.

The Palestine war of 1948 remains a formative event in the Middle East and especially for the immediately concerned parties, Israelis and Palestinians. Notwithstanding the primary role of that war in shaping the contours of the Arab-Israeli conflict for generations and its impact on processes of socialization and politics in Israel and the Arab neighboring countries, the study of memory and historiography of 1948 is still in its infancy. The last three decades witnessed a major surge in the production by both Israelis and Palestinians of historical research and memory of the 1948 War along with the shifting focus of the Arab-Israeli conflict from one between Israel and its Arab neighboring states to its original inter-communal Arab-Jewish dispute within historic Palestine. Whether the result of intensified conflict or peace negotiations, or the timed release of archival documents, the dialectic of politics and self-legitimation accounted for mutually encouraged efforts to recover, rewrite, and disseminate particular historical narratives of the 1948 War concerned with issues of injustice, morality, and guilt, especially but not exclusively, the Palestinian refugee problem.

The increasing interest on both sides of the national divide in the background and consequences of the 1948 War parallels the incremental return of the Arab-Israeli conflict since the late-1980s to its origins as an inter-communal Jewish-Arab dispute within historic Palestine. Attesting to this interest is the ever-increasing body of printed and visual works, including critical research and oral histories, personal memoirs and novels, documentation and commemoration. Despite some parallels in the parties' approaches to their century of shared history, especially the cataclysmic events of 1948, their historical research, memory, and

---

1. Aziz Haidar, "The Different Levels of Palestinian Ethnicity," in *Ethnicity, Pluralism, and the State in the Middle East,* ed. Milton J. Esman and Itamar Rabinovich (Ithaca, 1988), 105–8; Mahmud Ghanayim, *The Quest for a Lost Identity: Palestinian Fiction in Israel* (Weisbaden, 2008), 1–3.

narratives represent major asymmetries of perceptions, concerns, and emphases. Moreover, the mutually frustrated hopes of the 1990s Oslo process and the unprecedented violence of the al-Aqsa Intifada seem to have aggravated mutual historical grievances and further deepened the abyss between the two parties' perceptions of the past. Seen through Israeli and Palestinian mainstream perspectives at its seventh decade of age, the legacy of 1948 reveals ever-polarized narratives about why and what had taken place then and since, bestowing ever-evolving symbolic and moral values onto interpretations of the past as well as providing substance for discussions on the war's relevance to the present.

Memories, Histories, and Narratives

"Memory is life," contended Pierre Nora.

> It remains in permanent evolution, open to the dialectic of remembering and forgetting, unconscious of successive deformations, vulnerable to manipulation and appropriation, susceptible to being long dormant and periodically revived.... History, because it is an intellectual and secular production, calls for analysis and criticism ... Memory is absolute, while history can only conceive the relative.[2]

Whereas the professional academic study of history represents, ideally at least, an enlightened and critical approach to the past and is thus universal, collective memory reflects the reality and spirit of time, the impact of internal and external factors such as changing ideological emphases, international politics and discourses, and social and group needs.

All these elements take part in shaping collective identity amidst inclusion and exclusion of individuals and groups and in self-justification and de-legitimation of the "other," feeding on embedded fears of past and present. Nonetheless, while far from synonymous, history and memory are neither contradictory nor entirely separate from each other but rather maintain close interaction and mutually constitute each other. Like memory, history as a discipline also draws on perceptions of past events and is often influenced by present processes as triggers for historical analogies and interpretations, which in turn may influence the constant reproduction of "collective memory."

Memory, both individual and collective, is elastic in nature, spontaneous, sentimental, and susceptible to psychological factors, lacking "scientific" or rational rules, and concerned with the public rather than the small community of professional historians. Collective memory is constructed and maintained by means of social interaction, discourse, and popular culture such as commemorative monuments, rituals, mass media, and literature as well as by storytelling of

---

2. Pierre Nora, "Between History and Memory: Les Lieux de Memoire," *Representations* 26 (1989): 8–9.

individuals, families, and other social groups. Remembrance, however, is selective in nature, susceptible to forgetfulness and repression as well as to self-imposed silence, especially about a painful or ugly past, which individuals maintain for as long as they live as part of their obligations to their identity group and collective needs.[3] Unlike individual memory, however, which can be directly experienced only by the individual and cannot be transferred from one person to another, collective memory is a distinct verbalized form of a narrative in which individual memories become part of an intersubjective process mediated by language: ". . . they can be exchanged, shared, corroborated, confirmed, corrected, disputed, and even appropriated."[4] In this process, the boundaries between one's own experience and what one has "experienced" through hearing, reading, or watching in pictures and films, are often blurred.

Since the 1980s, oral history and memory attained increasing respectability, no longer perceived inferior in comparison to critical history. Largely due to the growing use of Holocaust survivors' testimonies by leading historians, interest in the past shifted from focusing on explaining "what happened and why" to far more experiential aspects of those who lived through the events:

> How is an event, and especially a traumatic event, experienced and remembered? What kind of shadow does the past cast over the present? What are more or less adequate modes of representing the past events? How can the memory of a historic event be preserved in public commemoration and personal memories?[5]

These questions call for more attention to memory of past events as a factor shaping the perceptions and choices of those who "remember" (directly or indirectly) and as such represent a significant element in their common identity.

Due to the significance of collective memory in shaping collective identity, leaderships invest discernible efforts in shaping and inculcating this memory, and in guarding its exclusivity. Especially in cases of conflict between ethnic and national groups, collective identity shapes the public discourse and defines its

---

3. Jay Winter, "Thinking about Silence," in *Shadows of War: A Social History of Silence in the Twentieth Century,* ed. Efrat Ben-Zeev, Ruth Ginio, and Jay Winter (Cambridge, 2010), 3–31. On the silence in Israel's Jewish society on 1948, see Efrat Ben-Zeev, "Imposed Silences and Self-Censorship: Palmach Soldiers Remember 1948," in *Shadows of War,* 181–96.

4. Aleida Assmann, "Transformations between History and Memory," *Social Research* 75.1 (2008): 50. On the relations between the individual and collective memories see Paul Ricoeur, *Memory, History, Forgetting* (Chicago, 2004).

5. Aleida Assmann, "History, Memory, and the Genre of Testimony," *Poetics Today* 27.2 (2006): 263. An early example of nostalgic rewriting of the past based on oral history is the studies by George E. Evans of the pre-industrialization English village, especially his *Where Beards Wag All: The Relevance of the Oral Tradition* (London, 1970).

boundaries by fostering concrete contents of collective images and patterns of conduct about "self" and "other" ostensibly based on the group's historical experience. The elements of collective and conscious identity translate into collective narrative, which encompasses stories, myths, perceptions, and attitudes understood as undisputable historic truth. Particularly in cases of national conflict, such narratives assume various forms and means from textbooks, political discourse, and media to memorial events, rituals of commemoration, and monuments, all of which render national consciousness tangible for the members of the group. National narratives function as a conscious anchor that constructs and legitimizes the basic assumptions of the national existence and its conduct and as such, shapes both the internal relations between national individuals as well as their and external relations with, and attitudes towards the "others."[6]

Historians, and especially anthropologists, have challenged the literature concerned with manifestations of hegemonic forms and contents of collective memory, primarily national memory and its change over time, suggesting that people constantly construct their past, creating "micro-social remembrance."[7] Variations of historical memory are found at all levels from family and kin groups to national communities representing different levels of involvement and proximities to the narrated past that may complement, differ from, or even contrast other narratives. The more heterogeneous a society the more diverse and nuanced the versions about the past. This, however, does not preclude the existence of a master unifying narrative whose primary assumptions and arguments serve as the core of collective identity and under which local and small group narratives can exist without contradicting each other. As a product of social and political discourse and as a functional mechanism, social groups create variations of narrating the stories about past events as well as the practices of their commemoration, selecting particular contents and emphases in accordance with the social and political context and relation between narrator and audience.

Contours of Israeli and Palestinian Historiography and Commemorative Narratives

In line with this understanding of the dynamic nature of memory, its various contents and entwinement with social and political influences, both intra- and extra-societal, the chapters included in this volume represent varied aspects of memory and historical narratives of specific time and circumstances. For various

---

6. Uriel Abulof, *The Mortality and Morality of Nations: Jews, Afrikaners and French-Canadians* (Cambridge, 2015).

7. Efrat Ben-Ze'ev, *Remembering Palestine in 1948: Beyond National Narratives* (New York, 2011), 3–4.

reasons Israeli and Palestinian historiography and discourses of memory have developed at a different pace and in different directions. Nonetheless, in a historical perspective the highly volatile history of the Arab-Israeli conflict in general and the Israeli-Palestinian conflict in particular since 1948 represents more continuity than change in terms of the reproduction of memory and historiography by Israelis and Palestinians alike regarding their shared histories.

In recent decades the unifying narrative adopted by the Palestinian national movement has increasingly mirrored the Israeli one in both structure and contents. Similarly to the Zionist-Israeli framing of Jewish historical narrative along contrasting gravities of destruction (*hurban*) and redemption (*ge'ula*), Holocaust (*shoah*) and rebirth (*tekuma*), exile (*galut*) and return to Zion, the Palestinian historical narrative draws on catastrophe (*nakba*) and defeat as well as on rebellion/revolution (*thawra*) and resistance (*muqawama*), exile (*ghurba, shatat*), and return (*'awda*). These parallels culminated in the growing Palestinian tendency since the late 1990s to draw an analogy between the Holocaust and the *nakba* in their claim for international recognition of their collective trauma, suffering, and the historical injustice Israel had done to the Palestinians.

Israeli Perspectives

The shaping of a collective Israeli memory, especially in its first four decades of independence, was the realm of the state institutions and semi-official public media, largely representing a continuation of the pre-state Zionist narratives and the political rivalries they reflected. Even later, Israel remained largely committed to those narratives upholding the Jewish people's historical bonds to the land of Israel and contribution to its redemption from centuries of neglect and wilderness. Underlying these claims was always the haunting traumatic Jewish historical experience on Israeli policymakers, before and after the advent of the state of Israel, in which the "Holocaust was merely the latest and most brutal chapter in a long history."[8] Israeli political discourse repeatedly associated Arab threats to Israel with the memory of the Holocaust. Especially against the backdrop of the second Palestinian uprising and recurrent Palestinian suicide bombing attacks on Jews, frequent employments of the Holocaust and its related memories significantly underlined Israeli-Jews' self-image as victims.

At the same time, Israel kept silent about its role in causing the exodus of more than half of the Palestinian population from the area that came under its control, as a necessary strategy of nation building and protection of the state's international reputation.[9] The official and censored history of the War, written by

8. Alan Dowty, "Israeli Foreign Policy and the Jewish Question," *MERIA*, 3.1 (1999): 1–13.
9. Anita Shapira, "On Silence," *Kivunim Hadashim* 28 (2013): 20–33.

the IDF's History Department and first published by the Ministry of Defense in 1959, remained unchanged in subsequent editions published ever since,[10] despite the wealth of memoirs of high ranking military and civilian officials and individuals, accounts of veterans associations of pre-1948 main Jewish underground movements and regular brigades, and most of all, academic studies. This literature presented a much more diverse picture, including Israeli expulsion of Palestinian civilians and massacres. The Israeli dominant narrative thus avoided admittance of acts of expulsion of Palestinian Arabs during the 1948 War, let alone atrocities committed against them, with the exception of Deir Yasin for which the rival dissident groups of Etzel and Lehi were blamed and denounced by the Zionist leadership. Regarding the Arab mass exodus, the State of Israel's narrative essentially blamed the Palestinians as a collective for rejecting the UN Partition Resolution, which the Jews accepted as a compromise, and initiating a bloody war as of late 1947. Furthermore, the Arabs of Palestine were convinced by the Arab states to leave their homes in order to return with the victorious Arab armies that were about to invade Palestine immediately after the Mandate expired, stressing the voluntary nature of the Arab exodus. Thus, the Palestinians brought on themselves the tragedy of mass displacement and consequent suffering as refugees.

The release in the late 1970s of hitherto classified official wartime archives enabled the rewriting of Israel's early history, but it was the emergence of a new generation of leftist historians eager to challenge standard Zionist narratives that underpinned the advent of Israel's "New History." Notwithstanding its revisionist claims and new factual revelations, the public significance of the studies published in the late 1980s and early 1990s was derived from the rising significance of the Palestine question throughout the 1980s due to the Lebanon war and the Palestinian uprising in the Occupied Territories, and the questions and historical analogies it triggered. The convergence of historical and public discourses over the past was further affected by the resumed international efforts in pursuit of peace in the Middle East in the early 1990s, culminating in the Israeli-Palestinian Oslo Accords.

Benny Morris's systematic study of the evolvement of the Palestinian refugee problem[11] clearly revealed the active role played by the Jewish forces, before and after the proclamation of the state of Israel, in the displacement of the Arabs from their villages and urban centers. His conclusions that this was a result of war, not of a premeditated plan notwithstanding, triggered apologetic responses by

10. Israel Defense Forces, History Branch, *The History of the War of Independence* (Tel-Aviv, 1959) [Hebrew].

11. Benny Morris, *The Birth of the Palestinian Refugee Problem* (New York, 1987).

established Israeli historians reiterating Israel's principal arguments, albeit with more sophistication and use of historical data.[12]

Social and macro-economic changes as well as the fashion of academic revisionism, such as "critical sociology" and "new history," were at the root of the new Israeli historiography. Sociologists and historians alike thus questioned Israel's founding myths while opening avenues to better understanding of Arab and Palestinian narratives, mostly without completely renouncing core Zionist beliefs or "crossing the lines" toward the Palestinian national narrative. Indeed, despite the energetic debates the new historians aroused, mostly within the academic community, the impact it made on Israeli official institutions or public discourse on 1948 in general and the Palestinian refugee problem in particular, was minor even during the 1990s Oslo process.[13]

Within Israel's Jewish society, the symbolically endowed 1948 War as one fought against all odds leading to Jewish national rebirth and the fulfilment of the dream of generations, rendered inevitable partisan and sectorial struggles over shaping the Israeli national memory of the war already during, and mainly after it ended. The political struggle over memory and commemoration of the war has largely reflected the historical rivalry between the labor and the revisionist movements before and after 1948, taking the forms of competing historiography, commemoration, and myth making.[14] In contrast to the leftist-led historiography that denied the expulsion of the Arabs and described it as voluntary, revisionist historiography took pride in fulfilling a leading role in bringing about the mass exodus of the Arabs. It was only in the course of the 1980s, following the rise of the right wing Likud Party to power in 1977, that the revisionist groups' narratives of the 1940s, including the 1948 War, and contribution to Zionist statehood, obtained official recognition. Attesting to the incorporation of the dissident groups' narratives into the mainstream one, some of the books previously published by Etzel and Lehi veterans in the 1950s and 1960s were reprinted and published by the Ministry of Defense, culminating in combining the histories of the latter groups with those of the Haganah in one publication.[15]

---

12. Shabtai Teveth, Review of Benny Morris, "The Palestine Arab Refugee Problem and its Origins," *Middle Eastern Studies* 26.2 (1990): 214–49.

13. Anita Shapira, "Hirbet Hiza: Between Remembrance and Forgetting," in *Making Israel,* ed. Benny Morris (Ann Arbor, MI, 2007), 81–123.

14. See for example Udi Lebel, *Politics of Memory - The Israeli Underground's Struggle for Inclusion in the National Pantheon and Military Commemoralization* (London and New York, 2013).

15. Haim Lazar, *The Conquest of Jaffa,* 4th edition (Tel-Aviv, 1981); Shlomo Lev-Ami (Levi), In *the Struggle and Revolt: The Hagana, Etzel and Lehi 1918-1948* (Tel-Aviv, 1979) [both in Hebrew].

Rafi Nets-Zehngut, Bosmat Garami, and Ofer Boord discuss these trends of (mainly) continuity and change in Israel's historical narratives of 1948 as represented in official publications, public television, and museums, respectively. As it turned out, changes in the dominant narrative were not only minor, but also temporary. As Ofer Boord shows, the historical rivalry between the pre-state revisionist Etzel and mainstream Haganah remains apparent in the narratives presented by their respective museums in an obvious effort to preserve their legacies in the collective memory of the struggle for Jewish statehood. Similarly, Dror Greenblum sheds light on the construction of the Kfar Etzion myth by the religious-Zionist movement as a means to secure its place in Israel's national memory.

Palestinian Perspectives

Palestinian historiography, especially since the reemergence of Palestinian nationalism and institutions in the mid-1960s and their nation-building efforts, largely addressed the 1948 War as the culmination of a long and heroic struggle against the British Mandate and the Zionist enterprise.[16] Compared to the wealth of individual memoirs and historical accounts of this struggle, commemorative surveys of the pre-1948 Palestinian political institutions and leadership, land, and population, and analyses of the causes and remedies of the disaster (*nakba*) of Palestine,[17] apart from the comprehensive history of the war by 'Arif al-'Arif, Palestinians produced relatively scarce critical studies of Palestinian history in which the 1948 War is only briefly discussed.[18] What exists, are a few critical essays about the causes of the Palestinian exodus during the War aiming to refute the Israeli narrative about its voluntary nature.[19]

---

16. For a broader discussion of Palestinian historiography of 1948, see Avraham Sela, "Arab Historiography of the 1948 War – The Quest for Legitimacy," in *New Perspectives on Israeli History*, ed. Lawrence Silverstein (New York, 1991), especially 140–5.

17. Such as Muhammad Nimr al-Hawwari, *The Secret of the Nakba* (Nazareth, 1955); Bayan Nuwayhid al-Hut, *The Palestinian Leaderships and Institutions 1917-1948* (Beirut, 1981); al-Dabbagh and Mustafa Murad, *Our Country Palestine* (Beirut, 1973), 6 Volumes [all in Arabic]; Walid Khalidi, ed., *Before Their Diaspora: A Photographic History of the Palestinians, 1876-1948* (Washington, DC, 1984); ed., *All that Remains: The Palestinian Villages Occupied and Depopulated by Israel in 1948* (Washington, DC, 1992); ed., *The 1948 Nakba: Its Causes and Ways of Handling*: Qustantin Zurayq, Qadri Hafiz Tuqan, Musa 'Alami, George Hanna (Beirut, 2009) [Arabic].

18. 'Arif al-'Arif, *The Catastrophe (al-Nakba) of Jerusalem and the Lost Paradise, 1947-1952* (Sidon and Beirut, 1959) [Arabic]. In contrast, see Issa Khalaf, *Politics in Palestine, Arab Factionalism and Social Disintegration 1939-1948* (Albany, 1991); Rashid Khalidi, *The Iron Cage, the Story of the Palestinian Struggle for Statehood* (Boston, 2006).

19. Especially Walid Khalidi: "Why did the Palestinians Leave?" *Middle East Forum* 35:7 (1959); "The Fall of Haifa Revisited," *Journal of Palestine Studies* 37.3 (2008): 30–58; Nafez Nazzal, *The Palestinian Exodus from Galilee 1948* (Beirut, 1978).

From the outset, Palestinian historiography remained markedly apologetic, explaining the disaster as inevitable considering the overwhelming weight of colonial, Zionist, and Arab adversaries.[20] With the establishment of the Institute for Palestine Studies in 1963, and the PLO a year later, Palestinian historiography took a new direction of emphasizing the ceaseless political and military struggle Palestinians had waged during the Mandate years for liberating themselves from British colonialism and defeat of Zionism.[21] Apart from lamenting the "lost paradise" and repeated affirmation of the cause of the dispossessed Arab refugees and their standing right to return to their homes, this self-glorification was a critical necessity in the face of "empty arguments and lies, incriminations and inventions that had prevailed in certain times."[22] In addition to Israel's refusal to allow the return of the Arab refugees, blaming them for their exodus and denying the very existence of a distinct Palestinian people, the new historiography had to also defy the Arab discourse of blaming the Palestinians for selling their lands to the Jews and failing to fight for their national rights, holding them responsible for their disaster.[23]

The reshaping of Palestinian history largely consists of a romantic idealization of rural life, with a special emphasis on the peasant as a national signifier carrying the banner of resistance to the British Mandate and Zionism/Israel and for those who did not become refuges the steadfastness (*sumud*) to the land.[24] A typical example in this context is the attempt to link history and memory through the genre of "historical drama" telling the story of a peasant community in Mandatory Palestine. The story of this community serves as a representation of the Palestinians' collective history from the Mandate through the 1948 disaster and consequent humiliation of refugee life and the fate of those who came under

20. Avraham Sela, "Israeli Historiography of the 1948 War," in *Shared Histories: A Palestinian-Israeli Dialogue*, ed. Paul Scham, Walid Salem, and Benjamin Pogrund (Walnut Creek, CA, 2005), 205–15; Jamil Hilal, "Reflections on Contemporary Palestinian History," in *Across the Wall: Narratives of Israeli-Palestinian History*, ed. Ilan Pappe and Jamil Hilal (London, 2010), 177–215.

21. See 'Abd al-Qadir Yasin, *The Struggle of the Palestinian People Before 1948* (Beirut, 1975); Naji 'Alush, *The Arab Resistance in Palestine, 1914-1948* (Acre, 1979) [both in Hebrew].

22. Hasan Abu Raqaba, *Flowers and Thorns, Memoirs of a Palestinian Officer* (Beirut, 2005), 5 [Arabic].

23. For these allegations and their refutation, see Qustantin Zurayq, Meaning of the Nakba (Beirut, 1948), 33. See also a series of four articles by Bayan Nuwayhid al-Hut, refuting the historical allegations about voluntary sales of land by Palestinians to Jews before 1948, *al-Hayat* (London), 14–17 June 1997, 18 [both in Hebrew].

24. Meir Litvak, "A Palestinian Past: National Construction," *History and Memory* 6.2 (1994): 45; Ted Swedenburg, "The Palestinian Peasant as a National Signifier," *Anthropological Quarterly* 63.1 (1990): 18–30; Khalid A. Sulaiman, *Palestine and Modern Arab Poetry* (London, 1984), 33–34.

Israeli rule, to the rise of a Palestinian resistance movement in the 1960s. Analyzing an Arab television drama series on this history, Mustafa Kabha's chapter reveals a novel approach of self-critique of Palestinian social and political fragmentation and factional feuds which peaked during the 1936–1939 revolt and had a disastrous impact on the Palestinians' fate in the 1948 showdown with the Jews.

Although a proto-national Arab-Palestinian movement had emerged already under the Mandate, the advent of the Palestinian resistance movement necessitated new narratives for nation building, of heroism, sacrifice, and determined commitment to the homeland. Hence, "many of the commemorative narratives and practices that have become emblematic of Palestinian nationalism originated in the refugee camps of Lebanon during the *thawra*"[25] (revolution) of 1965–82. Not all Palestinians shared those commemorative narratives and practices because not all of them experienced displacement, exile, and refugee life under the leadership of a resistance movement, which explains the development of particular practices of commemoration of the *nakba* along geographical and political divides.

Apart from the apologetic nature of much of the literature of memoirs and autobiographies of prominent Palestinians of the Mandate generation, Palestinian scholarship on 1948 tends to be tautological in nature, drawing a direct causal link between end results and ostensibly initial intents. According to this deterministic approach, the causes of the *nakba* were rooted in the Balfour Declaration of 1917 and the Zionist project's vision, taking little or no in-depth interest in the volatile and unpredictable nature of the historical process. Hence, although Palestinian historiography of the early 2000s indicated a slight shift towards a critical approach in tackling new issues and aspects of the 1948 War and its consequences,[26] it remained largely concerned with the preservation and reaffirmation of its master collective narratives revolving on victimhood. A case in point is the discernible avoidance of Palestinian biographers of Haj Amin al-Husayni, the unchallenged Palestinian leader during the Mandate and 1948 War, of any critique of his disastrous post–WWII politics and responsibility for the tragic consequences of the 1948 War for his people.[27] Even in the case of a critique of the Palestinian leadership's ineptitudes and ill-advised policies during the Mandate up to the 1948

25. Laleh Khalili, *Heroes and Martyrs of Palestine, The Politics of National Commemoration* (New York, 2007), 8.

26. Apart from Issa Khalaf, *Politics in Palestine*, and Rashid Khalidi, *The Iron Cage*, see also Mustafa Kabha, ed., *Towards a Historical Narrative of the Nakba: Complexities and Challenges* (Haifa, 2006), especially 1–23 [Arabic].

27. See Taysir Jbara, *Palestinian Leader Hajj Amin al-Husaini, Mufti of Jerusalem* (Princeton, NJ, 1985); Philip Mattar, *The Mufti of Jerusalem: al-Haj Amin al-Hussaini and the Palestinian National Movement* (New York, 1988).

disaster, the final analysis is that these failures were of no significance in the overall historical account.[28] Thus, the Palestinian *nakba* narrative is infused with a sense of fatalism, of Palestinian helplessness vis-à-vis not merely superior, but insurmountable, almost cosmic, forces. Especially in poetry and literature, the moment of displacement and exodus in 1948 is often portrayed as an event whose magnitude stands above and beyond the ability of the individual or the collective to resist, one with no reasonable explanation, hence the Palestinians cannot be held responsible for their fate.[29]

Ironically, contrary to the re-writing of Palestinian history during the Mandate, which emphasized resistance and sacrifice by the Palestinian Arabs against the Mandate and the Zionist enterprise, Palestinian historians entirely ignore the attacks launched by Arab irregular and volunteer forces against the Yishuv, describing the Haganah offensive of April 1948, which triggered a major wave of Arab exodus, as an independent initiative, unrelated to the Arab irregular attacks.[30] While appreciating the discernible departure of the "new history" studies from the Israeli traditional narratives, especially on the origins of the Palestinian refugee problem, Palestinian historians effectively portrayed the Haganah's Plan D offensive as integral to the concept of "transfer," said to be deeply rooted in the Zionist ideology from its very inception. This is because a connection exists between the imperative to "transfer" the Arab population and seize its lands and the imperative to accommodate the hundred thousands of Jews it was planned to bring to the new Jewish state.[31]

The relative paucity of Palestinian academic studies on the 1948 War is particularly salient in view of the flourishing production of memory. Especially salient among Israeli Palestinians, the press, literature and poetry, cinema, television, and the Internet all have become highly influential in the public sphere as

---

28. Rashid Khalidi, "The Palestinians and 1948: The Underlying Causes of Failure," in *The War for Palestine: Rewriting the History of 1948*, ed. Eugene L. Rogan and Avi Shlaim (Cambridge, 2001), 16–17.

29. For representations of this motif in Palestinian poetry and literature about 1948, see Honaida Ghanim, "Poetics of Disaster: Nationalism, Gender, and Social Change Among Palestinian Poets in Israel After Nakba," *International Journal of Politics, Culture and Society* 22 (2009); Ahmad As'ad, *Children of the Dew, Novella* (London, 1990) [Arabic]; Ghassan Kanafani, "Returning to Haifa," in *Palestine's Children: Returning to Haifa and Other Stories* (Boulder, CO, 2000); Elias Khoury, *Gate of the Sun* (London, New York, 2006).

30. Walid Khalidi, "The Arab Perspective," in *The End of the Palestine Mandate*, ed. William Roger Lewis and Robert W. Stookey (Austin, TX, 1986), 121.

31. Walid Khalidi, "Plan Dalet: A Masterplan for the Conquest of Palestine," *Journal of Palestine Studies*, 18:1 (Autumn 1988), 4–33; Nur-eldeen Masalha, "On Recent Hebrew and Israeli Sources for the Palestinian Exodus, 1947–1949," *Journal of Palestine Studies*, 18.1 (1988): 134–5.

never before. A local, communal, and personal-familial dimension has increasingly marked the appetite for remembrance and commemoration of the 1948 War and its meanings, effectively appropriating it from the established elites, official institutions, and academic scholars. The "privatization of memory" has been imprinted on the academic research as well as represented in studies of professionals in the fields of history, sociology, anthropology, communication, and cinema.

The dialectic of memory and reality has been especially evident since the signing of the Oslo Accords in 1993, which seemed to have marginalized the hitherto sacrosanct Palestinian refugees "right of return," by postponing the discussion on refugees to the phase of permanent status negotiations. The Oslo process indeed shifted the emphasis of public discourse from "Palestine" to "Palestinians,"[32] representing the erosion of a core Palestinian national objective, and thus stimulated strong popular sentiments over the trend towards privatization of Palestinian memory.[33] It thus triggered fierce Palestinian criticism and the rise of grass-root advocacy groups, research centers, documentation projects in historic Palestine and Lebanon, and web-based international social coalitions aimed at keeping the principle of "return" of the refugees high on the Palestinian and international political agendas.[34] These new initiatives document and disseminate information about the human and material reality of the Palestinian refugees and their individual experiential memory of 1948, stressing their full right of return to their homes and properties.

The *nakba* has thus been constructed as a central national myth explaining not only the Palestinians' past and present, but also serving as a powerful mobilizing force for collective action and integration as a national community.[35] With the celebration of Israel's 50th anniversary in 1998, Palestinians collectively

32. Fouad Moughrabi, "A Year of Discovery," *The Journal of Palestine Studies* 27.2 (1997): 5–15.

33. See for example, Ghada Karmi, "Only Palestinian Refugees Can Give Up Their Right of Return," *The Guardian*, 24 January 2011; "Has the Message Arrived?" *Haq al-'Awda* 3 (January 2004), 2–3, presented a long list of all PLO organizations, the Islamic groups, leading prisoners, and the PLO Department of refugees – all rejecting the Geneva Initiative's article on the refugees; "Palestinian refugees reject Bush declaration," *al-Majdal* 22 (June 2004), 43–4.

34. Such as the Bethlehem-based Badil, www.badil.org, which publishes two magazines – *al-Majdal* (in English) and *Haqq al-'Awda* (in Arabic), and *The Palestine Right to Return Coalition al-'Awda*, www.al-awda.org. *For similar associations in Lebanon, see* Ahmad al-Haj, "The Palestinian Research Centers in Lebanon: Partnerships in the Preservation of the Identity and Demands of the Refugees"], *al-'Awda* (Lebanon), 53 [Arabic], February 2012 http://alawda-mag.com/default.asp?issueId=54&contentid=2073&MenuID=8

35. Michael Milstein, "The Memory that Never Dies: The Nakba Memory and the Palestinian National Movement," in *Palestinian Collective Memory and National Identity*, ed. Meir Litvak

commemorated the *nakba* as never before, holding demonstrations and marches, ritualized visits to destroyed villages in Israel, and issuing special publications by research institutions about the 1948 experience of displacement and exile. In the following years, the *nakba* developed into a primary signifying symbol of Palestinian history and identity perceived as a continuous sequence of traumas, a perpetuation of victimhood manifested in repeated massacres, suffering, and misery.[36] In this narrative, Zionism/Israel is the main culprit perpetuating the Palestinian *nakba* through terror and massacres while the helpless Palestinian victims are repeatedly betrayed by the Arab world and the international community. The reconstruction of the *nakba* became the blood extract of the Palestinian claim for statehood and historical justice to the refugees through fulfilment of the right of return.

In addition to the organized effort of focusing on the traumatic memories and narratives of exile of the 1948 refugees, Palestinian institutions and NGOs have increasingly targeted Israel's official and public attitudes to the origins of the Palestinian refugee problem, demonstrating Israel's total denial of the very existence of and responsibility for the *nakba*.[37]

The new trend of Palestinian memory reflected the changing focus of the political agenda from armed resistance and heroic sacrifices to an increasing effort to mobilize the international arena in support of the Palestinian claims for statehood and justice to the victims of Israeli wrongs. Hence, Palestinian institutions, especially the Institute for Palestine Studies, grassroots organizations, and individual academics, conducted systematic efforts of collecting social and demographic data about the Palestinian refugees and their lost properties, as well as the pre-1948 Palestinian visual landscape.[38] Similarly, academic studies discussed the case of Palestinian refugee right of return in the international law as well as of the feasibility of their return to their homes.[39]

(New York, 2009), 48. See Esther Webman, "The Evolution of a Founding Myth: The Nakba and its Fluctuating Meaning," ibid., 27–45.

36. Jawad al-Hamad, *The Zionist Massacres against the Palestinian People 1948–2001* (Amman, 2001) [Arabic]; Adel Manna, "The Palestinian Nakba and its Continued Repercussions," *Israel Studies* 18.2 (2013): 86–99.

37. Amal Jamal and Samah Bsoul, *The Palestinian Nakba in the Israeli Public Sphere: On the Forms of Denial and Responsibility* (Nazareth, 2014) [Arabic].

38. See Salim Tamari, *Palestinian Refugee Negotiations: From Madrid to Oslo II* (Washington, DC, 1996); Iliya Zureik, *Palestinian Refugees and the Peace Process* (Washington, DC, 1996); Salim Tamari, ed., *Jerusalem 1948, The Arab Neighborhoods and their Fate in the War* (Jerusalem, 1999); Salman H. Abu-Sitta, *The Palestinian Nakba 1948: The Register of Depopulated Localities in Palestine* (London, 2000).

39. Ghada Karmi and Eugene Cotran, eds., *The Palestinian Exodos 1948-1998* (London, 1999).

Noteworthy among these projects are the ethnographic documentation series of the ruined villages, Jerusalem 1948, remapping of Palestine, and Internet websites recording oral testimonies of Palestinian refugees (such as www.palestiner emembered.com and others). The late 1990s also witnessed a popular adoption of the key as the ultimate symbol of the Palestinian refugee's unbroken tie and quest for return to the original home. This has been epitomized by the Palestinian woman wearing it on her neck underlining the longing for the original domesticity.[40] These activities and others clearly shifted the focus from the Palestinian national history to the local and private accounts, underlining the multiplicity of memory, commemoration, and different foci of interests among Palestinian communities, especially between refugees and non-refugees and between Israeli-Palestinians whom the Oslo Accords entirely ignored, and residents of the West Bank and Gaza Strip.

Fig. 1. Marching in Kafar Miske with a key to the non-existent House
Courtesy of AFP

40. Jihad S. al-Misri, *The Symbolism of Return Keys in the Culture of Palestinian Refugee Woman and its Reflection in the Works of Palestinian Artists* (Bethlehem, 2011); Salim Daw,' dir., *Mafatih* [Keys] (Israel, 2003). For images of the key among Palestinian refugees, visit for example www.palestineremember.com and https://www.google.com/search?q=Palestinian+refugee+camp+al-%60aida+Key

Fig. 2. Lifta, February 25, 2002
(Photo by Jacob Katriel)

Although largely assuming a local nature of one's village or neighborhood and lacking an all-Palestinian perspective,[41] oral testimonies of 1948 Palestinian refugees came to constitute the backbone of Palestinian memory of the 1948 War and, no less important, the main building blocks of the historical meaning of the *nakba*. For Palestinians this effort was especially significant due to decades of relatively muted voice and inability to attain international attention to their tragedy and the historical injustice done to them by Israel. Retrieving the memory of those who experienced it became essential not only to enable a necessary healing process of the traumatic events but also to construct a powerful symbol of national identity revolving on victimhood. Above all, the Palestinian "claim of memory" consciously aims at presenting a necessary alternative to the dominant Jewish-Israeli historical narrative of the 1948 War. By bringing the victims' memory into the open, the Palestinians are less interested in its historical accuracy. Rather, its significance is rooted in the very exposure of the Palestinian narrative through human experience and perspectives, to give room to the silent victims and break

41. Salim Tamari, "Narratives of Exile," *Palestine-Israel Journal* 9.4 (2002).

the wall of indifference of the world to the Palestinian plight.[42] A recent genre of memory writing, affected by the frustrated hopes among Palestinians for fulfilling their yearned statehood, has gone as far as claiming "to imagine rather than represent," including the longing for past Palestinian revolution and resistance.[43]

The reproduction of the *nakba* as a primary strategy in the campaign for international recognition of their victimhood and traumatic past and present, and the Oslo process in the late 1990s, brought about a new Palestinian direction by linking together the Holocaust and the *Nakba*. Edward Said's public call in 1998 for a mutual acknowledgement of Israelis and Palestinians of each other's past trauma and suffering, though admitting their incompatibility in scope and context, suggested that Israelis should issue an apology for "the wrong done by their government against a relatively innocent people."[44] A common theme in Palestinian self-perception in the conflict even before 1948 is of being "victims of the victims," pointing to the horrific and unjust cost *they* were forced to pay by the international community due to the victimization of the European Jews by the Nazis.[45]

Unlike the emergence of a revisionist Israeli historiography and Jewish "memory activist" groups committed to commemorate the Palestinian *nakba*,[46] the Palestinian collective perceptions of the past did not evolve in tandem with these changes on the Israeli side of the hill but remained, by and large, unchanged with the exception of shifting emphases. Especially since the 1990s, Palestinian narratives of the conflict took the form of increasing efforts to construct a mobilizing collective narrative revolving on continuous injustice and victimhood and cultivation of the refugees' indefatigable longing for the homes and places from which they had been exiled. The hegemonic Palestinian version of the past thus keeps drawing primarily on memory and ideology rather than contextual and critical scrutiny of the social and political causes of the Palestinian community's tragedy of 1948, in which the latter, and the Arab states involved, failed to back up

42. This is bluntly stated in Ahmad H. Sa'di and Lila Abu-Lughod, eds., *Nakba: Palestine 1948, and the Claims of Memory* (New York, 2007), 5–13. For a review of Palestinian oral history projects see Sherna B. Gluck, "Oral History and the Nakba," *Oral History Review* 35.1 (2008): 68–80.

43. Penny Johnson, "Introduction," in *Seeking Palestine: New Palestinian Writing on Exile and Home*, ed. Penny Johnson and Raja Shehadeh (Northampton, MA, 2013), x; Karma Nabulsi, "Exiled from Revolution," ibid., 187–96.

44. Edward Said, *The End of the Peace Process: Oslo and After* (New York, 2000), 9.

45. Neil Caplan, "Victimhood in Israeli and Palestinian National Narratives," *Bustan* 3 (2012): 1–19. For a broader discussion on the historical causal link between the Holocaust and the *Nakba*, see Gilbert Achcar, *The Arabs and the Holocaust: The Arab-Israeli War of* Narrative (New York, 2009), 5–29.

46. Most saliently, *Zochrot ("Remembering"): To Commemorate, Witness, Acknowledge, and Repair* (www.nakbainhebrew.org).

militarily the posturing of their political intransigent resistance to the UN Resolution of Partition.

This brief presentation of Israeli and Palestinian 'master narratives' on 1948, the focal event of their century-long conflict, is significant in view of the growing research literature emphasizing the importance of historical narratives and collective memory in the processes of conflict resolution and reconciliation, especially in protracted conflicts marked by long and continuous ethno-religious violence, bereavement, and displacement. This literature underlines the need to recognize the other's burdening memory of past traumas and injustice, and the potentially healing effect of collective apology for historical wrongs.[47] The stalemated Israeli-Palestinian Oslo process provided the Palestinians with suitable international atmosphere to adopt these post–Cold War trends of seeking historical justice and apology for the catastrophe that befell them by Israel's hands. The reconstructed meaning of the *nakba* thus became a powerful spearhead in the Palestinian struggle for international recognition of their 1948 national disaster and subjection ever since to continued occupation, persecution, and suffering wherever they reside.

Memory, however, especially one saturated with symbols and constituting the core of collective identity, is undisputable and hence immune from criticism. Hence, historiography dialogues between Jewish-Israeli and Palestinian scholars held since the 1990s revealed that the Palestinians were not prepared to openly question their master narrative of 1948 or render it susceptible to historical critique.[48] During the Oslo process, with its multitude of "people to people" activities often supported by generous foreign funding, Palestinian academics, filmmakers, and peace activists joined ranks in applying fashionable theoretical assumptions of promoting peace through mutual presentation of each of the parties' particular narratives.[49] While these efforts resulted in important co-productions of narrative studies, they failed to find their way into textbooks and programs of the educational systems of either of the parties. In any case, these efforts were short-lived and remained largely confined to small elite groups, leaving little impact on the respective societies.

47. Elazar Barkan, *The Guilt of Nations. Restitution and Negotiating Historical Injustices* (New York and London, 2000); Alexandra Barahona De Brito, Carmen Gonzalez Enriquez, and Paloma Aguilar, eds., *The Politics of Memory* (Oxford, 2001); Mark Amstutz, *The Healing of Nations* (Lanham, MD, 2005).

48. Bruce Maddy-Weitzman, *Palestinian and Israeli Intellectuals in the Shadow of Oslo and Intifadat al-Aqsa* (Tel-Aviv, 2002); Scham, Salem, and Pogrund, *Shared Histories*; Edward Said, "New History, Old Ideas," *Al-Ahram Weekly*, 21–27 May 1998.

49. Paul Scham, "Arab-Israeli Research Cooperation 1995–1999: An Analytical Study," *Middle East Review of International Affairs* 4.3 (2000): 1–16; *Yes PM: Years of Experience in Strategies for Peace Making* (Jerusalem, 2002), http://www.ipcri.org

The wide gap between Palestinian and Israeli-Jewish historians, notwithstanding the latter's limited impact on the Israeli dominant narrative on 1948, further questions the possibility of an historical compromise, let alone conciliation, between the two peoples. The epilogue by Avraham Sela and Neil Caplan further illustrates the post-Oslo Israeli-Palestinian efforts to attain legitimacy, both domestic and international, for their respective national narratives of the past, fully understanding their implications on mutual claims in the present. Indeed, the compelling weight of national narratives of self-righteousness and victimhood, denial of one's responsibility for wrongs of the past, and mutual projection of full responsibility for them on the other seriously disable the parties to consider a compromise capable of attaining legitimacy of their respective constituencies.

Israeli Palestinians' Memory of 1948 and After

Most Palestinians who remained in Israel and became its citizens did not experience displacement, refugee life, and exile from their homeland, though many of them remained separated from relatives who did go to exile across the political borders. Apart from the traumatic wartime experience of the horrors of hostilities and absence of institutionalized social and political support systems, thousands of them became refugees within Israel following the expulsion or flight from their homes and prohibition from returning to their original places. A small minority of this group experienced both displacement and temporary exile, spending a short time in Lebanon as refugees and returning to Israel on their own or through family unification, a frequent motif in Israeli Palestinian fiction and biographies.[50]

Remembrance of the experiences of hostilities and displacement in 1948 is shared by Palestinians whether they remained in Israel or became refugees living away from their homes. This memory is typically represented in fiction and poetry rather than memoirs, apparently due to repression, describing the exodus as a flood, an unsolved puzzle, a story shrouded in fog, "a moment when time stopped moving."[51] The remembrance of those who remained in Israel, especially in the first two decades after the war during which "Israeli Arabs" lived under military government, underscores two particular strands that simultaneously existed and

---

50. See documentary film *Zahra* (Muhammad Bakri, dir., Israel, 2009); Ben-Ze'ev, *Remembering Palestine 1948*, 24–5. This is also the story of the hero in Emile Habibi, *The Strange Events Concerning the Disappearance of Sa'id Abi al-Nahs the Pessoptimist* (Haifa, 2006 [1974]). For an English version of the novel see Emile Habiby, *The Secret Life of Saeed: The Pessoptimist* (translated from the Arabic by Salma Khadra Jayyusi and Trevor LeGassick) (London, 1985).

51. As'ad, *Atfal al-Nada*. For similar descriptions in poetry see Ghanim, "Poetics of Disaster," 23–39.

interacted in their life. They experienced the post-war years as both traumatic and humiliating and, at the same time, of steadfastness and survival in the face of isolation from the Arab world, restrictions on movement, confiscation of land and impoverishment, and other means of control imposed by the Israeli military government (1948–1966). The poet Mahmud Darwish described the Palestinians in Israel after the *nakba* as "living in the peak of the volcano."[52]

During the years of military government, Israeli Arabs manifested adherence to their Arab national identity parallel to preserving their local and traditional attachments, and were bound to strike a fine balance between their Israeli citizenship and Arab political and cultural identity. They developed a particular perspective by which they "simultaneously treated the state as present and absent in their lives while emphasizing the traumas they had to endure in the aftermath of the war, and the steadfastness they had to employ in order to sustain their dignity and survive."[53] In addition to surviving the traumatic experience of 1948 and consequent Israeli military government, these Palestinians take pride in challenging the newly demarcated borders that had abruptly separated villagers from their farmed lands, and divided families and clans.[54]

A major manifestation of this defiant attitude was the "resistance literature"[55] of Israeli-Palestinian poets and writers, many of whom were influenced, both before and after 1967, by Marxist Socialist Realism infused by the Communist Party and its political and literary magazines.[56] The post-1967 years saw an increasing shift in the collective conduct of Israeli Arab citizens towards a strategy of adjustment and political struggle for their civil rights and for receiving a fair share in the national resources, amidst renewal of social and cultural contacts with the Palestinians in the West Bank and Gaza Strip. Israeli Palestinian sociologists and writers often described their community as doubly peripheral, once versus the Jewish majority and again vis-a-vis the Arab world and Palestinian people

52. Ghanim, ibid., 31.

53. Iris Nusair, "Gendering the Narratives of Three Generations of Palestinian Women in Israel," in *Displaced at Home: Ethnicity and Gender among Palestinians in Israel,* ed. Rhoda Ann Kanaaneh and Isis Nusair (New York, 2010), 83; Honaida Ghanim, "Being a Border," ibid., 109–15.

54. Such as the symbolic "return" of the displaced villagers of Kafr Bir'im and Ikrit to their homes, Nur Masalha, "Present Absentees and Indigenous Resistance," in *Catastrophe Remembered: Palestine, Israel and the Internal Refugees, Essays in Memory of Edward W. Said,* ed. Nur Masalha (London, 2005), 36–41, The memories of this experience are typically represented in Bakri's documentary *Zahra*.

55. Ghassan Kanafani, *The Literature of Resistance in Occupied Palestine 1948–1966* (Beirut, 1970) [Arabic].

56. Ghanim, "Poetics of Disaster," 19–27. See also Hunaida Ghanim, *To Rebuild the Nation: Palestinian Intellectuals in Israel* (Jerusalem, 2009) [Arabic].

at large,[57] with a third peripheral level, represented by the "internal refugees."[58] Assaf Peled and Tal Ben-Zvi refer to these trends before and after 1967, seen through the works of two typical Israeli Palestinian representatives of Marxist realism namely, the political activist and writer Emile Habibi and artist Abed Abdi, respectively.

Israeli Palestinians received the Oslo Accords with double frustration because not only had the agreement entirely ignored their cause as a minority lacking collective rights, it also lacked a clear statement about the 1948 refugees, relegating the issue to the permanent status negotiations, and thus interpreted as a deliberate marginalization of the refugee issue. The latter sentiment was especially salient among the 150,000–250,000[59] Israeli citizens who became "internal refugees," defined by Israel as "absent present" regarding their "abandoned" homes and villages within Israel. In many cases, they became refugees because of their expulsion by the Israeli authorities from their villages and neighborhoods during 1948 or shortly after. In response, the post-Oslo years witnessed a growing grass roots agitation and propagation of the Palestinian refugees' rights, especially their right of return to their homes in Israel.

For Israeli-Palestinian internal refugees, practices of commemoration and preservation in the forms of individual and family ritualized pilgrimages to their ruined villages and restoration of churches have been a matter of routine since 1948. The 1967 War enabled Palestinian refugees from the West Bank and Gaza Strip to adopt similar practices, albeit more infrequently. Parallel to the growing emphasis among Palestinian refugee associations in the West Bank and Gaza in the post-Oslo years on the *nakba* and the refugee problem, Israel's Palestinians grew active in their effort to bring the memory and meaning of the 1948 War to Israeli and international awareness, manifested by public ceremonies and commemorations. The 1990s witnessed a particular pattern of conduct of the Israeli Palestinian community, namely organized efforts especially of the Islamic Movement and other voluntary organizations to renovate neglected Islamic sites, such as mosques and cemeteries in urban and rural areas, as a way of reclaiming

---

57. Majid al-Haj, "Whither the Green Line? Trends in the Orientation of the Palestinians in Israel and the Territories," *Israel Affairs* 11.1 (2005): 183–206. As well described by Emile Habibi in, *The Hexad of the Six Days* (Cairo, 1984) [Arabic].

58. Majid al-Haj, "The Arab Internal Refugees in Israel: The Emergence of a Minority within the Minority," *Immigration and Minorities* 7.2 (1988): 149–65.

59. According to Palestinian estimate, by the early 2000s there were 250,000 internal refugees in Israel. See Leila Farsakh, *Palestinian Labour Migration to Israel: Labour, Land, and Occupation* (London, 2005), 201. For a lower estimate of 150,000–170,000, see Hillel Cohen, "The State of Israel versus the Palestinian Internal Refugees," in *Catastrophe Remembered,* ed. Nur Masalha, 56–72.

the right of possession by assuming continuous presence in them in a private and family ritualistic manner, as a semi-practical "return."[60]

This trend culminated on 15 May 1998 when Israel's Palestinian citizens publicly commemorated the fiftieth anniversary of their 1948 catastrophe (*nakba*) parallel to Israel's national celebrations of its own jubilee, setting a new form of differentiation by adopting two national commemoration dates and narratives expressing their particular collective identities and political claims. For Israel's Palestinian citizens, the commemoration of the *nakba* on May 15 and not on Israel's independence date celebrated on the 5th of Iyyar (according to the Jewish calendar) represents their autonomous political identity and memory. An especially salient element of the Palestinian commemoration of the *Nakba* Day since 1998 has been gatherings and marches to the remains of destroyed villages. That same year the first memorial monument was built to embed the victims of the 1948 War in the Palestinian national narrative. Despite the cautious and modest act taken by the Arab initiators, it triggered strong antagonistic responses of Israeli public figures including government members.[61] The reconstruction of 1948 as a catastrophe in which the Palestinians were the ultimate victims and the Zionists the utter victimizers sparked hostile Israeli responses by individual commentators, grass roots organizations, and the legislature, culminating in the *Nakba* Law of 2011, denying public funding for Israeli Palestinian institutions commemorating this event. One may perceive the Foreign Ministry's campaign regarding "the Jewish refugees" of the Arab countries as an attempt to balance the Palestinian claims related to 1948.[62]

Underlying the stern Israeli response to the growing public commemoration of the *nakba*, is the "nightmare of return,"[63] namely, the threat of masses of Palestinians returning to Israel and the broad consensus among Israeli Jews that the "right of return" is nothing but a euphemistic strategy for the elimination of Israel as a Jewish state. The haunting return of the Arabs is amply represented in biographies and novels of both Arab and Jewish writers as well as in documentary films in which Palestinian refugees practically return (especially after 1967) to

---

60. Efrat Ben-Ze'ev and Issam Aburaiya, "'Middle Ground' Politics and the Re-Palestinization of Places in Israel," *International Journal of Middle East Studies* 36.4 (2004): 639–55; Masalha, "Present Absentees and Indigenous Resistance," 41–55.

61. Tamir Sorek, "Cautious Commemoration: Localism, Communalism, and Nationalism in Palestinian Memorial Monuments in Israel," *Comparative Studies in History and Society* 50.2 (2008): 337–68.

62. Raphael Ahren, "Changing Tack, Foreign Ministry to Bring 'Jewish Refugees' to Fore," *The Times of Israel*, 3 April 2012 http://www.timesofisrael.com/foreign-ministry-promotes-the-jewish-refugee-problem/

63. Miron Benvenisti, *The Dream of the White Sabra* (Jerusalem, 2012), 162. For examples of unofficial Israeli responses to the *Nakba* commemoration and demands that Israel admit responsibility for its occurrence, see Jamal and Bsoul, *The Palestinian Nakba*, 116–28.

their homes currently inhabited by Jews.[64] Israel's systematic efforts since 1948 of obliterating the traces of pre-1948 Palestinian landscape[65] typically represent the Jewish wishful forgetfulness and claim for reconstruction of its Jewish identity. The flattening of depopulated Arab villages and urban neighborhoods, land appropriation, renaming of nature objects and localities, resettlement of displaced Arab villages and towns by Jewish migrants, and turning former Arab inhabited areas into nature preserves and national parks that largely deny their pre-1948 Palestinian past[66]—all could hardly conceal the remains of the pre-1948 Palestinian physical landscape. Israeli-Jews are thus constantly reminded of the land's Arab past by the very presence of Arab forms of landscape such as ruined stone buildings, wells, agricultural terraces, olive tree orchards, and cacti fences. At least to those who remember and understand their origins and meaning, these remnants trigger fears of the expelled Arab who returns to vindicate his disaster or reclaim his property rights.[67]

Not only the presence of the Arab-Palestinian past is still salient in Israeli Jewish consciousness and routine discourse, especially since the early 1990s Israeli-Palestinian citizens have begun challenging Israeli practices of ignoring the Arabic language on traffic signs, parallel to Hebrew and English, resuming the use of the original Arab names of natural sites.[68] Hence, Israeli and Palestinian commemoration, repression, forgetfulness, and silence keep interacting with each other, attracting some Jewish groups and individuals to challenge core Zionist narratives. Ziva Kolodney discusses this struggle in the case of Haifa where grass roots groups comprising Israeli Jews and Palestinians endeavor to commemorate and reclaim the city's Arab past.

The Oslo Accords of the 1990s witnessed a wave of film production, mostly documentaries revolving on personal, familial, or local memories and experiences of Palestinian refugees of 1948. Often funded by European foundations as a contribution to the Israeli-Palestinian Oslo process, many of the documentaries

64. This is a repeated motif in Habibi's novels, Seraje Assi, "Memory, Myth and the Military Government: Emile Habibi's Collective Autobiography," *Jerusalem Quarterly* 52 (2013): 91. See Sandy Tolan, *The Lemon Tree: An Arab, a Jew, and the Heart of the Middle East* (New York, 2007); Badil, *Documentary on Refugees of Jerusalem* (Bethlehem, 1998).

65. Aharon Shai, "The Fate of Abandoned Arab Villages in Israel, 1965–1969," *Cathedra* 105 (2003): 151–70 [Hebrew].

66. Noga Kadman, "Roots Tourism—Whose Roots? The Marginalization of Palestinian Heritage Sites in Official Israeli Tourism Sites," *Teoros* 29.1 (2010): 55–66.

67. Gil Hochberg, "A Poetics of Haunting: From Yizhar's Khirbeh to Yehoshua's Ruins to Koren's Crypts," *Jewish Social Studies* 18.3 (2012): 55–69. See As'ad's response to A.B. Yehoshua's story, *Atfal al-Nada*, 4–5; Ben-Ze'ev and Aburaiya, "Middle Ground," 645–6.

68. In 1997 the Israeli Palestinian advocacy association 'Adala, appealed to the court on this matter and won the case.

revolved on Palestinian longing for the "lost paradise" and myriad forms of remembrance, memory, and commemoration of 1948, and co-produced by young Israelis and Palestinians, in addition to many others produced separately by Israelis and Palestinians.[69] The films address issues of guilt and responsibility, justice and injustice, memory and longing to "land," "homeland," "place," and "home."[70] To an extent, during the Oslo process the mental borders separating Israeli-Jews from Palestinians grew blurred by this genre of Israeli-Palestinian co-produced films related to 1948. As reviewed by Bosmat Garami, a handful of Israeli documentary and feature films on the Palestinian refugee issue appeared as early as the late 1960s and the 1970s—some of which were screened by Israel's only television channel. These films addressed hitherto taboo issues, such as the expulsion of Palestinian "internal refugees" and their original place, about which they continue to dream and yearn to return to, even temporarily. The growing genre of such films on the 1948 Palestinian refugees in the following decades, more than other products of popular culture, played a pioneer role in introducing this issue to Israeli public debate.[71]

AVRAHAM SELA is Professor Emeritus of International Relations and a senior research fellow at the Truman Institute of the Hebrew University of Jerusalem. Among his publications are "Arab and Jewish Civilians in the 1948 Palestine War" in *Caught in Crossfire: Civilians in Conflict in the Middle East*; *The Palestinian Hamas: Vision, Violence and Coexistence* (with Shaul Mishal); and "Myths and Historiography of the 1948 Palestine War Revisited: The Case of Lydda," *Middle East Journal* (with Alon Kadish).

ALON KADISH is Professor in the Department of History at the Hebrew University of Jerusalem and Director of the Institute for the Study of the Land of Israel and its Settlement at the Yad Izhak Ben-Zvi in Jerusalem. His recent publications include "The Jewish Victory in Tzfat during the War of Independence (April–May, 1948)," *Ariel* (with Avraham Sela); and "Myths and Historiography of the 1948 Palestine War Revisited; The Case of Lydda," *Middle East Journal* (with Avraham Sela).

69. Examples are Nizar Hassan, dir., *A Saga* (Mashhad films, 1998); Ra'anan Alexandrovich and Ra'id Andoni, dirs., *The Internal Journey* (Israel, 2001); Sahira Dirbas, dir., *Haifa* (Israel, 2002); Salim Daw', dir., *Mafatih*; Dan Bar-On, dir., *Haifa* (Israel: 2002); Michel Khleifi and Eyal Sivan, dirs., *Route 181* (Paris, 2004).

70. Nurith Gertz and George Khleifi, *Palestinian Cinema: Landscape, Trauma, and Memory* (Bloomington, IN, 2008).

71. Shapira, "Khirbet Khiza," 88–113.

Part 1: Israeli-Jewish Narratives:
Continuity and Change

1 The 1948 Palestine War on the Small Screen

A Comparative Analysis of Its Representation in Two Israeli Television Series

Bosmat Garami

Introduction

Televised history has become the focus of growing academic research, which examines its uniqueness compared to the tradition of written history, and emphasizes its significant role in shaping collective memory. Film and television became central mechanisms of memory construction during the second half of the twentieth century and Western scholarship has long been emphasizing the power of fictional as well as documentary film in the representation of history[1] and defending television's capabilities to "mediate" history successfully against those who doubt it.[2] According to Edgerton, televisual characteristics such as immediacy, dramatization, personalization, and intimacy, all shape the medium's interaction with the past. Sorlin mentions the potential of television's serials to expose "long durations," describe mental and social processes, and create meaningful encounters with historical figures.

Wars have been particularly attractive as a central subject of prominent television series, both documentary and fiction. From the 1940s' *Why We Fight*, through the 1970s' *The World at War*, to Ken Burns's *The Civil War*, the drama,

---

1. Marc Ferro, *Cinema and History* (Detroit, 1988); Robert Rosenstone, "History in Images/History in words," *The American Historical Review* 93.5 (1988): 1173–85; "Introduction," in *Revisioning History*, ed. Robert Rosenstone (Princeton, 1995), 3–13; Shlomo Sand, *Film as History: Imagining and Screening the Twentieth Century* (Tel-Aviv, 2002) [Hebrew].

2. Gary Edgerton, "Introduction: Television as Historian," in *Television Histories: Shaping Collective Memory in the Media Age,* ed. Gary Edgerton and Peter Rollins (Lexington, KY, 2001), 1–16; Pierre Sorlin, "Television and Our Understanding of History: A Distant Conversation," in *Screening the Past,* ed. Tony Barta (Westport, CT, 1998), 205–20.

The War of 1948 (2016); 27–50, DOI: 10.2979/warof1948.0.0.03

visuality, and extended impact of war inspired the creation of series that became landmarks in the history of television documentary.[3]

The two Israeli historic-documentary series examined here also have war as a central subject: the 1948 War, a major signpost in the Arab-Israeli ongoing conflict. The series are *Amud Ha'esh (Pillar of Fire*[4]) and *Tkumah (Revival*[5]). The series were produced by the state owned Israeli Television Channel One, a generation apart. *Pillar of Fire (POF)* is a product of the late 1970s, at the apex of Israel's most agonizing years following the traumatic 1973 Yom Kippur War and sense of growing international isolation, which culminated in the 1975 UN Resolution that "Zionism is a form of racism." Its creators' express goal was to explain and justify the Zionist ethos and celebrate the Zionist enterprise.[6] The series covers the period of 1896–1948, from the beginning of political Zionism to the founding of the State of Israel. Each of its 19 chapters is one hour in length. When it was first broadcast in 1981 it earned an 89 percent rating (high even when considering that there was only one channel then).

Tkumah (TK) was produced in the mid-1990s, toward the state's jubilee celebration in 1998, when it was first broadcast. In an era of multi-channel television it still earned a 30 percent rating. Despite the time gap between them, *TK* was a continuation of *POF* in that it sought to encompass the first 50 years of Israel. It covers the period from the 1930s, the prologue to the 1948 War, until the assassination of Prime Minister Rabin in 1995, which the series perceived as a breakdown of the Oslo process and the loss of hope for its further development. It reviews this period with a critical eye, its creators' declared wish being to express the state's multi-vocality and introduce to the Israeli public hitherto silenced counter-narratives.[7]

The production processes of the two series largely correspond to their ideological approaches. *POF* is practically the unified creation of its main editor and scriptwriter Yigal Lossin, then director of programming and creator of news magazines and documentary programs and series on Channel 1. *TK*'s 22 one-hour chapters, on the other hand, were created by 19 of the country's leading documentary directors. The series' chief editor, Gideon Drori, was a producer, director, and editor of Channel 1, who had participated as a director-editor in the production of *POF* at the time. Drori, who passed away in 2005, was also a known civil rights activist. He drew-up general guidelines for *TK*, but the directors had enough artistic freedom to put together a complex, multi-vocal view of the period.

3. Jack Ellis and Betsy McLane, *A New History of Documentary Film* (New York, 2005).

4. Yigal Lossin, *Pillar of Fire* (Jerusalem, 1981) [Hebrew].

5. Gideon Drori, *Revival* (Jerusalem, 1998) [Hebrew].

6. Yigal Lossin, *Pillar of Fire: Chapters in the History of Zionism* (Jerusalem, 1982) [Hebrew].

7. Anat Balint, "The Selection is the Conception," *The Seventh Eye* 14 (1998): 10–13.

During the 20-year gap between the two series significant changes affected the Zionist hegemonic master-narrative: its dominant status weakened, especially with the emergence as of the late 1980s of a "new history" of Israel's early years represented by critical young historians, who challenged the Zionist-Israeli foundational assumptions and mythical ethos, especially policies and practices in and around the 1948 war. Drawing on newly released official archives, these historians pointed to Israel's active role in the creation of the Arab-Palestinian refugee problem,[8] triggering broad academic and public controversies.[9]

These changes were expressed in the cultural scene, notably in film and television. Researchers offered the following periodization of Israel's cinematic history:[10] Films about pioneers made before the establishment of the state and the nationalist-heroic cinema that followed the state's birth adhered to the Zionist narrative, including adoration of pioneering and negative approach to Arabs and their narrative. Significant change began in the 1970s and peaked in the 1980s, with what Gertz referred to as "the cinema of the stranger and deviant" or what Shohat called "the Palestinian wave," that gave voice to the Arab-Palestinian and additional "other" protagonists, like new immigrants and Sephardic (Oriental) Jews. Although early harbingers of a different and critical approach were produced much earlier,[11] it took more than a decade before films critical of the Zionist ethos and its realization were proliferating and screened in cinemas and on television. Films such as *Khirbat Khiz'ah*, *Khamsin*, and *Behind Bars*, produced in 1978, 1982, and 1984, respectively, exhibit a new approach to the Arab-Israeli conflict and to the position of the Arab in the Zionist narrative. Simultaneously, history textbooks began to give more expression to the Arab point of view and negative Arab stereotypes diminished.[12]

---

8. Benny Morris, *The Birth of the Palestinian Refugee Problem, 1947-1949* (Cambridge, 1988); Avi Shlaim, *Collusion Across the Jordan* (New York, 1988).

9. Shabtai Tevet, Review, "The Palestine Arab Refugee Problem and Its Origins," *Middle Eastern Studies* 26.2 (1990): 214–49; Avi Shlaim, "The Debate About 1948," *International Journal of Middle East Studies* 27.3 (1995): 287–304; Anita Shapira, "Politics and Collective Memory: The Debate About the 'New Historians,'" *History and Memory* 71 (1995): 9–40; Ben-Josef M. Hirsch, "From Taboo to the Negotiable: The Israeli New Historians and the Changing Representation of the Palestinian Refugee Problem," *Perspectives on Politics* 5.2 (2007): 241–58.

10. Nurith Gertz, *Motion Fiction: Israeli Fiction in Film* (Tel-Aviv, 1993); Ella Shohat, *Israeli Cinema: East/West and the Politics of Representation* (Tel-Aviv, 1991); "Overarching Narrative/ Critical Readings: The Politics of Israeli Cinema," in *Fictive Looks on Israeli Cinema,* ed. Nurith Gertz, Orly Lubin, and Judd Ne'eman (Tel-Aviv, 1998), 44–66 [both in Hebrew].

11. Ram Levi (producer), *Me, Ahmed* (Tel-Aviv, 1966).

12. Ruth Firer, *Agents of the Zionist Education* (Tel-Aviv, 1985) [Hebrew]; Elie Podeh, "History and Memory in the Israeli Educational System: The Portrayal of the Arab-Israeli Conflict in History Textbooks," *History & Memory* 12 (2000): 65–100.

The 1948 War and the Palestinian Arab refugee problem were central subjects of these critical tendencies.

The comparative study here places *POF* and *TK* within this changing Israeli reality. It uses narratological-semiotic research tools for analysis of the televisual text, with the purpose of showing that different constructive means are used to represent the different ideologies of the two series. The chapter examines four major aspects of the 1948 War as represented by both series. It first describes the place of the 1948 War in the serial narrative of each series, concentrating on temporal and plot structures. It then proceeds to exhibit the modes each series uses to represent the Arab side. The third aspect it examines is the representation of the Palestinian refugee problem, while the last one shows the difference between the series in the treatment of major aspects of the Zionist ethos of the War. The chapter thus aims to give full insight into the concept each series presents of the War, as well as to illustrate the total inseparability of "form" from "content."

The 1948 War in the Serial Narrative of Each Series

The 1948 War is a central topic in both series but functions differently in each of them: while in *POF* it is the final and ultimate phase toward the yearned goal of a Jewish state, in *TK* it is an initial, traumatic event, with far-reaching implications for the years to come.

The Jewish/Israeli-Arab conflict is a central theme in *POF*. Its presence is gradually magnified as the series progresses. The Conflict is described as a total conflict between two sides: the Jewish community (Yishuv), which struggles to realize the Zionist vision of Jewish statehood, and the Arabs—of Palestine and the neighboring countries—and their leaders, whose purpose is to destroy the Zionist enterprise. The Conflict is present from the very start of the series' narrative. In chapter 2, "The Arabs Awaken," the attack on the Tel-Hai settlers in March 1920 is described, as well as the April 1920 Arab riots in Jerusalem, the first major violent attack perpetrated by Arab-Palestinians against Jews recorded in the series. The developing violent conflict is the central axis of the complex political struggle described in the series, which revolved on Jewish immigration and settlement and the emerging option of dividing the country between the adversaries.

The series elaborates on the Arabs' 1921 and 1929 riots and the 1936–39 revolt. It describes in detail the suffering and victims of Arab violence on the Jewish side, such as the massacre of 67 members of the historic Hebron community in August 1929. The Zionist legitimate response to the Arab violence, according to the series, was the creation of Jewish defensive organizations: Ha-Shomer (The Watchman) in 1909, the Haganah (Defense) in 1920—and within it the Palmach (abbreviation of Strike Companies) in 1941—which later transformed into the Israel Defense Forces (IDF). Representation of the Conflict culminates in the series' last three chapters: the Arabs' refusal to accept the November 29, 1947, UN Resolution on the partition of Palestine into Jewish and Arab states and the declaration of war against its implementation. The series ends in May 1948 with the proclamation of the State of Israel. The war is still raging, but Israel's victory is imminent.

In *TK* the 1948 War is the first round in the swelling Israeli-Arab conflict, which is the central axis of the series. It is situated right after the prologue in chapter 1. Chapters 2 and 3 describe the battles of the war: the first presents the coping of the Yishuv and its defense forces with the first stages of the war—the November 1947 UN resolution on partition until May 1948—while chapter 2 shows the continuation of the war after the establishment of the state and de-scribes its heavy price in human losses (constituting one percent of the current Jewish population). Unlike *POF*, *TK* does not emphasize the story of two morally opposite parties, i.e., the Jewish one preoccupied with construction while the Arabs sought destruction. Rather, it depicts the War as the case of two sides entangled in a fatal struggle, for which both share the responsibility and from which both suffer heavily.

The temporal structure of the two series further clarifies the different func-tions of the 1948 War in each of them. The basis for the analysis here is Genette's typology,[13] which analyzes what he entitles "tense," by showing the author's choices in the categories of "order," "duration," and "frequency." *POF* is found to be chron-ological and diachronic, as far as the order of events is concerned. It presents a complete linear narrative from beginning to end, which serves its overarching plot—"from Diaspora to National Revival." A discernible tendency of deceleration is identified from chapter 14 onward. Instead of the "summary" characterizing the first part of the series, with chapters covering periods of about ten years, a "slow-down" is observed toward the end. Chapters 17 and 18 cover about half a year each, and the final chapter 19 describes a period of less than two months. Thus the events between the UN resolution and the declaration of the State of Israel gain extra significance. The political victory of Zionism combined with the ultimate military struggle to protect the newly born state receive considerable "commemorative time"[14] and are emphasized as the result and the objective of a long historical process.

TK's temporal structure is different and more complex: it is chronological and thematic at the same time. Chapters of the chronological axis deal with primary episodes in the Israeli-Arab conflict, starting with the 1948 War, then the 1956 Sinai War, the 1967 Six-Day War, the 1973 Yom Kippur War, and so on. The thematic axis consists of chapters dealing with social and cultural processes, for example the great wave of immigration during the state's first decade, relations

13. Gerard Genette, *Narrative Discourse* (Oxford, 1980), 33–160; *Narrative Discourse Revisited* (Ithaca, 1988), 21–40.

14. Yael Zerubavel, *Recovered Roots: Collective Memory and the Making of Israeli National Tradition* (Chicago, 1995), 9.

between Oriental and European Jews, religious and secular, Left and Right politics, etc. These chapters are integrated among those describing the Israeli-Arab conflict, but do not form a chronology. This complex structure portrays the constant interaction between the Israeli-Arab conflict and the socio-cultural processes in Israel. Ideologically it points to the fact that the main events of the conflict shaped Israeli society and identity and were influenced by it at the same time.

The period of 1947–49 is stretched out over two consecutive chapters, which form one dramatic unit. Moreover, analysis shows that about half of the series' chapters deal with the period around 1948 or start their narrative at that time. This highlights *TK*'s perception of the 1948 War not only as a major turning point in Jewish-Israeli history but also as a formative event to which later developments can be traced back. Hence, while *POF* is teleological, aiming forward to the end of the narrative, to the attainment of the Zionist goal right after the awesome event of the 1948 War, *TK* is deterministic in that it repeatedly relates to that war as the source and point of departure, accounting for most of what followed in the coming decades.

A final aspect that concerns the serial narrative is the plot structure of each series, that is, the shaping of a series of historical events according to familiar plot structures, an act White names "emplotment."[15] The creators of *POF* perfectly shaped it according to the classic plot structure, as described by Aristotle and others since. As mentioned, it consists of linear progress from beginning to end. It is basically a problem-solving structure: the protagonist, the Jewish people, looks for an answer to the situation of ever-present anti-Semitism and the destructive negativity of the Diaspora, culminating in the Holocaust. It overcomes many obstacles in seeking the goal of the renewal of sovereignty in its ancient homeland. Along the way, its chief antagonists are the Arabs. The protagonist and its goal are presented in chapter 1, entitled "Destination-Jerusalem"; the antagonist is immediately introduced in chapter 2. Throughout the series this binary opposition between Jews and Arabs, "good" and "evil," right and wrong, is emphasized.

The role of the "villain" does not remain faceless. By personalization of the evil the drama is strengthened, and the feelings of the spectators are directed as to whom to fear and hate and with whom to identify. The personality that arouses the strongest negative feelings is the leader of the Palestinian Arabs, the Mufti Haj Amin al-Husseini. He is connected in the series only to harassment and killing of Jews, while his role in the Palestinian national movement is hardly mentioned. A devil in disguise, his "delicate" external appearance is described as totally contradictory to his "murderous" personality. He is repeatedly referred to as "the

---

15. Hayden White, "The Historical Text as a Literary Artifact," *Clio* 3.3 (1974): 277–303. See also Elazar Weinryb, "History as Literature," in *Historical Thinking: Issues in Philosophy of History* (Tel-Aviv, 1987), Vol. 1, 389–453 [Hebrew].

most fanatic, dangerous enemy of Zionism." His demonization is also carried out visually, by the use of slow-motion and freeze-frame. He is accused of tirelessly intensifying the Conflict, being the spirit behind the 1920 and 1929 riots against the Jews, and an uncompromising opponent of the partition of the country.

A most effective dramatic device used to strengthen the "villainy" of the Arabs is emphasizing their connections with the Nazi regime. The series elaborates on the sympathy and assistance offered by certain Arab leaders in the region to the German war effort. Palestinian Arabs are said to have hoped for the arrival of "Abu-Ali"-Rommel from the south. The Mufti offered himself as an ally to Mussolini and Hitler. He not only named Hitler "defender of the Islam" but, the series emphasizes, planned to solve "the Jewish problem" in Palestine using the Fuhrer's methods. The series emphasizes that the Mufti was later declared a war criminal. The great emphasis on those aspects of unity between the Nazis and the Arabs serves to further de-legitimize Arabs' national claims and mark them as absolute evil.

The movement of *POF*'s plot toward solution is gradual. It includes both the political and the military victory of the protagonist, the Jewish people. Chapter 17 describes the political solution and presents all the maneuvers on both sides toward the UN vote on partition and the establishment of a Jewish state. The Arabs' state of unpreparedness and disarrayed efforts to prevent a pro-Zionist vote is admitted by their own representatives, as a member of the Saudi delegate sums up: "The Arabs counted on luck and good will, while for the Jews' politics was not a gamble but a science . . ."

The most violent showdown in the Arab-Jewish conflict, the 1948 War, bursts out powerfully immediately after a majority of the UN member states supported the establishment of a Jewish state in Palestine, which was rejected and forcefully resisted by the Arabs. In order for the Jewish military victory to be even more impressive than the political one, the series emphasizes the great advantages of the opponent. Here the ancient Jewish mythical plot structure of "The few against the many" or "David against Goliath"[16] is fully employed. Chapter 18 quotes, among others, the American secretary of defense who prophesizes: "45 million Arabs will definitely push the 350,000 Jews into the sea, and end of story!"[17] In chapter 19 the antagonist grows even stronger, with all the neighboring Arab countries joining the fight. Just as in a Hollywood movie, where toward the end of the plot the protagonist is in the greatest danger but then comes out victorious, here too the few, being good, right, and ready to sacrifice everything for their lofty goal, manage to overcome their powerful, villainous opponents.

16. Zerubavel, *Recovered Roots*, 217.
17. By late 1947 the Jewish community in Palestine numbered 600,000.

The War is described as a series of heroic Jewish resistance in response to Arab attacks: the siege and bombing of Jerusalem, the offensive by Qauqji[18] on Kibbutz Mishmar Ha'emek, the slaughter on the convoy to Mount Scopus, etc. The Arabs are the vicious aggressors but the Jews manage to sustain the Arab attacks and pass from defense to offense. The conquest of the Arab village Qastel, a strategic stronghold that dominates the road to Jerusalem, and the breaking through (though temporarily) the siege on Jerusalem's Jewish part are described in detail, and become a symbolic harbinger of the imminent victory. So is the liberation of Tel-Aviv from "the nightmare of its aggressive neighbor, Jaffa." The road is now open to the "happy end" of the plot.

In *TK*, no classic plot structure is evident, but rather a far more complicated construct than *POF*'s. There is no overarching linear story leading to a clear ending, but instead a multi-dimensional, fragmentary dramatic structure, where the thematic chapters serve as "satellites," surrounding the chronological axis describing the Israeli-Arab conflict. No serial goal is presented in the first episode, as in *POF*, but rather a query is posed: Will the generation of native-born Israelis succeed in developing an Israeli society that will live in peace and security? In addition, no binary oppositions between Zionists and non-Zionists, Jews and Arabs, "good" and "bad" are posed. The conflict is described as a complex, bloody, vicious, ongoing struggle between two peoples, which in turn is further aggravated by the kind of choices and decisions made by the two sides.

Thus the two chapters 2 and 3 dealing with the 1948 War portray a complex picture. The many faces of the War are presented, from the Jewish as well as the Arab points of view. There is even some parallelism drawn between the efforts and sacrifices of the two sides. The war is described as a series of attacks and counter-attacks of both sides while atrocities were committed by both. The Jewish advantage was achieved slowly, in a costly process of trial and error, victories and failures, at the price of many losses. The ecstatic unity characterizing the Jewish side in *POF* is not present here. Field commanders criticize the military head-quarters, newly arrived immigrants tell of their estrangement from Israeli-born soldiers, etc. Chapter 3 criticizes decisions made by higher military ranks, which claimed a heavy toll from both citizens and soldiers in battle.

Problematic aspects of the war are raised again in several other chapters that do not deal with it directly. Chapter 4, for example, describes the difficulties of new immigrants and Holocaust survivors to be accepted into the fighting units of the Palmach; chapter 11, dealing with Israeli Arabs, describes harsh war

18. Fawzi al-Qauqji was the commander of the "Army of Deliverance," a semi-regular force of volunteers from the neighboring Arab countries, backed by the member states of the Arab League, aiming at supporting the Arabs of Palestine in their resistance to partition and establishment of a Jewish state.

experiences of Arab villagers; chapter 20 discusses the problematic issue of participating in the war for Yeshiva religious Jews; and chapter 19 tells about the war from the viewpoint of American Jewry, the pride of which rose at the sight of Jewish fighters. In this way the 1948 War gains a multi-faceted presentation. The difference in details and points of view creates a "Rashomon"-like description, which escapes the uniform, single-voice presentation of *POF*.

Unlike *POF*, which ends when the war is still raging, *TK*'s chapter 3 describes the end of the war and the post-war situation as well. The victory is celebrated, but not with the enthusiasm of *POF*. "The young State survived the test," says the narrator, but participants in it testify to feelings of shock and mourning, mixed with satisfaction that the Yishuv and the dream of Jewish statehood prevailed. The chapter praises the decision of Ben-Gurion not to continue the war with the option of widening the borders, but to turn to the major task of absorbing the massive waves of immigrants. The 1948 War, according to these chapters, strengthened the connection between Israelis and their country, and consolidated their values. Although Ben-Gurion wrote in his diary: "The Arab people was defeated by us; will they forget it?," and with the threatening shadow of the refugee problem—the chapter closes with optimism and a true hope for peace. It ends with the symbolic picture of a girl looking up to a white dove flying above.

TK presents the 1948 War as the first and only "no-choice" one of the wars yet to come. Plot-wise it is the first round in what would prove to be a protracted conflict, which becomes more intensively violent with every round. The total victory of the "good" and the "right" is thus absent here, unlike *POF*'s happy end.

Modes of Representation of the Arab Side

Both series use a full array of means resulting in representing completely opposite ideologies: Whereas *POF* largely ignores the Arab-Palestinian point of view *TK* offers a relatively extensive representation of their narrative.

Interviews

TK has twice the percentage of Arab interviewees as *POF*: 16.3 percent and 7.8 percent, respectively. *POF* is not eager to give voice to the "other," "negative" side, while *TK*'s goal is to represent the conflict in its full complexity, giving voice to all parties concerned. Most Arab interviewees in *POF* are representative figures, and not ordinary individuals with whom one can identify. Thus Anwar Nusseiba, a 1948 combatant and scion of a Jerusalemite notable family and later a minister in a number of Jordanian governments, reappears in six chapters, always in the role of senior commentator on the Arab moves. Muhammad Nimr al-Hawari, founder and commander of the Arab para-military organization al-Najada, represents and speaks for the "Arab military field commander" in three different chapters. Very few interviewees in this series are involved in a continuous, personal story within the chapter in which they appear. This privilege is reserved only for representatives of the Zionist narrative, like pioneers or Holocaust survivors. In *TK*, half of all interviewees portray an ongoing, personal life story, including Arabs. Such is the case of Na'um Sam'an, the refugee from Sukhmata village, who, in chapter 3, tells the story of his forced exile, and is shown returning to the site of his deserted village with fellow refugees. In addition, in this series, meetings with interviewees, including Arabs, are often held at a site where past events took place or against the background of the person interviewed. This way Arabs are often presented as attached to their original villages, families, the land they farmed, the olive groves—all emphasizing their historical roots in the country.

Interviews "mediation," i.e., their integration among other components of the text, also differs in the two series, following their different approaches. *POF* employs a variety of means in order to mark the interviewee as "right" or "wrong." Such means are voice-over narration, archival selections, other contradictory interviews, reports of connected events, etc. By combining the interview with these other components it acquires the desired meaning. This way Arabs expressing opinions contrary to the Zionist position can still be interviewed in *POF*, though not many such cases occur. *TK* adopts a different approach represented by many cases in which the "official" Zionist position, sometimes expressed in propaganda films or newsreels, is countered by testimonies of interviewees, including Arabs. Such is the case when a newsreel that boasts of the first happy Independence Day celebrations everywhere is followed by a powerful testimony of an Arab named 'Ali Hamid, originally from al-Ghabissiyya village in the Galilee, who tells how their loyal participation in those celebrations did not prevent the traumatic expulsion of his people from their village more than a year after the war had ended[19] (chapter 11). Generally, the series does not justify one side or the other, but rather juxtaposes interviews to present the complexity of the historical situation.

Iconography

POF's iconography expresses the Zionist ethos to which it adheres: landscapes of an "empty land," prominence of pioneers working the land, and images of Jewish victimhood. Images of Arabs manifest several dimensions. One is the Arab as the authentic native, a living version of the people of the Bible. Arabs are presented in their authentic wear, on their horses or camels, as nomadic shepherds living in tents and women in long veils carrying jugs on their heads. Enchanting romantic paintings of Arabs were made by Bezalel Academy artists from the early decades

19. See Benny Morris, *The Birth of the Palestinian Refugee Problem Revisited* (Cambridge, 2004), 515–16.

of the Zionist enterprise. These images represent the Zionist self-portrayal as a continuation of the Biblical era, with pioneers dressed like Arabs. This also strengthens the concept of the "empty land" ascribed to Zionist founders and connoting that the country was not historically inhabited by Arabs but "waited" for the Zionist pioneers to be redeemed. Similarly, the Arab inhabitants are presented in the series as members of a backward society in need of enlightenment and progress brought by the Jews. This coincides with Western, romantic, orientalist concepts of Arabs as exotic, yet uncivilized "men of the desert,"[20] which is prominent in *POF.*

The series shows that with time, the Zionist settlers tended to be less romantic toward Arabs, as the latter manifested their utter resistance to the Zionist enterprise. Hence another character trait of the Arabs, most relevant and dominant in the context of the 1948 War, is their violent and murderous nature. Throughout the series accumulating images present them as a violent, armed mob setting out to kill Jews, operating in gangs on the hills or along the roads. These images are usually presented in long-distance group shots, sometimes taken from above or from behind, thus rendering Arabs into a faceless mass, dehumanized, estranged in their ethnic attire, suiting the role of the hated, vicious antagonist they play in *POF.* The series reflects the gradual transformation in the Zionist image of Arabs, from the romantic to the violent. These aspects of the iconography of Arabs are typical of the pre-State "pioneers" Israeli cinema of the 1930s (films like *Tzabar, Oded Ha-noded, To a New Life, Work*) and the "national heroic" period of the 1950s and 1960s (*Hill 24 Does Not Answer, They Were Ten, Rebels of the Light*), as well as of Hollywood films about Israel (*Exodus, Cast a Giant Shadow*).[21]

TK's visual representation of Arabs is totally different, practically opposite. Arabs are not seen at all as "people of the Bible," wandering tribes, or primitive villagers. In the very few cases that such imagery is used, it is done to ironically contradict such concepts and those who hold them. Adversely, in chapter 11, when Palestinian poet Mahmoud Darwish, then in exile, reminiscences about his father's home village and mode of life, it is presented as a lost paradise of close connection to nature and the land, a real and pure existence, not at all backward or primitive. Here the series expresses the typical Arab-Palestinian perception of their pre-1948 war existence. Jewish "progress" is criticized in this chapter as supplying modern supermarkets, cars, and villas, but not civil rights to Arabs. Israeli rule is described as paternalistic and orientalist.

The most dramatic contradiction between the two series in the visual representation of Arabs involves the Arab-Jewish conflict and particularly the 1948

---

20. Edward Said, *Orientalism* (New York, 1978).
21. Gertz, *Motion Fiction;* Shohat, *Israeli Cinema.*

War. *TK* presents Arabs as a legitimate party in this conflict, whose voice is heard, whose attachment to the land recognized. *TK* shows Arabs as victims, a role reserved solely for Jews in *POF*. In that series images of Jews wounded or lying killed are common, and Jews are seen training for battle, or fighting, but not as aggressors. In *TK* the roles are often reversed. Thus in chapter 3 it is the Jews who are armed, attacking, faceless inside their jeeps, while the Arabs are shown as human victims: sitting on the ground, covering their faces, old wrinkled men crouching, children running away, men raising their hands in surrender. In chapter 11 descriptions of the war also include Israelis shooting at Arab villages, soldiers herding scared refugees, etc. More imagery of Arab victimhood will be described later, when discussing the Refugee Problem and the Zionist ethos of "Purity of Arms." *TK* portrays Arabs as a suffering, human side in a tragic conflict.

Editing

Adhering to the Zionist ethos, *POF* tends to present binary contradictions between Jews and Arabs. Arab "inferiority" and "backwardness" are thus stressed by juxtaposing them with Jewish mobilization, diligence, and modernity. In chapters 4 and 8, for example, images of Jews energetically tilling the land or erecting buildings are preceded by images of Arabs sitting passively in the field or the old town's native quarter, or performing some agricultural work in an old fashioned way. Similarly, images of peaceful Jewish settlements are followed by those of menacing armed Arabs (chapter 9); Jewish widespread enlistment to the "Jewish Brigade" under British command in WWII is followed by a ridiculed presentation of non-motivated, meager Arab recruitment to the British war effort, and Jewish joy and dancing following the UN resolution on partition of Palestine is juxtaposed with Arab violent riots. Such contrasting editing strengthens the concept of "good," positive Jews, versus "bad" Arabs.

In *TK*, juxtaposing editing is often used not to contrast but to present similarities between Jews and Arabs. The description of the 1948 War shows damage to both sides as well as fear, casualties, and sorrow for losing friends. This similarity represents the series' intent to present an evenhanded approach with a view toward understanding and reconciliation.

Terminology

POF adopts the Zionist terminology: "aliya" (immigration to Israel, literally meaning "ascension"), "settlement," "pioneers," "redemption of the land." The terms "Arabs" and "Jews" are used for a clear separation between the two peoples. Arabs are often termed "aggressors," "enemies," "murderous," "gangs," "rabble," or "mob." The text avoids referring to the connection between Arabs and the land, does not use the terms "Arab settlement" or "Palestinians," and the country is named "Eretz Israel" (the Land of Israel). In chapter 2 the narrator entirely overlooks any Arab attachment to the land by ironically stating: "Palestine was wherever Jewish aspirations were." *TK*'s terminology, by contrast, is more objective and promotes an equal attitude toward Jews and Arabs. Here the "Jewish settlement" and the "Arab settlement" are used. Similarly, "Palestine" and "Palestinians" are frequently used, recognizing the identity of Arabs who had lived in Palestine long before the 1948 War and the refugee problem resulting from this war. Chapter 15, which describes the history of the post-Six-Day War Palestinian terrorism, uses "Palestinian terrorists" but also "Palestinian fighters." The Arab citizens are termed "Israeli Arabs."

Point of View

This category, entitled "focalization" by Genette,[22] refers to the focus of perception, or the perspective from which the story is told. It is most important in directing the spectator to the desired meaning and to identification with the "right" side. The overarching perspective in *POF* is that of the Zionist narrative and Arab interviewees, as shown above, are subjected to this ideology. Paradoxically, by their self-criticism Arab representatives sometimes strengthen the Jewish-Zionist perspective. Thus, Anwar Nusseiba tells in chapter 19 of the disagreements among his colleagues, and how they were even willing to cooperate with the Jews so as to hurt each other. Nusseiba smilingly describes how Arab fighters deserted the Qastel in order to participate in the funeral of their commander Abd al-Qader al-Husseini, enabling its conquest by the Jews without a fight. Arab interviewees testify to fear, personal revenge, murders, and anarchy, which characterized the long Arab strike of 1936 and the three-year long revolt against the Mandate. Thus the image of Arab-Palestinian leadership as disoriented and Arabs as inferior, reckless, ill-advised, treacherous, and murderous is promoted in the series by "reliable witnesses" who know best—the Arab leaders themselves.

The absence of a genuine Arab perspective is conspicuous in all reports of the war events. Thus in chapter 19 the death of the top Arab commander of the Jerusalem front, 'Abd al-Qader al-Husseini, and the deep mourning over him are described by the narrator, with no internal Arab perspective, i.e., a testimony of the Arabs themselves. "Many Arabs felt that an irreplaceable commander was lost, and from now on everything will deteriorate," presumes the omniscient narrator. Reports of other traumatic events of the war, like conquests, killings, and deportation, completely ignore the Arab point of view—perceptual, emotional, or ideological.

In *TK*, the issue of focalization, like other aspects, is more complex. While the overall perspective is basically Zionist, Israeli, and Jewish, the chapters express multiple perspectives. It is essentially a "Rashomon"-like focalization, in which

---

22. Genette, *Narrative Discourse*, 185–211.

events are presented from various points of view, representing narratives of different Israeli social and political groups, including Arabs.[23] Thus, chapters 2 and 3 describing the 1948 War, give voice to the experiences of several representative Israelis, including the Arab deportee Na'um Sam'an, who represents the calamity of the Palestinian refugees. The battle of Haifa and its conquest by the Haganah is an example of a description using a variable, Rashomon-like focalization. It is presented alternately by a Jewish witness, Shraga Har-Gil, who tells of the painful disruption of the Jewish-Arab co-existence in the city, and by the Arab Abd al-Majid 'Alqam, who tells of the traumatic war experiences of Arabs in Haifa.

A surprising example, even shocking to the Jewish spectator, is the report of the fall of the 35 Jewish fighters (known as the Lamed-Heh Platoon) in January 1948, who were assigned with reinforcing the besieged Gush-Etzion south of Bethlehem, killed to the last one by Arab villagers before fulfilling their mission. This traumatic, mythologized event in the Jewish narrative of the war is told, with all its cruel details, by an Arab who took part in the battle. The choice of the enemy's focus of perception here is ideological: it expresses the series' stand that the enemy is human, and his motives, feelings, and point of view should be recognized. It also deliberately avoids emphasizing the Zionist "Few against the Many" theme.

Another case is the occupation of Jaffa, which is described only from the Arab point of view. "Jaffa's fate was determined," states the narrator, followed by a detailed description of the collapse of the town's defense, the massive desertion of the inhabitants, and the pillage by the conquering Jews. The tragedy of the Arabs is the focus here, and not the salvation of nearby Jewish Tel-Aviv, as in *POF*. Building the story from an alternative perspective, *TK* emphasizes parallelism between the fighting parties, as well as the tragic misunderstanding at the basis of the conflict.

Chapter 11, dedicated to the Israeli Arab citizens during the State's first 50 years, also elaborates on issues of the 1948 War and its long-lasting effects. It interviews many Arabs but only three Jews, who, similarly but opposite to the role of Arab interviewees in *POF*, strengthen here the Arab point of view and manifest Jewish incompetence. The chapter fully adopts, and gives considerable space, to the Arab-Palestinian perspective and critical viewpoint toward the Israeli military and political establishment, accompanying it by Arab music thus increasing the

---

23. The delicate balance of perspectives in the series can be exemplified by the case of chapter 15, which describes Palestinian guerrilla and terror acts in the 1970s. The chapter was originally entitled "My country, My country" in Arabic, the title of the Palestinian anthem, a title expressing the Palestinian viewpoint. Due to a vigorous public protest and dispute, the title was changed to "On the path of terror – Biladi, Biladi," thus giving expression and priority to the Israeli viewpoint.

emotional involvement and identification of the spectators. In chapter 11, for example, the singer Amal Murqus appears, singing about Palestinian dream of building a house, in the shade of the vines and the fig tree. Chapter 15 goes further to end with PLO's hymn, "Biladi, Biladi," as the organization's members leave Beirut on a boat in the summer of 1982.

Representation of the Refugee Problem

The refugee problem remains the most crucial issue in the Israeli-Palestinian conflict and, by far, the most traumatic event in the Palestinian memory of the 1948 War. As such, it keeps nurturing Palestinian identity of victimhood and controversial versions of memory and historiography between Israelis and Palestinians as to the causes of the Arab-Palestinian exodus or expulsion from their cities and villages. Here too the different ideological positions of the two series are clearly manifested: while *POF* tries to minimize, even to ignore, any Jewish responsibility for the creation of the refugee problem, *TK* dedicates much more commemorative time to it, and depicts it as a major, complex, painful issue, which the Jewish side should acknowledge.

POF chapter 18 shows groups of both Arabs and Jews in Jerusalem packing and leaving the town as the war breaks out. Despite this similarity the narrator emphasizes that while the Jews "sought shelter in rear areas," the Arabs "left to find shelter in neighboring countries." Thus the connection of those Palestinians to their homeland is minimized, as is their will to stay and defend it. Chapter 19 presents the only documentary film footage in the series of escaping Arab refugees. It illustrates the escape from Haifa following its conquest by the Haganah. The narrator says: "Many escaped even before the first shot was fired, for fear. There was no clear policy: in certain places they were expelled, in others, encouraged to stay." Separating the massive flight from descriptions of traumatic events, such as the massacre in the Arab village of Deir Yassin described earlier in the chapter, the series portrays this phenomenon as voluntary, pointless, and even cowardly. Claiming the absence of clear Jewish policy and yet admitting that there was also expulsion, however, is immediately followed by a tacit denial of such acts by Yigael Yadin, chief operations officer of the Haganah and later the IDF (practically acting-chief of staff for most of the wartime). He testifies that many efforts were made to stop the Arab flight from Haifa, and that his men were ordered to act as "the most humane conquering army." Thus the issue is sealed with the position of the Zionist narrative, which totally denies any responsibility of the Israeli leadership for the creation of the refugee problem.

In *TK* the refugee problem gains much more prominence, addressed in five of the series' 22 chapters. In addition to its extensive discussion as part of the story of the 1948 War in chapters 2 and 3, it is also brought up in chapter 5, describing the attempts of Palestinian refugees to return to their homes in Israel in the 1950s.

Chapter 11 also addresses this issue as part of the experience of Israeli Arabs, and chapter 15 adds the point of view of the Palestinian resistance groups in the 1970s, infrequently defined as guerrilla but more often as terror organizations. It should be noted that the series, focusing on life and events inside Israel, does not address the refugee problem at large, i.e., those living in the neighboring Arab countries.[24]

It is not only the extent of the coverage that makes *TK*'s treatment of this issue so unique in its depth and critical approach but the subjects and imagery chosen to be displayed. Convoys of escaping refugees are repeatedly shown in chapter 3, particularly as part of the descriptions of Jewish occupation of Lydda (Lod), Ramla, and the Galilee. These refugees are not just figures in a crowd; they have faces and voices. Frightened children, old wrinkled men and women sitting on the ground, raising their hands in despair—all shown in close-ups or medium-shots, with some interviewed about their traumatic experience. Unlike *POF*, here the massive escape is clearly connected to Jewish conquests and events such as the Deir Yassin massacre, albeit without explicitly placing the blame on the Jewish forces for the Arab exodus. Not only Arab but Jewish interviewees as well express the perspective of the Palestinians and focus on their disaster. Yaakuba Cohen of the Palmach laments in chapter 2 the end of the bustling, lively Arab community of Haifa, and a commander of a Jewish squad remembers in chapter 3 harsh sights of the thirsty refugees fleeing from the Galilee.

The series draws a comparison between the plight of the Arab refugees and that of Jews in wartime Europe. An excerpt from Golda Meir's diary is read, describing how she found pitas and hot coffee on the table in a deserted house in Haifa, and how it brought back to her memories of similar sights in Jewish towns in Europe. Describing the conquest of Jaffa the narrator explains that deserted Arab houses were seized by Jewish refugees from Europe. Visuals here document Arabs in a wire-fenced camp begging for water, connoting black-and-white images from the Holocaust. Though not explicit, this reflection calls for emotional identification on the part of the Jewish spectator, as well as for moral reconsideration.

The many images of extreme distress of the refugees are accompanied by narration that does not belittle the Arab tragedy or avoid placing much of the blame on the Jewish side. "Conquest was accompanied by many cases of killings, pillaging and massive expulsion of the civilian population," says the narrator in chapter 3. Lydda and Ramla suffered "the first organized expulsion of the war, and though no direct order was issued, the political leadership knew and agreed." "The traumatic memories of the expulsion and the feeling of the homeland rooted

---

24. TK's chapters 15 (Terrorist Organizations) and 21 (The Intifada) refer indirectly to the refugees in the West Bank and Gaza Strip.

in your heart—cannot be erased," says the narrator, representing the Palestinian point of view. *TK* fully displays the complexity of the issue: Jewish responsibility exists, but not always, and not to the same degree everywhere. The overall perception here is that history has turned one people, which had experienced genocide, expulsion, persecution, and exile, into a perpetrator of the expulsion of another people, albeit without clear intention. The two peoples are thus condemned to sustain their respective tragedies.

A major aspect of *TK*'s treatment of the refugee problem is its emphasis on the strong ties between Palestinians and their land. While *POF* avoids as much as possible showing Palestinian life on their land and promotes the image of "The empty land" waiting for its Jewish redeemers, *TK* presents Arab villages and towns, and places interviewees against the background of their family homes and farms. Arabs are shown tilling their fields, picking olives, and talking about their ancestors. The series follows the Palestinian image of the olive tree as a symbol of their deep roots in the land. The series thus dedicates considerable space to the representation of Palestinian post-1948 ethos of rural life as a national symbol.[25]

These "signposts of memory," as Benvenisti[26] defines them, appear in *TK* not only as archival material, but in scenes filmed especially for the series. Hence, in chapters 2 and 3 we watch Na'um Sam'an and his fellow villagers, expelled at the time from Suhmata village in the Galilee, weeding the deserted cemetery and holding a memorial ritual among the ruins. In chapter 11 refugees from Ghabissiyya village hold a similar ritual; 'Ali Hamed and his friends visit the ruined village and point to the sites of their former houses. Refugees from Ikrit in Upper Galilee hold a protest gathering in their empty village, to which, even after 50 years of legal struggle, they are still not allowed to return. These images, accompanying harsh stories about the cruelty of the expulsion, show despairing and helpless men, women, and children, sitting passively in the ruined sites, surrounded by the green scenery. The many individual stories and faces, together with the images that connote an abruptly disrupted historical tradition of attachment to the land, by and large represent the Arab-Palestinians' narratives of their 1948 disaster in the overall story of *TK*.

Representation of Zionist Ethos of the War

The two series treat main aspects of the Zionist ethos differently, which influence their perceptions of the 1948 War. *POF* adheres to the ethos of "the empty land,"

25. Ted Swedenburg, "The Palestinian Peasant as a National Signifier," *Anthropological Quarterly* 63.1 (1990): 18–30.

26. Meron Benvenisti, *Sacred Landscape* (Berkeley, 2000).

thus affirming the legitimacy of the Zionist enterprise: the Jews redeeming the land are fulfilling their right and, since they do not dispossess anyone, any attempt to destroy them or their work is villainous. At the same time the series perpetuates "Jewish victimhood," presenting images of Jews massacred in 1929 in Hebron in an almost identical manner to those of Jews murdered and injured in the Kishinev pogrom of 1903 in Russia. It is always a result of causeless, blind hatred. Victimhood, also in the 1948 War, is reserved almost entirely for Jews: they are killed by the "bad," murderous Arabs.

TK, on the other hand, rejects the concept of "empty land" and extends the concept of victimhood to Arabs as well, describing the Jewish role in the war as one that inflicted on the Arabs injury, death, and expulsion. The two series differ also in their treatment of two central concepts related to the fighting itself: "The few against the many" and "purity of arms."

The Ethos of Heroism: The Few Against the Many

The mythical plot structure of "the few against the many" as the ultimate manifestation of heroism is central to Zionist narrative. Modeled on the Biblical story of David and Goliath, it is connected to the national revival and return of the Jewish people to their land. In *POF* the legitimacy and righteousness of the "few" are unquestioned. It is clear that the Zionists always sought peace with the Arabs and their resort to arms is defensive, an inevitable response to Arab aggression.

The building of the Yishuv's military force is proudly narrated at the end of chapter 6: "The fathers of Zionism refused to believe their eyes; none of them had foreseen that the noble dream of the Jews' return to their homeland means war with the Arabs." Reiterating the military superiority of the Arabs in numbers and arms, the series glorifies the heroism of the Jews in the 1948 War, from bus drivers to inhabitants of towns, kibbutzim, and settlements, and the fighting forces themselves. Uncommitted to the Zionist ethos, *TK* presents a non-binary, complex view of the war, bereft of the ethos of Jewish heroism.

This difference between the two series is clearly demonstrated in the following two cases.

Breaking the Siege Over Jerusalem

POF pays much tribute to Jerusalem, the city of David, the eternal holy city, the symbol of Jews' yearning for their fatherland over the generations, and the core of Zionism. The desperate battle for Jerusalem and its results are therefore particularly meaningful in the narrative of the war. The last chapter of the series elaborates on the harsh realities of the siege and the battle—hunger, people killed by constant shelling, deadly Arab attacks on the convoys to the city, failures of attempts to break through, all of which is reported separately from the Haganah's "Nahshon" operation, which freed the city, albeit only temporarily.

This way a "thematic distance" is opened between the successful operation and anything that can blur its glory. Another element here is forming a block of successful events "building up" toward the imminent victory, regardless of their chronological order: the conquest of the Qastel, the killing of 'Abd al-Qader al-Husseini, and organizing a huge supply convoy to the city. Such structure is meant to create feelings of pride and excitement toward the successful operation at the end of the sequence.

The operation's success is demonstrated by Palmach fighters entering the city on their trucks, waving and smiling, while a nostalgic 1948 war song, "Hen Efshar" (It May Be) is played in the background. They are received with much warmth by the city's Jewish population. The narrator sums up: "The fighters realized just then: they have saved Jerusalem!" Only later in the chapter, within a group of other short war reports, is it mentioned that Jerusalem fell under siege again, this time by the Jordanian army. The series thus presents glorious heroism, reinforcing the audience's emotional identification with it.

In *TK*, the events related to the battle for Jerusalem are described in chronological order, including losses and failed operations as well as victorious moments, like the conquest of the Qastel. They are interrupted by other events that happened in the country during those months, and do not form a thematic block of any kind. *TK* employs the same film as *POF* to show the Palmach's successful breakthrough into the besieged city. It also introduces an emotional moment, as one of the fighters who entered the city describes the event, choking with tears. Yet the narrator immediately cools the excitement down saying: "but operation 'Nahshon' did not achieve all its goals; the road to Jerusalem was blocked again." Heroism is recognized, but not turned into a glorious myth.

The Battle of Mishmar Haemek

This kibbutz in the Jezreel Valley was attacked by the Army of Deliverance commanded by Fawzi al-Qauqji in early April 1948. Here too the two series use the same archival color film that was shot by one of the members of the kibbutz during the attack. The film shows the ongoing battle, shots and explosion of shells, ruined houses, the defenders, men and women running for shelter in the trenches, playing chess or making coffee in moments of intermission. The different messages the two series derive from the film disprove the common saying that photos speak for themselves. *POF* dedicates considerably more time to the event than *TK*. Its description is composed of extensive narration and a long interview with one of the defenders, with illustrations and highlights from the film. "We had the feeling that this battle would decide the fate of Israel," tells the interviewee and adds, "We decided: we do not move from here!" The narration emphasizes the drama of the struggle of the poorly equipped few against the heavily armed many: "In Mishmar Ha-'Emek there were no shelters, nor arms to counter the Arab artillery; so the solution was to get out there and assault the aggressors face to face!" The description is concrete and emotional. The courage of the kibbutz members defending their home is fully displayed. "After pushing Qauqji away they went to bury their dead; while mourning they learned of the victory in Jerusalem," the narrator sums up. By using drama, contrasts and pathos, *POF* turns the battle into a glorious myth promoting the ethos of Zionist national heroism.

TK, in contrast, is content with a much shorter and objective report of the battle. There are no eye-witness testimonies, just the film and narration: "Battles over Mishmar Ha-'Emek lasted for ten days and the heavy shelling completely destroyed the houses. Positions changed hands—Arabs [capturing them] in the day and Jews at night. Eventually, Qauqji withdrew." Narration is factual, devoid of any emotional drama. Instead of contrasts, there is even some symmetry between the adversaries. The Jewish perspective is not emphasized (although the film itself does promote it). The final victory does not express the heroism of the "few against the many," as the choice of "withdrew" and not "was pushed away" clearly shows.

In its complex and multi-focal presentation of the 1948 War, *TK* examines the realities behind the myth of Jewish heroism and gives voice to the horror and existential anxiety defenders and fighters felt. This is attested by the descriptions and testimonies of the evacuation of the children from Nitzanim in the south, the desperate fight in the Jewish Quarter in the Old City of Jerusalem, or during the battle of Degania against the invading Syrian army. Settlements such as Yad-Mordechai and Nitzanim fought heroically and sustained heavy losses but had to evacuate their positions and surrender, respectively. Other settlements, like Degania and Negba, stood the fight and became heroic myths. However, in all cases the price was heavy and the trauma immense. Heroism won the war, but the pathos, enthusiasm, and unanimity that characterize its presentation in *POF* are lacking here.

The Ethos of "Purity of Arms"

The total binary perception of the two fighting sides in *POF*, describing Jews as just and inferior in men and arms, and Arabs as the complete opposite, excludes the possibility of presenting Jewish fighters as anything but noble, humane, and moral in employing their arms. Aggression, cruelty, and atrocities are associated only with Arabs. *TK*, on the other hand, presents complex war circumstances, and allocates extensive space to acts of conquest, killing, expulsion, and looting performed by Jews, particularly in the later period of the war. "Who talks of purity of arms?" asks Meir Davidson, a senior commander in the Givati Brigade and adds: "There are no pure arms. In war you fight to survive and you shoot anything that moves." "Soldiers of the young army had to cope with issues of morality and conscience, without directions from the political leadership . . . sometimes they broke the moral code of 'purity of arms,'" admits the narrator in chapter 3.

Jewish awareness of this problem already existed at the time. In that chapter, which shows the harsh realities of the expulsion of Arabs from Lod, Ramla, and the Galilee, it is told that Ben-Gurion, worried about the rumors of massacres and looting, ordered to distribute to the soldiers a poem by Nathan Alterman, written in the wake of the conquest of Beer-Sheva, denouncing any such breach of morals. He himself read the poem aloud in the Knesset.[27]

A test case of the different way each series adopts about the "purity of arms" is their treatment of the Deir Yassin massacre, which has since become the symbol of Jewish victimization of Arabs in that war. In *POF,* visuals show a map of the area where the village of Deir Yassin was located and headlines of newspapers with the following narration: "Of all the events of spring 1948 it is the conquest of the small village of Deir Yassin which won publicity. In that operation performed by the dissenter organizations of Etzel and Lehi, 250 Arabs lost their lives. Newspapers in Israel and abroad reported an indiscriminate massacre of men, women, and children. The official Jewish leadership strongly denounced the perpetrators of the Deir Yassin massacre. Etzel and Lehi rejected the accusations and insisted that all Arabs had been killed in the heat of the battle."[28]

This description is condensed, summarizing the event without revealing human feelings. The place and its past inhabitants are merely named, and no witness is heard. Arab perspective is completely missing. The rhetoric minimizes the importance of the case and tacitly doubts whether it took place at all with the official Zionist leadership acquitted of any responsibility. The denial of the conquerors closes the report and remains unanswered.

In *TK,* the report opens with an illustrative film of the place today (Givat Shaul in west Jerusalem), then an archive excerpt showing escaping refugees. In between, the refugee Sam'an is interviewed, sitting in a green field by the side of a woman and an old man wearing a Kufiya (Arab head dress). At the end Yigal Naor, then a junior commander in the Palmach, speaks. A whining, sad Arab music accompanies the images. The narration and the testimonies of the interviewees support each other, and create a grim picture of the event. Narration: "120 men, women and children were shot in cold blood during the conquest of the village . . . the horrifying descriptions of the massacre . . . increased the panic flight of Arab residents." Underlining that Deir Yassin was not an exception, Sam'an, an Israeli Palestinian from the Galilee, speaks of other massacres: "On such a day,

27. Museum of Eretz Israel Exhibition Catalogue, *Alterman/A Poet in His Town: His 100th Anniversary* (Tel-Aviv, 2010), 15, 108.

28. Early reports published by Jewish, British, and Arab media based on the Red Cross mentioned 254 dead Arabs. In fact, the real scope of Arabs killed in the village was far lower: 100-120 according to Morris, *Birth of the Arab Refugee Problem,* 238, which was adopted by *TK;* and even lower according to a Palestinian documentary: Muhammad Bakri (producer), *1948* (1998).

when they come and slaughter 50–60 of us . . . and in Safsaf they shoot 40 people—a man is scared!" Naor: "We had instructions not to hurt women and children, but they could not know it. As for men—everyone was a fighter as far as we were concerned."

The extensive commemorative time dedicated by *TK* to this event, and the variety of materials used in its construction, testify to its importance for the series' representation of the 1948 War. The horrific realities of the massacre are not questioned but emphasized. The internal perspective of the Arab refugee creates a strong identification on the part of the spectator, and the background chosen for the interview strengthens the perception of Arabs as helpless victims who were uprooted from their land. In this case, those who are to blame are far from being humane, just, or of pure arms.

Conclusion

The 1948 War is a central subject of both series, *POF* and *TK*. In the first, it is treated as proof, in the spirit of Zionist ideology, of the transformation of the Jewish people from victimhood to heroic, national revival in its homeland. In the latter series it is a formative and heroic event, albeit traumatic, the consequences of which still shape, for better or for worse, political, military, and social processes in Israel. A central question posed above concerns the place each series' presentation of the 1948 War occupies in the changing Israeli social and ideological scene, from a dominant monolithic Zionist narrative to a multi-vocal Israeli perspective connoting less or no commitment to the master-commemorative Zionist narrative.

This study shows that *POF* fully adheres to the classical Zionist narrative, employing all available constructive means to promote it. Surprisingly, at the time of its first broadcast in 1981, the series evoked critical voices, opposing its "extensive expression of the Arab standpoint." Moreover, both Katzburg, a historian and one of the series' advisors, and Rosenthal, one of its chief producers, justified that criticism. Katzburg admitted that the series had indeed made an effort to present a fair and balanced picture,[29] and Rosenthal opined that the Arab point of view was over-emphasized in the series and praised "the high objectivity of the series and openness of its approach," which "allows us to correct certain stereotypes of Israelis and Arabs" and "lets us think in a deeper way about the plight of the Arab refugees."[30] These responses evidently ignore the negative role of Arabs in the series and the complete de-legitimization of their perspective.

29. Netanel Katzburg, "Following the Series 'Pillar of Fire' on Israeli Television (an interview),"*History Teacher Discourse* 14 (1981): 7.

30. Alan Rosenthal, "Israel Documentary and 'Pillar of Fire,'" *Studies in Visual Communication* 8 (1982): 80–2.

It is also a clear example of how much reception of televised texts is dependent on time and context.

It is possible that the general state of "historical consciousness" prevalent at the time of the series' production, in which the Zionist enterprise had to be re-justified, can explain how such a cinematically anachronistic text could be produced in the late 1970s. *POF* connects itself in fact to the early national-heroic cinema characterizing the pioneers' films of the pre-state period and the heroic films of the 1950s and 1960s. In that cinema the working and fighting Israeli collective is at the center, while Arabs are assigned the role of the "other" and the "villain." It should be also noted that *POF* was produced just as national collective norms were weakening, the "Palestinian Wave" appeared in cinema and films about the "other," and the "different" began to express a variety of critical narratives, all of which is absent from the series' text.

The creators of the series must have been aware of these processes though it remains unclear how they perceived the impact of these tendencies on their audience. Describing the road of Zionism to statehood the text they created fully adhered, as if on a pedestal, to the ethos of the Zionist enterprise. This they realized by producing a series that is a model of academic expertise and archival research, combined with dramatic construction and emotional intensity. In retrospect, it was a last opportunity for Israel's single television channel to enable its spectators to experience the same unbridled enthusiasm and pride that was strongly cultivated by the 1948 generation that witnessed the horrors of the war and the birth of the State of Israel.

TK's starting point is obviously different. Its goal is to critically examine central aspects of the Zionist ethos and its realization over the years. Of these aspects, the 1948 War and the treatment of the Arabs received extensive and multi-faceted scrutiny. The series presents a perfect mirror-image to that presented in *POF*. All the constructive means—plot structure, temporality, interviews, iconography, narration, and perspective—are consistently used to criticize the Zionist ethos of the war and to express side by side the Arab-Palestinian narrative. This line of presentation characterizes the attitude of *TK* not only to the 1948 War, but all along the series' chapters related to the conflict. *TK* accuses both Israel and the Arabs of adopting a militant stand, ignoring the other side's point of view and making wrong choices, which time and again missed the chances for a solution of the conflict and achieving peace. The context that enabled *TK* to do that includes the "new history" debate in the late 1980s to the early 1990s, the Oslo process, and the rise of a Labor-Meretz government in 1992, which not only signed the Oslo Accords and led a process of Israeli withdrawal from parts of the West Bank and Gaza Strip, but also tried to acknowledge—without success—new historical narrative of the conflict with the Palestinians.

Precisely because the Arab-Israeli conflict is still raging and the Palestinians perceive their 1948 catastrophe (*nakba*) as deliberately perpetrated by the Zionists—hence their demand that Israel take full responsibility for it—any

discussion of the war, and especially the origins of the Palestinian refugee problem, is bound to be controversial and ideologically loaded with ethical questions
of justice, legitimacy, and guilt. *TK*'s attitude indeed aroused a heated public
debate among Israeli Jews. Not only was the series screened at the height of the
Oslo process, which tore Israeli society apart along ideological lines, the debate
was further fueled by the introduction, almost at the same time, of new history
textbooks for high schools inspired by the "new history."

Particularly rightwing spokesmen and periodicals fiercely criticized the books
and the series, raising complaints similar, though on a larger scale, to those made
against *POF* at the time. The debate was conducted in the daily newspapers, in the
Executive Board of Israel Broadcasting Authority, the Ministry of Education, on
radio and television, and in partisan periodicals such as the rightwing *Ha-'Uma*
(The Nation) and the leftist *Mitzad Sheni* (On the Other Side), particularly around
March 1998, when controversial chapters of *TK* were screened. Indeed, giving
space to elements of the Palestinian narrative of 1948 on an official TV channel
could hardly take place without provoking a public controversy, even at the apex
of the Israeli-Palestinian Oslo process. Interestingly enough, despite being nearly
two decades apart, both series came under similar critique and protests over 1948.
Still, the concept of what "expressing the Palestinian narrative" means has changed radically. Israel's "historical consciousness" has indeed evolved significantly in
time, as represented by the very production of *TK*, yet the debate it triggered
exemplified how mythical memory competes with historiography in the process of
forming "collective memory."

TK's bold critical attitude toward the 1948 War and its impact on the conflict
notwithstanding, it does not question the legitimacy of Israel or the Zionist vision.
It is thus depicted by radical non-Zionist critics,[31] as still remaining within the
boundaries of the Zionist narrative. Nonetheless, the series does challenge Zionist-
Israeli founding myths and reexamines the process of Jewish national revival in a
way that defines it as a pioneer on the small screen and a true revisionist historical
documentary.

BOSMAT GARAMI is author of "Chronology and Ideology: Temporal
Structuring in Israeli Historical Documentary Series," *Journal of European
Television History and Culture*, and "The Duality of 'Normality': Representations
of Tel-Aviv in Three Historic-Documentary Series," *Kesher*.

31. Ilan Pappe, "Israeli Television's Fiftieth Anniversary '*Revival*' Series: A Post-Zionist
View?" *Journal of Palestine Studies* 27.4 (1998): 99–105.

2   Israel's Publications Agency and the 1948 Palestinian Refugees

Rafi Nets-Zehngut

Introduction

Nations involved in an intractable conflict usually present a biased *official memory* of the conflict. To fit their interests, such memory portrays these nations positively and their rivals negatively. As such, it plays an important role in the conflict by affecting the psychological and behavioral reactions of the parties toward their rivals. Therefore, such memory is of importance for scholarly research as attested by the blooming research literature in recent years on memory, especially in the context of conflict, war, and peace.[1]

Israel's intractable conflict with the Palestinians and the Arab states is by no means exceptional in Israel's quest for legitimacy and self-righteousness, among others, by producing and disseminating its own memory about the causes and development of the conflict. One of Israel's major official institutions endowed with the production of such a memory for the Israelis is the Information Center (*merkaz ha-hasbara*),[2] specifically the Publications Agency (*sherut ha-pirsumim*), one of the Center's units. The displacement and exodus of more than half of the Arab population from their homes during the 1948 Palestine War has remained the core issue shaping the conflict and the identities and policies of the parties concerned with far-reaching implications on its possible resolution. No other issue in the Israeli-Palestinian conflict has so strongly shaped the parties' collective image of "self" and "other" and become identified with Palestinian claims of victimhood, injustice, and historical wrongdoing on Israel's part.

This chapter differs significantly in both data and analysis from an earlier version of this study. See Rafi Nets-Zehngut, "The Israeli National Information Center and Collective Memory of the Israeli-Arab Conflict," *The Middle East Journal* 62.4 (2008): 653–70.

1. Patrick Devine-Wright, "A Theoretical Overview of Memory and Conflict," in *The Role of Memory in Ethnic Conflict*, ed. Ed Cairns and Michael Roe (New York, 2003), 9–33; Jay Winter, "Thinking about Silence," in *Shadows of War—A Social History of Silence in the Twentieth Century*, ed. Efrat Ben-Zeev, Ruth Ginio, and Jay Winter (Cambridge, 2010), 3–31.

2. Apart from informative publications and movies, the Center also conducted national events and internal journeys.

The War of 1948 (2016): 51–74, DOI: 10.2979/warof1948.0.0.04

In view of the perpetuation of the Palestinian refugee problem, the growing international recognition of the Palestinian claims for statehood after 1967, and, as of the late 1980s, the broadening awareness of Israel's active role in the 1948 Palestinian disaster and its ominous significance for the self-righteousness of the Israeli society, and no less, Israel's moral standing and international legitimacy, the question arises: how did Israel shape its own official memory about this issue? More specifically, how did the state cope with new claims—both political and academic—challenging its own Zionist memory concerning the 1948 exodus? These questions are addressed here by scrutinizing the publications produced and disseminated by the Agency, Israel's official instrument for producing public knowledge about the state's political and social history and identity. The chapter explores the Agency's narrative of the 1948 Palestinian exodus from its advent to the early 2000s, as well as the institutional and political factors that shaped the dynamics of its construction.

Methodologically, the research period encompasses approximately 50 years—from the early 1950s to 2003—when the Agency was transformed into the Information Headquarters [hereafter "the Headquarters"] and its activities were significantly reduced. The findings are based on the Agency's publications as well as interviews with its senior officials. The interviews were conducted mostly as in-depth, semi-structured interviews,[3] in order to explore the modus operandi of the Agency and the production of the official version. All surviving directors and two former employees of the Center/Agency and the authors of two of its publications were interviewed.[4]

Twenty publications were examined for this study, all in Hebrew; they were traced in the Headquarters' offices and in various archives, as well as in private and public libraries. Their content analysis[5] mainly focused on narrative about the causes and process of the exodus. The historical narratives on the 1948 Palestinian exodus are largely represented by a continuum with the Zionist and Palestinian contradictory master-narratives on each end, and others, comprised more or less of elements of each of those in between. For the purposes of analysis in this chapter, we discern two such mixed types of narrative namely, a Zionist-critical narrative, close to the Zionist one, and a *critical/balanced* narrative somewhere in the middle.[6] According to the Zionist narrative—the Palestinians fled voluntarily, mainly because of public appeals of their leadership and of Arab states to leave

---

3. Sarah Tracy, *Qualitative Research Methods* (Chichester, 2013), 130–56.

4. See list of interviewees in Appendix.

5. Kimberly Neuendorf, *The Content Analysis Guidebook* (Thousand Oaks, CA, 2001).

6. Rafi Nets-Zehngut, "Major Events and the Collective Memory of Conflicts," *International Journal of Conflict Management* 24.3 (2013): 209–30.

their localities to facilitate the invasion by the Arab armies.[7] According to the Zionist-critical narrative, the vast majority of the Palestinians left voluntarily, with only an insignificant number of them expelled.[8] According to the critical narrative (often titled, since the late 1980s, "post-Zionist"), some of the Palestinians left voluntarily (e.g., due to societal collapse, fear and helplessness, and calls of leadership for temporary departure), while many others were expelled by the Jewish militias and later by the Israeli military forces.[9] According to the Palestinian narrative, the Palestinians were forced by the Zionist/Israeli forces to leave their homes as part of a pre-meditated ethnic cleansing.[10]

Other aspects of the Agency's narrative addressed in the content analysis are, for example, the type of localities discussed (e.g., large or small), the extent of discussion of the exodus (e.g., length), how the expulsions were addressed (e.g., using euphemism or diminishing their importance), and the sources that were mentioned in support of the narratives presented.

The chapter begins with a discussion of relevant theoretical aspects of collective memory and conflict, followed by an overview of the inclusive Israeli collective memory of the exodus. It then describes the *modus operandi* of the Agency followed by the main part of the chapter, namely representations of the causes and process of the exodus. The conclusions discuss some insights about the dynamics of this memory.

Collective Memory and Conflict

Collective memory is generally defined as representations of the past of a group that are collectively adopted.[11] These representations relate to major events, which are of special importance to the collective,[12] and they take the form of narratives.

7. Shmuel Katz, *Land of Contestation—Reality and Imagination in the Land of Israel* (Tel-Aviv, 1972), 24 [Hebrew].

8. Aharon Liskovsky (Layish), "The Present Absentees in Israel," *Hamizrach He-Hadash* 10.3 (1960): 186–92; Mary Syrkin, "The Arab Refugees—A Zionist View," *Commentary* 40.1 (1966): 23–30.

9. Benny Morris, *The Birth of the Palestinian Refugee Problem 1947–1949* (Cambridge, 1987), 286–96.

10. Walid Khalidi, "Why Did the Palestinians Leave?" *Middle East Forum* 35.7 (1959): 21–4; "Why Did the Palestinians Leave, Revisited," *Journal of Palestine Studies* 34.2 (2005): 42–54; Nur Masalha, *Expulsion of the Palestinians: The Concept of "Transfer" in Zionist Political Thought 1882–1948* (Washington, DC, 1992); Rafi Nets-Zehngut, "The Israeli and Palestinian Collective Memories of Their Conflict: Comparing Their Characteristics, Determinants and Implications," *Journal of World Affairs* 20.2 (2014): 103–21.

11. Wolf Kansteiner, "Finding Meaning in Memory: Methodological Critique of Collective Memory Studies," *History and Theory* 41.2 (2002): 179–97.

12. Nets-Zehngut, "Major Events," 212.

Collective memory consists of two main types. First, the *popular* memory, defined as representations of the past held by the society members[13] including tribes and ethno-national communities without their own state, which is often expressed via public opinion surveys. It significantly influences the psychological (e.g., emotions, attitudes, motivations, and national identity) and behavioral reactions of the people holding it, and therefore accorded great importance.[14] The second, the *official* one—defined as representations of the past adopted by the formal institutions of the state. This memory is manifested via formal outputs such as state publications, national celebrations, national anthems, sites and monuments, curriculum and textbooks in the educational system, and museums.[15] Political leaders and state officials are aware of these products' potential impact on the popular memory and, regardless of the regime they serve—authoritarian or democratic—they employ vast state resources to attain this purpose. They aim to encourage the societal institutions to produce publications and other outputs, which may impact the popular memory of the citizens.[16]

Collective memory relates, inter alia, to political conflicts with which scholarly research is most interested. Collective memory of a *conflict* consists of the narratives that describe the events that led to the conflict and its course. Typically, its dominant narrative is selective, simplistic, and biased, and portrays in a dichotomous manner righteous "self" versus evil "other."[17] This typical narrative is functional during the climax of intractable conflict, since it provides each party with the socio-psychological basis needed to meet the enormous challenges that such a conflict poses. It explains to the people why they are asked to sacrifice during the conflict, justifies the conduct of their country, delegitimizes the rival, and motivates the people to be patriotic and support the state during the conflict. Such narrative, however, also inhibits de-escalation of the conflict, its peaceful resolution, and reconciliation between the parties.[18] The discussion regarding

13. Konstantinos Nikoloutsos, "Reviving the Past: Cinematic History and Popular Memory in the 300 Spartans," *Classical World* 106.2 (2013): 261–83.

14. Dario Paez and James Liu, "Collective Memory of Conflicts," in *Intergroup Conflicts and Their Resolution: A Social Psychological Perspective,* ed. Daniel Bar-Tal (New York, 2011), 105–24.

15. James Wertsch, "Blank Spots in Collective Memory: A Case Study of Russia," *The Annals of the American Academy of Political and Social Science* 617 (2008): 58–71.

16. Nets-Zehngut, "Israeli Information Center," 655.

17. Daniel Bar-Tal, Neta Oren, and Rafi Nets-Zehngut, "Socio-Psychological Analysis of Conflict-Supporting Narratives: A General Framework," *Journal of Peace Research* 51.5 (2014): 662–75.

18. Daniel Bar-Tal and Gavriel Salomon, "Israeli-Jewish Narratives of the Israeli-Palestinian Conflict: Evolvement, Contents, Functions and Consequences," in *Israeli and Palestinian Narratives of Conflict: History's Double Helix,* ed. Robert Rothberg (Bloomington, IN, 2006), 19–46; Robert Rotberg, "Building Legitimacy through Narrative," ibid., 1–18.

collective memory in general, and of conflicts in particular, is by and large true also regarding *official* memory of *conflicts*.[19]

The research literature about official memory of a conflict is broadly interested in official institutions and authorities, rarely conducting a systematic study of the products of official agencies in charge of disseminating information to the wide public. Moreover, the explanatory aspect of studies regarding such memory is often based on narrow circumstantial and external evidence without first-hand information from the figures determining the modus operandi of the given official institution. Thus, the findings are somewhat invalidated, questioning the extent to which the examined publications, or the staff behind them, represent the institution's entire product of official memory.[20]

This section addresses these lacunas and analyzes the narrative fostered by Israel's main official institution assigned to produce knowledge for the public about the 1948 exodus. The study examines *all* the Agency's publications produced throughout its period of operation and, in addition, uses interviews with the Agency's senior staff whose contribution to our understanding of the findings was irreplaceable.

Israel and the Palestine Conflict

The Israeli-Arab/Palestinian conflict has lasted for about a century while causing severe human and material losses to the parties involved. Following the 1936–39 Arab Revolt it became the uppermost factor shaping the Jewish (and later Israeli) existence, ideology, and identity. From the outset, Israel's leaders were aware of the important role of their people's popular memory of the conflict, hence the state undertook to disseminate the Zionist narrative about the conflict among its citizens.[21] Generally, this was a typical self-serving narrative of conflict, selective and biased, presenting a simplistic manner of events in a black-and-white way. It blamed the Arabs/Palestinians for the outbreak of hostilities in the wake of the 29 November 1947 UN Partition Resolution and its escalation to an all-out war while portraying Israelis positively as peace-loving, morally superior, and victims of the conflict.

A central element in Israel's historical narrative of the conflict refers to the causes of the 1948 exodus and the Palestinian refugee problem. This issue is,

19. Taner Akcam, "Facing History: Denial and the Turkish National Security Concept," in Ben-Ze'ev, Ginio, and Winter, *Shadows of War*, 173–80; Brian Havel, "In Search of a Theory of Public Memory: The State, the Individual, and Marcel Proust," *Indiana Law Journal* 80.3 (2005): 605–726.

20. Carolyn Boyd, "The Politics of History and Memory in Democratic Spain," *The Annals of the American Academy of Political and Social Science* 617 (2008): 133–48; Catherine Epstein, "The Production of 'Official Memory' in East Germany: Old Communists and the Dilemmas of Memoir-Writing," *Central European History* 32.2 (1999): 181–201.

21. Mordechai Bar-On, "The Struggle Over the War Memories," in *The War of Independence 1948–1949—Revisited, Part II*, ed. Alon Kadish (Tel-Aviv, 2004), 967–1003 [Hebrew].

especially due to its deliberate preservation by the Arab world, of great political, psychological, and social importance for both parties.[22] Since 1948, the Zionist narrative not only took no responsibility for the exodus, but also attributed it solely to the Palestinians themselves and the Arab states.[23] This narrative was widely disseminated by all available means including the educational system,[24] the mass media—most of which represented political parties until the early 1990s, the academic institutions, newspapers, publishing houses, and the IDF.[25]

Early Israeli testimonies about expulsion of Palestinians were published in limitedly circulated forums already during the war,[26] and non-Israeli Jewish scholars published critical studies of the 1948 War as early as the late 1950s.[27] Some Israeli-Jews published memoirs of 1948 along similar lines in the late 1960s[28] but it was notably as of the late-1970s that challenges to the dominant Zionist narrative became increasingly apparent in Israel, ascribed, inter alia, to the shocking impact of the 1973 War on Israeli consensus on national security. The critical discourse on 1948 in Israel came in the form of memoirs,[29] some of which

22. Ian Lustick, "Negotiating Truth: The Holocaust, Lehavdil, and Al-Nakba," *Journal of International Affairs* 60.1 (2006): 52–77; Rafi Nets-Zehngut, "Palestinian Autobiographical Memory Regarding the 1948 Palestinian Exodus," *Political Psychology* 32.2 (2011): 271–95.

23. Rafi Nets-Zehngut, "The Israeli Memory of the Palestinian Refugee Problem," *Peace Review* 24.2 (2012): 187–94.

24. Ruth Firer, "The Presentation of the Israeli-Palestinian Conflict in Israeli History and Civics Textbooks," in *The Israeli-Palestinian Conflict in History and Civics Textbooks of Both Nations,* ed. Ruth Firer and Sami Adwan (Hanover, 2004), 21–96; Eli Podeh, *The Arab-Israeli Conflict in History Textbooks (1948–2000)* (Westport, CT, 2002), 105–10.

25. Daniel Bar-Tal, *Living in Conflict: A Psychological-Social Analysis of the Jewish Society in Israel* (Jerusalem, 2007), 62 [Hebrew]; Nets-Zehngut, "The Israeli Memory."

26. Avi Yiftah [Shmariahu Gutman], "Lod Goes to Exile," *Mi-Bifnim* 13.3 (1948): 452–61.

27. Don Peretz, *Israel and the Palestine Arabs* (Washington, DC, 1958); Ronny Gabbay, *A Political Study of the Arab-Jewish Conflict—The Arab Refugee Problem (A Case Study)* (Geneva and Paris, 1959).

28. Uri Avnery, *The Seventh Day War* (Tel-Aviv, 1969); Yitzhak Tischler, *Last on the Ridge* (Tel-Aviv, 1970).

29. For a review of such memoires, and newspaper articles containing testimonies of Jewish 1948 War veterans, see: Rafi Nets-Zehngut, "The Role of Direct-Experience People in Promoting Transitional Justice: The Israeli Case," in *The Performance of Memory as Transitional Justice,* ed. E. Bird and F. Ottanelli (Cambridge, 2015), 115–32. See, Gil Keisary, "I was the Operation Officer who Issued the Operation Order in Hirbet Hazaz," *Ma'ariv,* 17 February; Moshe Carmel, "The Distorted Face of the War of Independence," *Davar,* 19 February; "Who was Expelled, How and Why," *Davar,* 10 March 1978 [all in Hebrew]. Most notable was Yitzhak Rabin's memoirs attesting to the expulsion from Lydda and Ramla, the largest single case in the war. The description of the expulsion was censored from the 1979 version of the book but leaked to the media. It was only published in a new edition after Rabin's assassination. Yitzhak Rabin, *The Rabin Memoirs* (Berkeley, 1996), 383–4.

appeared in the printed media,[30] including revelations made by small ultra-leftist groups.[31] The growing exposure of Israelis to the critical narrative was also nurtured by the public controversies triggered by the publication of fictional literature. A notable case is the debate on S. Yizhar's story "Khirbet Khiz'ah," describing a deliberate expulsion of Palestinians from their village in 1948, following its publication in 1949, and again over the screening of a cinematic version of the story in late 1978 by Israel's single state-owned television channel.[32] By the late 1970s, the Zionist narrative of "no-expulsion" had been increasingly challenged by a rather complex version of the Palestinian exodus—the critical narrative.

The late 1980s witnessed the commencement of a revisionist history of the birth of Israel commonly identified with the "New Historians." Employing the newly released Israeli official archives on 1948 and adopting a critical approach to the Zionist narrative of the 1948 War, the new historiography targeted central elements of this narrative defined as "myths," a primary one of which was the causes for the 1948 exodus, adopting the critical narrative. Hence, a 1987 comprehensive study by historian Benny Morris presented a critical narrative regarding the exodus. While refuting the Arab claims that the exodus was the result of a Zionist master plan to expel the Palestinians, Morris provided ample evidence that the exodus of Arab-Palestinians was at least partly the result of expulsion. Furthermore, as of June 1948 Israel adopted a policy, which was only partly implemented, of preventing the return of the refugees to their homes in the territories under its control.[33] The new historiography, especially Morris's study, triggered an intense debate in Israeli academia, media, and the public in general touching on foundational issues of the morality and legitimacy of the state, succinctly phrased by Morris's piercing question "Was Israel born in sin?"[34] The juxtaposition of the new historiography with the Intifada, which broke out in late 1987, rendered this debate all the more critical implying a direct line of Israeli unjust policies toward the Palestinians between 1948 and the present.[35]

---

30. Especially salient, since the 1950s, was the maverick weekly *Haolam Hazeh*, edited by Uri Avnery.

31. For example, Matzpen and the Alternative Information Center.

32. Anita Shapira, "Between Memory and Forgetting," in *Making Israel*, ed. Benny Morris (Ann Arbor, MI, 2010), 88–113.

33. Morris, *The Birth of the Palestinian Refugee Problem*, 286–96.

34. Morris, "The New Historiography: Israel Confronts its Past," *Tikkun* 3.6 (1988): 19–23, 99–102.

35. Shapira, "Between Memory and Forgetting," 94.

The critical societal publications—mostly those of the New Historians— strongly challenged the official Zionist narrative of the exodus, challenging the state apparatus under discussion to cope with it.[36]

The Publications Agency—Objectives, Role, and Performance

The Information Center, with the Agency as part of it, was founded in the early 1950s as part of the Prime Minister's Office. Between 1967 and 1977, the Agency was affiliated with various ministries, and from 1978 a part of the Ministry of Education. Since the early 1990s, the Center's budget was reduced due to budget-ary restrictions determined by the Ministry of Finance. In 2004, its title was changed to the Information Headquarters. Its staff was drastically reduced (from 80 people to only 6), as well as its responsibilities[37] and its editors reduced from 11 in the 1970s to 2 in 2003.[38]

The Center's main aims were to provide the Israeli public with information about the activities of the various ministries, to nourish the Jewish and democratic character of the state, to enhance the connection between the Jewish citizens and the Diaspora, and to strengthen the attachment and the contribution of the citizens to the state (mainly in the context of the conflict). To achieve these aims, it dealt mainly with the topics related to the Israeli society, science development, the history of the Jewish nation, the Zionist movement, Israel's foundation, and the conflict.[39] A paragraph from one of the Agency's 1971 publications typifies the official attitude to the conflict:

> Parallel to the hot war the Arabs are conducting against us, along the borders and in terror activities against civilians, an Arab propaganda war is taking place around the world. This Arab propaganda . . . is aimed against the State of Israel and the Jewish nation . . . [T]he purpose of this booklet is to strengthen the recognition of the Israeli youth in the justness of our basic standpoint, also so that he can cope with the "propaganda war" when he will be required to do so.[40]

The Center used various units, which dealt with organizing tours, producing films, holding exhibitions and events, and producing publications.[41] The publications— books, booklets, and flyers were produced by the Agency, written by its staff or by

---

36. Rafi Nets-Zehngut and Daniel Bar-Tal, "Transformation of the Official Memory of Conflicts: A Tentative Model," *International Journal of Politics, Culture and Society* 27.1 (2014): 67–91.

37. Interviews with Braverman, Shatz; Doron Shohet, "The Information is on its Way," *Me'et Le'et* 2 (1996): 1.

38. Interviews with Braverman, Ofaz, and Shatz.

39. Interviews with Ofaz and Braverman; *Government Yearbooks*, "The Information Center," *1960–61* (1961), 151–4; *1997–98* (1998), 235–40.

40. Rafael Ruppin, *Us, Them, and the Land of Israel* (Jerusalem, 1971), 5.

41. Interviews with Braverman, Shohet; "The Information Center," 1997–8, 235–40.

external authors (e.g., scholars, war veterans, or journalists), who were chosen, among other criteria, on the assumption that they will write in an "appropriate manner" (from the standpoint of the state). They were distributed among students and teachers in the educational system, tour guides, journalists, institutions of higher education, lecturers, the IDF, Israelis traveling or living abroad, the Jewish Agency, and the public in general (different types of publications were distributed to different audiences during different periods). There are no data on numbers of copies of these publications or on their scope of distribution to specific sectors.

The Rigidity of Official Memory

From its foundation to 2004, the mode of operation of the Agency/Center remained unchanged. In the first decades after the Center's foundation, including a long period when Ya'acov Shatz served as the Director of the Agency and later the Center (1961–96), the Agency strictly adhered to the Zionist line. Shatz attested: "Usually we were very very loyal . . . to the official line of publicity . . . so it is true that we got a reputation of 'writing on behalf of' [the state . . .]. Everybody that works in the Information Center works for the state. There is nothing to do about this."[42] In 1996, Doron Shohet became the Center's director. During his tenure the Center's policy partly changed due to his approach. He disapproved of biased official publications and maintained that in a democratic state like Israel the public should be informed as much as possible by objective sources, preferably academic, with no political or ideological identification. The interpretation of information should be made by every citizen on his/her own.[43] Despite the "change of mind" represented by Shohet, the line of publications, especially regarding the exodus, remained unchanged.

In the years 1968–88, 20 publications were produced, dealing, directly or indirectly, with the 1948 exodus, representing Israel's growing need to cope with the increasing military and international diplomatic activities of the PLO in the wake of the 1967 War, which culminated in the eruption of the 1987 Intifada. Two of the publications addressed Israel's War of Independence, three on foreign affairs, and another three were part of the "Know What to Reply" Series.[44] This series began at the end of the 1960s as a response to the growing awareness of the need to address the Palestinian and Arab international diplomatic campaign against Israel, demanding, inter alia, the return of the 1948 Palestinians into Israel. It was meant to provide Israelis abroad with proper ready-made responses to criticism of Israel, as well as to

42. Interviews with Shatz, Braverman, Ofaz, Rosner, and Falk (telephone interview).

43. Interview with Shohet.

44. Respective examples are *The War of Independence*, I (Tel-Aviv, 1968) and Pt. II; (ibid., 1978); *Know What to Answer—Questions and Answers for Clarification of Israel's Opinions on Diplomatic Matters* (Jerusalem, 1969) [Hebrew].

strengthen their internal belief in Israel's just and moral conduct. Three additional publications dealt with the Palestinians, four more reviewed operations of IDF brigades in the 1948 War, and one was about the famous debate between the British scholar Arnold Toynbee and Israel's ambassador to Canada Yaacov Herzog.[45] The other four publications deal with various aspects of the conflict.

The publications on 1948 often focused on the military and political conduct of the Jewish side with relatively brief discussion of the Arab-Palestinian community in the War, its political objectives, and military conduct, emphasizing its collapse and mass exodus.[46] As of the early 1970s, other publications specifically addressed the Arab refugee problem, its origins and significance in the broader context of the Arab-Israeli conflict, indicating the growing international attention to this problem and support for the Palestinian resistance movement.[47] Typically, earlier publications, from the late 1960s, dealt with the exodus briefly, while some of the later ones dealt with it at greater length. Most were written by the Agency's staff or senior figures of the 1948 War, veterans and less so by scholars (and one by an employee of the Prime Minister's Office). Publications written by other than the Agency's staff underwent considerable editing.

Except for minor differences, the vast majority of the surveyed publications (17 out of 20) presented the typical Zionist narrative regarding the 1948 exodus. Explaining the causes for the Arab exodus, the Zionist line of argumentation by and large emphasized the Palestinians' responsibility for initiating the 1948 War, hence their full responsibility for its outcomes: "The refugee problem is an outcome of the war that was initiated against us by the Arab countries."[48]

The surveyed publications reiterated that "The vast majority of them [the Palestinians] left on their own free will."[49] Other publications, especially those dedicated to the Palestinian refugee problem elaborated on the causes and circumstances of the Arab flight, emphasizing that the Palestinians left despite repeated Jewish efforts to convince them to stay. In fact, "The Jews observed with astonishment the scene of the Arab mass and panicked exodus. Arab clerics attested . . . about the uncontrolled flight of their people saying that had those fleeing wished to stay in their villages they could have done so but 'they listened to the Mufti.'"[50]

---

45. Government publication examples are: Marie Syrkin, *The Palestinian Refugees* (1970); Nadav Aner, *Refugees for Ever?—The Current Situation* and *Suggestions for Resolution* (1984); Meir Pail, *The Palmach Negev Brigade, 1947–1949* (1987); Yaacov Herzog, *On Israel and its Land—A Debate with Professor Arnold Toynbee* (1976).

46. *The War of Independence* (1978), 18–21.

47. Syrkin, *The Palestinian Refugees*, 1; Aner, *Refugees for Ever?* 7–9.

48. Herzog, *On Israel and its Land*, 8.

49. Ruppin, *Us, Them, and the Land of Israel*, 27.

50. Syrkin, *The Palestinian Refugees*, 4.

That the exodus was ordered by the Arab leadership was clearly manifest in the cases of the mixed cities, especially Tiberias and Haifa. In Tiberias, once the Arab majority (6,000) faced defeat at the hands of the Jewish minority (2,000), they fled the city with British transportation. In Haifa, the Arab leaders decided to leave despite Jewish efforts to convince them to stay in town and resume their normal life as equal citizens. The British military authorities perceived the Haganah conditions to the Arabs "reasonable" but the Arab leaders, who initially agreed to accept the Jewish offer changed their mind on the same day due to radio broadcasts from the Arab Higher Committee, [AHC] the political leadership of the Arab-Palestinians, ordering all of them to leave.[51] A 1970 publication provided an excerpt from a pamphlet produced in 1948 by the union of Jewish workers of Haifa asking the Arabs not to leave.[52]

The role of the AHC in instructing the latter to leave is repeatedly presented in specific cases, most significantly of Haifa, resulting in the exile of 70,000 Arab residents. Similarly, the Arabs of the coastal plain were instructed to leave their villages shortly after the citrus harvest, which preceded the Deir Yasin massacre, and thus refute the Arab argument about the impact of this event on the Arab exodus.[53]

The Arab exodus from Haifa was the rule rather than the exception. The city of Jaffa and many villages were abandoned before being threatened by war. Often times, thousands of Arabs ran away when confronting a handful of Jewish soldiers. The Jewish military impact on the Arab population, however, is rarely mentioned. Hence, in Safed, "In one night, 14,000 Arabs run away from 1,500 ultra-orthodox Jews," even though the Arabs had held the dominating strongholds in town.[54]

One publication referred to the existing explanations for the exodus: "The Arab leaders organized it; the British initiated it; the Mufti's horrific propaganda acted as a boomerang; the Deir Yasin massacre conducted by the Etzel and Lehi frightened the Arabs." Succinctly put, the mass Arab exodus was the result of the Arab military strategy of encouraging the exodus combined with panic. It was precisely the success of the Arab leadership's propaganda, which aimed to create an artificial problem of "refugees" to prepare the ground for, and justify the Arab states' military invasion, that the exodus turned into an unreasonable, uncontrollable flight which that leadership attempted to stem but to no avail.[55]

While this argument remained dominant in the Agency's publications, other explanations were offered, such as the negative impact of the Arab Army of

51. Ibid., 5–6.

52. Yehoash Biber, *Notes of Information* (13) (Jerusalem, 1970), 3.

53. Syrkin, *The Palestinian Refugees*, 5; Aner, *Refugees for Ever?*, 11.

54. Ibid., 6.

55. Ibid., 4.

Deliverance: "Improper behavior toward the local Arab population as a cause of the flight can be found in the attitude toward the local residents of the Arab volunteers that invaded the Land of Israel in order to 'free' it [. . .] the local population was afraid from its defenders more than from the Jews . . . hundreds preferred to run away."[56] Another explanation for the voluntary flight was the Arabs' unwillingness to live as a minority in a Jewish state: "No doubt that many Arabs that left the territory of Israel in 1948 . . . did it because they did not want to live under Jewish regime. It is a natural reaction of people who do not want to live as a national minority."[57]

Other publications offered a sophisticated structural explanation of the collapse of the Arab-Palestinians as a political and military factor and consequent mass flight, reiterating the complex and diverse nature of these events. Although the authors were apparently informed by recent historical studies, they entirely ignored the impact of the Jewish-Israeli policy and military operations on the exodus while highlighting built-in social and political weaknesses of the Arab-Palestinian society as opposed to the Jewish community's strengths:[58]

1. The absence of a central and authoritative political leadership and organized military force. The Arab-Palestinian leaders were divided; most of them ran away once the military course of events turned against the Arab side and conducted their policy from the neighboring Arab countries in disconnection with the reality in Palestine. The Arab military forces were organized as "gangs," or temporarily summoned villagers, that quickly collapsed when confronting the Jewish organized forces.

2. The lack of a constructive vision of a national movement based on shared territorial identity. The central national aspiration rallying the Arab population was the denial of Jewish existence in Palestine. Once the implementation of this aspiration faced difficulties, and in the absence of any constructive objective to continue staying in the country, running away was simple.

3. The demography of the Arab population, many of whom were originally from the neighboring Arab countries, whose flight was nothing other than "returning home."

4. The social structure and dependency on the leaders who were the first to leave, thus setting off their dependents to do the same.

5. Psychology of fear of Jewish atrocities as a result of projecting Arab behavioral norms onto the anticipated Jewish behavior.

56. Biber, *Notes of Information*, 2.
57. Ruppin, *Us, Them, and the Land of Israel*, 27.
58. Kadish, *The War of Independence*, 20–21; Aner, *Refugees for Ever?*, 12.

6. Belief in the final Arab victory as promised by the Arab states, which would facilitate the refugees' return to their homes and fear, among those who wanted to stay, lest they would be castigated as traitors once the Arab armies conquer the country.

7. The British policy of separation between the two communities by homogenizing the population—Jewish or Arab—in the mixed cities. In effect, this policy encouraged the Arabs to leave but failed to convince the Jews to abandon their homes knowing they could rely on the Haganah for their defense.

Beyond these underlying explanations and more immediate causes of the exodus, to explain its voluntary and early occurrence the official publications resorted to what might be defined as "meta-explanation," referring to built-in sense of reliance on, and belonging to, a broader Arab space in which the Arab refugees sought a safe haven. Hence, the early 1948 exodus of the Arab elite is presented as a repetition of the latter's voluntary and temporary exile during the 1936–39 Arab revolt.[59] While identifying with the painful loss of the Arab refugees' homes and lands, the exit from their towns and villages is described as relatively simple, like "going for a journey from one quarter to another in [the same] city." After all, most of the refugees remained within their homeland territory and among Arabs like them, and thus could not perceive their movement as going to exile.[60]

To further bolster the argument that the Arab exodus was voluntary, driven above all by fear rather than forced by Jewish violence, the Zionist narrative mobilized various Arab public statements expressing contempt toward the panicked flight and blaming the refugees themselves not only for their tragedy but also for inflicting heavy losses on the Arab armies.[61] Other statements, made mainly by Arab-Palestinians and published after the 1948 War, ostensibly validated the Zionist claim that the Arab states and the AHC had initiated and instructed the mass exodus: "The Arab governments told us 'leave so we can enter.' So we left, but they did not enter." Another Arab source stated that "Had the Arab leaders not disseminated horrific stories about Deir Yasin the residents of the Arab areas in Palestine would not have run away of their homes."[62] The conclusion drawn from these statements was that this Arab contempt toward the Palestinian refugees is precisely what explains the latter's need to forge a direct cause-effect connection between the Deir Yasin massacre and their mass exodus.[63]

59. Aner, *Refugees for Ever?*, 10.

60. Mary Syrkin, *The Palestinians* (Jerusalem, 1970), 4.

61. For quotations and their Arab sources, see Syrkin, *The Palestinians*, 7.

62. Ibid., 7.

63. Aner, *Refugees for Ever?*, 11.

A 1978 booklet concisely presented the Zionist narrative on Israel's War of Independence and underlined the core elements of the Zionist narrative. It was printed in the largest number of copies (including reprinted editions as late as 1996), and distributed to the public at least until 2006. Its continued dissemination across decades without any change, regardless of the Oslo accords, highlights the Agency's adherence to the original Zionist narrative about the Arab exodus. The following paragraph illustrates the essence of this narrative:

> Initially the local Arabs scored successes [in the War]. However, once their momentum was checked and the Jewish community took the initiative in the "Nahshon" operation and execution of Plan Daled, the Arabs of Eretz-Israel began collapsing quickly. This collapse combined with the calls of the Arab countries to the Eretz-Israel Arabs to leave their localities in order not to get in the way of the Arab armies' operations, and to [later] return as winners, which was most evident in the mass flight of the Arabs from their localities to the Arab countries . . . it is worth noting that the flight of the Eretz-Israel Arabs was contrary to the will of the Jewish community in the land, which on a few occasions called the Arab residents to stay in their localities.[64]

Only three publications, all by figures other than the Agency's staff, referred briefly to cases of expulsion of Arabs by the Jewish forces as exceptional and of insignificant scope, though still largely adhering to the argument of voluntary Palestinian exodus (i.e., presenting the *Zionist-critical* narrative). The limited reference to forced exile of Palestinians is the closest, albeit still a far cry from this critical narrative.[65] The first (1970), by Mary Syrkin,[66] a Jewish, Harvard University historian and a close friend and biographer of Golda Meir (prime minister in 1969–73), presented a detailed description of the Zionist narrative, while also asserting:

> Even though it was not the policy of the "Hagana" to encourage the flight of the Arabs, still a few hostile villages which threatened the road to Jerusalem were evacuated by the commanders of the Hagana. Lifting the siege on Jerusalem was one of the central operations in the war. Therefore, a few villages which served as bases for the enemy were forcibly evacuated . . . and their residents joined the flight. However, these were just a few incidents which took place at a later phase, and the number of people involved was too small to influence the scope of the mass flight, or to explain it.[67]

64. Kadish, *The War of Independence*, 20.

65. Syrkin, *The Palestinians*, 7; Meir Pa'il, *The Mobile Fighting in the Open Space in Light of the Restraint Policy, 1936–1948)* (Jerusalem, 1983), 8; *The Palmach Negev Brigade*, 6.

66. Syrkin, *The Palestinians*.

67. Ibid., 7.

The other two publications, of 1983 and 1987, on the 1936–48 Arab-Jewish conflict and the battles of the Negev Brigade in the 1948 War, respectively, were authored by Meir Pa'il, former Palmach commander, IDF colonel, historian, and a left-wing political activist. Referring to the Deir Yassin massacre in the 1983 publication he referred to the moral and political dilemmas of the war, expressing sorrow for "the occurrence of such an affair in our history," even if the Arabs had perpetrated more severe murders and terror activities. While largely ignoring the expulsion of the Arab villagers along the road from the coastal plain to Jerusalem, he however, underlined the insignificance of the massacre as a contribution to the Zionist interest or as a trigger for mass Arab exodus. Challenging the common argument about the link between this massacre and the mass Arab flight, he rightly points to the fact that most Arab neighboring villages within the radius of 10 km from Deir Yassin, from Beit Iksa and al-Nabi Samweel in the north, Qalunia in the west, and 'Ein Karim and Maliha in the south, remained in place. The Haganah had to fight for each of these villages and others, paying a heavy price which in some cases ended with scorching failure.[68] In this context, Pa'il refers to the village of Abu-Ghosh (west of Jerusalem) as another case in which the inhabitants remained in place after Deir Yassin, were expelled, but later allowed to return to their village.[69] One may argue that his reference to the expulsion of the Abu Ghosh inhabitants from their village and permit to return, one of a minute number of such cases in the country—is nothing but an attempt to show Israel's merciful face. His main argument is by far more comprehensive, minimizing the significance of Deir Yassin's massacre as a factor triggering the Arab exodus.

The 1987 publication contained only one sentence about the Arabs residing in the Negev Brigade's area of operations, stating that the residents of the villages conquered by the brigade—Burayr, Hulayqat, Kawkaba, Bayt Tima, Sawafir, Jammama, Huj, Simsim, and Najd—all were "evacuated" to the area of Gaza in the first half of May 1948.[70]

Even when these three publications referred to cases of expulsion as marginal and insignificant, their language was typically *euphemistic*.[71] The word "expulsion" was never used, but rather softer words such as "evacuation" (*pinui*), "forcibly cleared" (*punu be-ko'ah*), or "removal with consent" (*ha'avarah be-haskamah*). The use of such words was not coincidental and meant to reduce the damage

68. Such as in the case of al-Nabi Samweel and Beit Iksa. Ein Karim, Qalonia, al-Maliha, and two other nearby villages (Saris and Beit Mahsir, not mentioned by Pa'il) were conquered only after heavy battles.

69. Pa'il, *The Mobile Fighting in the Open Space*, 8.

70. Pa'il, *The Palmach Negev Brigade*, 6.

71. Miguel Gomez, "Toward a New Approach to the Linguistic Definition of Euphemism," *Language Sciences* 31.6 (2009): 725–39.

to Israel's image. This was another manifestation of the self-censorship that the Agency staff practiced,[72] which was a common phenomenon then in Israeli state institutions.[73]

These publications expressed *"Softening References"*—discussion of aspects that minimize the impact of the description of a difficult event. An example is the way Syrkin minimized the meaning of the expulsions emphasizing that the Haganah had no policy of encouraging the Arab flight, and that the "evacuations" (namely, expulsions) that took place were very important in order to win the war: "These were just a few incidents which took place at a later phase, and the number of people involved was too small to influence the scope of the mass flight, or to explain it."

Throughout the years, the publications presented the Zionist narrative of the causes of the exodus, for the most part. Only three presented a narrative that slightly deviated from the Zionist narrative (Zionist-critical), addressing insignificant expulsions, while using euphemism and Softening References.

Dynamics of the Agency's Performance

Until the 1967 War the Agency did not produce publications dealing with the 1948 exodus because the issue was until then of relatively little international interest even after the foundation of the PLO in 1964. The change in policy after 1967 was indicated, among others, by including the Palestinian issue in the Agency's publications. In addition to the exodus of some 250,000 refugees from the West Bank to Jordan, the 1967 war also brought a large population of refugees under Israeli rule and[74] boosted the prestige and the military activities of the Palestinian guerrilla groups, especially across the Jordan River, all of which necessitated the Agency's inputs. The impact of the 1967 War is clearly identified in the introduction of an 1970 Agency's publication asserting before discussing the 1948 Palestinian refugees that "The Six-Day War led the State of Israel to practically deal with the Arab refugees problem . . . now the State of Israel became a refugee 'Host Country,' with responsibilities. It is worthwhile examining a few questions regarding this matter."[75]

72. Interviews with Pail, Rosner, and Braverman (2006).

73. Rafi Nets-Zehngut, "Israeli approved textbooks and the 1948 Palestinian exodus," *Israel Studies* 18.3 (2013): 41–68; "The Israeli Army's Official Memory of the 1948 Palestinian Exodus (1949–2004)," *War in History* 22.2 (2015): 211–34; Rafi Nets-Zehngut, Ruthie Pliskin, and Daniel Bar-Tal, "Self-censorship in Conflicts: Israel and the 1948 Palestinian Exodus," *Peace and Conflict: Journal of Peace Psychology* 21 (2015): 479–99.

74. Syrkin, *The Palestinians*, 1; Aner, *Refugees for Ever?*, 7–9.

75. Biber, *Notes of Information*, 1.

The absence of the Palestinian refugee problem in the pre-1967 publications can be regarded as official amnesia, or silence, of the state. Since the end of the 1948 War Israel not only consistently denied its responsibility for the Palestinian refugee problem but also stifled all international efforts aimed at allowing the return of the refugees to their original homes or compensating them for their abandoned property. The regionalization of the conflict and its revision into one between Israel and its Arab neighboring states allowed Israel to frame the refugee problem as a component of the Arab-Israeli conflict, the perpetuation of which was but an Arab weapon against Israel. If there was any Israeli reference to the Palestinian refugees, both in the early 1950s and after the PLO's founding in 1964 except for some individuals' literary and poetic expressions—it was mainly in this context and, increasingly as a military threat represented by the guerrilla warfare waged against Israel by Palestinians across the borders with the Arab states.

Since 1968, the Agency's discussion regarding the Palestinians increased and as time passed more publications dealt with this issue, albeit in the wider context of the conflict and not in the specific context of the 1948 War. From the late 1970s the growing scope of Israeli critical narrative publications about the 1948 exodus obliged the Agency's staff to address this issue more directly. A key figure in the Center describes the early awareness of the critical narrative among the Agency officials: "Twenty years after 1948 there were here [in Israel] many people, thousands of people, that knew that there was expulsion [in 1948]. So what, did we live in a bubble? . . . The fact that we were working for the Information Center did not isolate us."[76]

The 1977 political turnover, namely the rise to power of the right-wing Likud party, the first after three decades of Labor-led governments, as far as the Agency's staff was concerned, inhibited their portrayal of the critical narrative. Whereas until 1977 there was full ideological identity between the directors of the Center/ Agency to the ruling party, underpinning a relatively harmonious relationship between the two, as of 1977 the Center's staff became "tainted" by the new ruling party as incapable of properly representing the state. The impact on the Agency was two-fold: first, its staff became more cautious in their conduct, in a manner that inhibited deviation from hitherto prevailing memory; second, the Government's secretary, amongst others, decreased the use of the Agency's services.[77]

Despite its familiarity with the critical narrative about the 1948 exodus, the Agency refrained from referring to it even though the interviewees in this research regarded it as the true story of the exodus. The reasons for this avoidance were diverse. The Agency was obliged to conform to the state's formal policy and to present Israel in a positive manner: "We had self-censorship about what can and

76. Interview with Rosner.
77. Interviews with Falk, Ofaz, Rosner, and Shohet.

cannot be written . . . with regard to disputed issues," as described by one of its former directors.[78] And a colleague explained: "We . . . were not going to publish anything that would doubt the Jewish right to establish a state in Eretz-Israel."[79] The Agency's raison d'être was to portray Israel's image as righteous as possible for both domestic and international purposes. Domestically, such image was necessary in the process of nation-building of the newly founded state, especially in view of the waves of immigrants from dozens of different countries, languages, and traditions, and the need to mobilize them to cope with the enormous security and economic challenges Israel faced. Internationally, portraying Israel positively would help to attain support and cope with the Arab/Palestinian diplomatic campaign. An excerpt from a 1971 publication of the Agency addresses these two rationales:

> Parallel to the hot war that the Arabs conduct against us along the borders and in terror attacks against citizens, an Arab propaganda war is being conducted around the world . . . The aim of the Arab propaganda is to divert the public opinion in various countries, and their governments, to accept the Arab argument and support the Arab fighting against Israel . . . The aim of this booklet is to strengthen the consciousness of the Israeli youth about the righteousness of our basic position, in addition in order to allow it to stand up against this "propaganda war" when it will have to.[80]

Three additional causes supported self-censorship: (1) Identification with the Zionist ideology—most of the senior officials of the Agency and Center during the research period supported the ruling Mapai party and later, "The Alignment" and "Ha'avoda," which remained committed to the founding Zionist-Israeli narratives of the 1948 War; (2) Abiding by institutional norms—the Agency's staff was cognizant of their duty to "present the state's point of view" as a basic civil service norm regardless of individual attitudes;[81] and (3) The personal cost of bureaucratic sanctions in case this norm is violated.[82]

The Agency/Center was ostensibly autonomous, without direct bureaucratic supervision. The themes and contents of publications were largely determined and authored by the Agency's staff or external contractors, with little or no coordination with other official agencies.[83] However, sensitive political issues such as the causes for the 1948 Palestinian exodus required self-censorship and top-down

---

78. Interview with Ofaz.

79. Interview with Rosner.

80. Rupin, *Us, Them, and the Land of Israel*, 5; Interviews with Braverman, Ofaz, Rosner, Shatz, and Shohet; Agency's publications: *Yehasey* (1968), 4–5.

81. Interview with Ofaz.

82. Ibid.

83. Interviews with Ofaz, Braverman, and Shatz.

restrictive mechanisms.[84] This included, firstly, the minister in charge of the Agency who often served as an active or passive watch dog of the latter's appropriate line. In the late 1960s, for instance, when the minister without portfolio, Israel Galili who headed the Center, insisted on reviewing every Agency publication, or someone on his behalf, before being published. The Agency's staff were aware to avoid deviation from the official policy, particularly following the 1977 political change of government. Second, the Agency's staff often voluntarily submitted their drafts to their superiors in the government for their inspection. Third, there was apprehension of retrospective criticism of publications by senior political figures such as the minister in charge due to contents that were inappropriate in their view.[85]

Consequently, the Agency's staff hardly ever considered presenting the critical narrative regarding the Palestinian exodus in their publications. One noted:

> The topic of expulsion [of Palestinians in 1948] was not mentioned [in the Agency's publications . . . they were not expelled. They left voluntarily or due to the pressure of the Higher Arab Committee. This was the publishing approach . . . It [the expulsions] was a taboo . . . the official position did not admit it.[86]

To avoid presenting the critical narrative in its publications and yet look credible, the Agency's staff referred to existing studies and records attesting to this type of narrative, though selectively adopting only those sections supporting the Zionist perspective and overlooking inconvenient sections about deliberate expulsions. This tendency is well represented in Nadav Aner's 1984 Agency publication on the Arab refugee problem and options for its solution.[87] However, since the late 1970s, the Agency's staff became aware of the increasing publications in Israel presenting critical narratives about the conflict (in general and specifically regarding the 1948 exodus). Since the late 1980s this awareness increased due to Benny Morris's publications on the origins of the Palestinian refugee problem, especially his 1987 book in English and its 1991 Hebrew version. The Agency's staff felt there was a need to produce a new and updated publication that would include the new findings.[88] Paradoxically, the 1977 political change of government made it

84. Interviews with Braverman, Falk, Ofaz, Shatz, and Shohet.

85. In 2002 Likud Minister of Education Limor Livant disqualified the Agency's publication, a guide to the Palestinian organizations, harshly reproaching the Center's staff and causing much unrest among them. Nurit Braverman, *Fatah, Tanzim, Hamas and Others: A Guide to Palestinian Organizations* (Jerusalem, 2002) [Hebrew].

86. Interviews with Ofaz and Shatz.

87. Aner, *Refugees for Ever?*, 55, refers to Ronny Gabbay (see note 27) and Arie Avnery, *The Jewish Settlement and the Banishment Claim, 1878–1948* (Tel-Aviv, 1980) [Hebrew].

88. Interviews with Braverman, Ofaz, Rosner, Shatz, and Shohet.

acceptable to admit that the Palestinians were expelled because this matched the line of the revisionist ideology about the essence of the Jewish-Arab conflict.[89]

In the first half of the 1990s the Agency approached Haifa University historian Motti Golani, considered not too critical on Israel's early history, to write an up-to-date booklet on the 1948 War of Independence, and to deal with the exodus. The Agency rejected his submitted draft and it was never published. A key figure explained:

> We talked with him [Golani] asking him to insert certain changes [in the draft], but he declined . . . As far as we were concerned, the conclusion was that this publication was impossible for the kind of audience we address. He tried to suggest a new concept, post-Zionist, but we did not think it was appropriate for our audience . . . because this audience is comprised of high school students. Maybe when they reach the university they will be able to read it, but not earlier.[90]

Later the Agency approached another scholar at The Hebrew University of Jerusalem, Avraham Sela, to write a concise book on the Arab-Israeli Conflict. Once again, the manuscript was rejected for being explicit about Israeli expulsions of Palestinians, especially as of July 1948.[91]

Nonetheless, three publications from both pre- and post-1977 did present the Zionist-critical perspective (i.e., voluntary flight accompanied by an insignificant expulsion). The reasons for this slight deviation from the typical Zionist narrative vary from one case to another, underlining the exceptional rather than a substantive change of mind about the Palestinian exodus.

The first, Mary Syrkin's article in 1970, translated from the original in English at the instruction of the PM's office, denied the Agency's staff any discretion for its contents. It carried Syrkin's name as the author, ostensibly indicating her sole responsibility for it.[92] The second, by Meir Pa'il in 1983, addressed the development of the Haganah mobile forces, refuting the common argument about the immense impact of the Deir Yassin massacre on the Arab mass flight and showing that most of nearby Arab villages remained in place and had to be fought for by the Haganah.[93] The third, in 1987, also written by Pa'il in cooperation with the

---

89. Daniel Gutwein, "Left and Right Post-Zionism and Privatization of Israeli Collective Memory," in *Israeli Historical Revisionism: From Left to Right,* ed. Anita Shapira and Derek Penslar (London, 2003), 9–42.

90. Interviews with Rosner and Braverman.

91. Interview with Ofaz. A Ministry of Defense book in 1996 includes a chapter with identical discussion about expulsions of Arab Palestinians in 1948. Avraham Sela, "The Arab Palestinians in the 1948," in *The Palestinian National Movement: From Confrontation to Reconciliation?,* ed. Moshe Maoz and Ben-Zion Kedar (Tel-Aviv, 1996), 115–203 [Hebrew].

92. Interview with Rosner.

93. Pa'il, *The Mobile Fighting in the Open Space,* 8.

Palmach Generation Association, addressed the battles fought by the Palmach Negev Brigade during the 1948 War, and was published for Israel's 40th anniversary as part of a publications series titled "In Warriors Footsteps."[94] It carried Pa'il's name co-produced with the Palmach Generation Association, thus reducing the Agency's responsibility as to its contents. This publication barely followed Morris's 1985–86 critical academic articles, though some of the Agency's staff were familiar with them.[95]

Even prior to Shohet's appointment in 1996, the Agency's staff were well aware of the critical narrative regarding the 1948 exodus, with which they largely agreed. Nevertheless, during Shohet's term the Center refrained from any publication on 1948 Arab refugees. This cannot be fully explained by Shohet's dovish orientation and objection to any government politically motivated publication, be it in line with Zionist narratives or not, or by the significant budget and manpower cuts that reduced the Center's scope of activities, especially of producing new publications. He explained that he was also guided by concern lest critically addressing the exodus by the Agency could provoke public controversies or meet the disapproval of his superiors at the Ministry of Education.[96] This concern was realized in 1996 with the return to power of a Likud-led government headed by Benjamin Netanyahu, which had not hidden its opposition to the Oslo process. Shohet perceived the Agency's publications as no match, or capable of competing with the media in disseminating information to the public, whose attention to official publications was minute. He recalled:

> I thought . . . that the period in which the state needs to disseminate and publicize its version was finished. Therefore I said that what is already on the shelf, and was published before my period, and some pupil can use it, I leave [intact]. No need to throw it away. But, to publish something new of such kind—it is not appropriate. And take into consideration that every critical journalist . . . is very critical about everything that the state publishes, and therefore I tried very much not to get into this whirlpool. . . . [F]or a child that reads it for the first time it is not that important whether [the 1948 Palestinians] were expelled or ran away.[97]

Thus, with no new critical publications of the Agency regarding the 1948 War as of 1996, only copies of a publication that dealt with it in a general manner[98] were re-printed and distributed, at least until 2006. This publication, as mentioned, presents the Zionist narrative.

94. Pa'il, *The Palmach Negev Brigade*, 6.
95. Interview with Rosner.
96. Interview with Shohet.
97. Interview with Shohet.
98. *The War of Independence.*

Conclusion

This study provides theoretical insights regarding collective memory in general and official memory in particular, as well as empirical information regarding the Israeli Information Center as a state agent producing and shaping public attitude.

During the 1950s to 2003, the official version produced by the Agency regarding the 1948 exodus largely represented the Zionist narrative. The responsibility for the exodus was exclusively put on the Arabs of Palestine, denying any responsibility of the Jews for their exodus, typically in line with other cases of intractable conflicts (i.e., biased in favor of the in-group, presenting dichotomous black-and-white narratives, with no grey areas).

The logic for formulating such memory was two-fold, internal and external, shaped by conditions of continued conflict and Arab efforts of delegitimization of the State of Israel. Internally, constructing a self-righteous popular memory of the conflict would promote solidarity within the Israeli society and sustainability under conditions of continued conflict. Such memory is an important attribute of the collective identity of the Israeli-Jews, one that would enable them to cope with the difficulties that such a conflict creates but also contributes to the conflict's perpetuation. Externally, such official memory serves Israel's efforts to obtain broad international legitimacy, to help Israel cope with the Arab/Palestinian diplomatic campaign demanding the return of the refugees into Israel. This external logic of memory construction should be emphasized, since it is often less discussed in the context of memory of conflicts, compared to the more discussed internal logic.

The findings reassert that collective memory is built around major events such as the 1948 War and its consequences for both Jews and Arabs. Within this context, the publications often emphasized and elaborated on conspicuous episodes, especially the Arab exodus from the mixed cities of Haifa, Safed, Tiberias, and Jaffa, due to their visibility and deeper imprint on popular memory than the peripheral localities, e.g., small villages, even though two-thirds of the Palestinian population on the eve of the 1948 War was rural.

The *modus operandi* of the Agency was only to a limited degree influenced by the party in power and of the minister in charge of the Center at any given time, regardless of the individual opinions of the latter's staff. Similarly, there was almost *no difference* in the way different parties in power, or the responsible ministers, supervised the Center.[99] Although until the 1977 elections most of the latter's staff, and surely the senior ones, supported the Labor led governments, the 1977 political turnover was of insignificant impact on their publications as far as the 1948 narrative was concerned.

---

99. Interviews with Shatz and Shohet.

Hence, despite the critical historical narratives published by various societal institutions since the late 1970s about the 1948 exodus, the Agency strictly adhered all along to the Zionist narrative. A major factor explaining this tendency was the Agency bureaucrats' awareness of their being an indivisible part of the state apparatus. They knew very well their boundaries and at the same time had been supervised by the political echelons. Moreover, regardless of their ideological gaps, both the "Labor" and the "Likud" parties favored the adherence to the Zionist narrative out of deep conviction that adopting a critical approach to the 1948 Palestinian exodus would be seriously harmful to Israel's fundamental interests domestically internationally.

This phenomenon reflects the difference between state and societal institutions concerning collective taboos on which the Center had less or no latitude compared to societal/non-official agents of memory, especially professional historians. For a state institution to officially admit expulsion in 1948 is tantamount to admitting responsibility for the Palestinian refugee problem, which would damage Israel more severely than if scholars or journalists do so. Theoretically, it is suggested that future analyses relate to different approaches—official and societal—to a given taboo, rather than treating taboos in general at any given national community.

This study underlines the gap, in fact rival relationship, between collective memory often represented by official institutions and critical history, and, more specifically, the former's sustainability regardless of the constantly developing historical research.[100] Contrary to institutionalized memory agents of ethnic, gender, and class collectives whose primary concern and loyalty are to their identity/interest group, historians and academic scholars are expected to elevate themselves above their political community's considerations in the service of objective truth even when it collides head-on with their own interest group. The extent to which these types of memory/history agents interact and affect each other is of universal relevance and must be examined along a historical span of time and in close consideration of the context in which such correspondence exists, if any. Although the Agency's staff was well aware of the new research literature on the 1948 War and Arab exodus, and capable of employing its findings in its products, as a state institution it was, by definition, obliged to produce and disseminate public knowledge of the past in accordance with what was continuously understood as the "national interest." Hence, the Information Center served as a gate-keeper assigned with preserving the conservative Zionist narrative about the Arab exodus while largely overlooking the critical studies published by historians about the birth of Israel despite, and presumably in contrast to, its growing prevalence both internationally and in Israel itself since the late 1950s.

---

100. Aleida Assmann, "Transformations between History and Memory," *Social Research* 75.1 (2008): 49–72.

No matter how credible and heavily documented the historical research on the 1948 War may be, adherence to the Zionist version of that war remained dominant, perhaps serving an essential need of the Jewish-Israeli community in its ongoing conflict, especially with the Palestinian national movements and its international supporters. It thus might be of no surprise to note that the impact of historical research of the 1948 exodus on Israeli public opinion still lags behind the Zionist narrative: although most studies by Israeli-Jewish scholars since the late 1970s presented the critical narrative of the exodus,[101] a field study conducted in 2008 found that only 39 percent of Israeli-Jews adopted this narrative.[102]

Interviewees

Nurit Braverman, Agency former employee since 1970, chief editor since the 1990s, director (2000–03).

Nahum Falk, Agency former employee, 1977–88.

Benny Morris, scholar.

Haim Ofaz, Agency employee since the mid-1950s, director (1973–2000).

Meir Pa'il, former Palmach commander, IDF colonel, historian, left-wing political activist.

Shlomo Rosner, Agency former employee since 1963, chief editor (1973–85), member of the Managing Board of the Center until 2003.

Yaacov Shatz, Agency former employee since 1958, director (1961–73), deputy director (1973–78) and (1978–96).

Doron Shohet, director of the Center, 1996–2003.

RAFI NETS-ZEHNGUT is Managing Director of the International Conflict Resolution Program at Bar-Ilan University. His recent publications include "The Israeli Army's Official Memory of the 1948 Palestinian Exodus (1949–2004)," *War in History*; "Self-Censorship in Conflicts: Israel and the 1948 Palestinian Exodus," *Peace and Conflict: Journal of Peace Psychology* (with Ruthie Pliskin and Daniel Bar-Tal); and "Approved Textbooks and the 1948 Palestinian Exodus," *Israel Studies*.

101. Rafi Nets-Zehngut, "Origins of the Palestinian Refugee Problem: Changes in the Historical Memory of Israelis/Jews 1949–2004," *Journal of Peace Research* 48.2 (2011): 235–48.

102. These findings are based on a representative public opinion poll examining the Israeli-Jewish popular memory of 23 major events of the Israeli-Arab/Palestinian conflict, by Rafi Nets-Zehngut and Daniel Bar-Tal, http://www.collective-memory.info/home (see second under Academic Publications).

3   The War of Independence Exhibited

A Study of Three Israeli Museums

Ofer Boord

Introduction

In the past three decades, Israel's history museums have gradually started to gain an important role within the public arena. Museums have attempted to compete with the teaching of history in schools, with the textbooks, as well as with TV programs and contents obtained through the Internet, by including short and focused captions, historic photographs, original items, reconstruction of buildings, and films. Many museums are currently successful in illustrating "boring" and distant historic issues in a captivating manner, and are thus a factor to be taken into consideration. The large number of museums as well as the scope of their visitors—mostly teenagers and soldiers during their compulsory military service—justifies an examination of the impact of these museums on their visitors.[1]

The current research on Israel's history museums is not extensive, mostly conducted by Israelis and published in Hebrew since the early 1990s. The various research topics include: the history museums in the Israeli public sphere and their relevance as reflections of collective memory,[2] interpretation of the Zionist-pioneer narrative at the museums,[3] the relationship between the exhibits and the history curriculum,[4] the impact of the Israeli commitment to nationalism

---

The author is the curator of two of the museums discussed (Etzel & Haganah). The chapter represents the author's private retrospective opinion about the displays.

1. Elad Bezalely and Dikla Liany, eds., *Guide of Heritage Sites* (Mikveh Israel, 2011); Society for Preservation of Israel Heritage Sites: www.shimur.org; Israel National Committee of ICOM: www.icom.org.il [Hebrew]. In 2009, approximately 2.7m visitors visited heritage sites and museums. This data is courtesy of the Society for Preservation of Israel Heritage Sites.

2. Ariella Azoulay, "Open Doors: History Museums in the Israeli Public Sphere," *Theory & Criticism* 5 (1993): 79–95; Maya Cohen-Mossek, *"Museums as Reflectors and Creators of Collective Memory: The Case of the Museums of the Israeli Ministry of Defence"* (MA thesis, Amsterdam University, 2009).

3. Tamar Katriel, "Performing the Past: Presentational Styles in Settlement Museum Interpretation," *Israel Social Science Research* 9.1–2 (1994): 1–26.

4. Sary Gal, "The Contribution of the Ministry of Defense Museums to the National Consciousness" (MA thesis, Tel-Aviv University, 1996).

The War of 1948 (2016): 75–98, DOI: 10.2979/warof1948.0.0.05

on the nature of the exhibits,[5] and the impact of the museums' structure and design on the nature of the historical display and collective memory.[6] Despite this variety of research foci, none have examined a specific issue within the studied museums or addressed the presentation of the 1948 War in the museums.

This chapter is based primarily on observation and examination of the exhibitions, supplemented by participating observation during guided tours and interviews with museum personnel. Clearly, the guide interprets and recreates the exhibits according to his/her perspective, pedagogic ability, and the nature of the group being guided. What is being told, ignored, or not told through guided presentations at these museums is equally important as a reflection of emotions, fears, and hopes of the Jewish community during the War as they have been formulated throughout the decades since the end of the war. The participating observations and interviews with guides were indeed necessary in order to reflect on the exhibition appropriately, since a history museum is, by nature, a very dynamic arena. Since these museums are educational centers, reviewing them through these assumptions and approaches is expected to enrich the current literature, offering new insights about the role historical museums play in shaping the outlook of the younger generation of Israelis visiting the museums.

The first two museums are sector-related, presenting the positions of two pre-state organizations that played an active, though by no means equal, role in the War. The 1947–48 Etzel Museum represents the underground National Military Organization (Irgun Zevai Le'umi, or Etzel) and is associated with the Revisionist Movement, which has been in opposition to the rule of the Labor Movement since the 1930s. With the proclamation of the State of Israel and establishment of the IDF, Etzel was dismantled and became a political party, Herut, led by its hitherto commander Menachem Begin, later Likud prime minister in 1977. Similarly, the Haganah Museum is associated with and represents the paramilitary organization, led by the labor movements, the mainstream current of the Yishuv, the pre-state Jewish community in Palestine, and of the State of Israel, until the Likud Party came to power in 1977. From the viewpoint of the organized Yishuv and Zionist Executive, the revisionists, including Etzel, were largely perceived as "secessionists" whose autonomous policies and practices undermined the Zionist enterprise. In Israel's first two decades, the national narrative was dictated by the ruling Labor movement, creating difficulty for the right wing to become part of the national narrative. The situation started to change in the 1960s, but the most

---

5. Nina Rudin, "The Settlement Museums of Israel and their Commitment to Zionist Messages" (MA thesis, Leicester University, 1998).

6. Orit Shaham Gover, "'Our Version': Designing the Palmach and the Begin Museums as Memory Fashioning Spaces'" (PhD diss., Haifa University, 2008); Inbar Kavenshtok, "The Historical Museum in the Historical Preserved Structure" (MA thesis, Bar-Ilan University, 2003).

significant change occurred only after Likud came to power in 1977. The two museums thus present two opposing, often clashing, narratives representing the decades-long and continuous political rivalry and competition over shaping the Israeli-Jewish collective memory.[7]

Unlike the Etzel and Haganah museums, the Israeli Museum is part of the Yitzhak Rabin Center, a central commemoration site for Israel's prime minister from the Labor Party who was assassinated by a Jewish zealot on November 4, 1995. Rabin's assassination took place during the fierce conflict between the right and left political currents in Israel over fundamental issues related to the Oslo process between Israel and the Palestinians. The museum does not address the left-right dispute but rather endeavors to bridge the gap between the two rival camps. It strives to present the Israeli story in its entirety, including all of its clashing sectors and narratives, in order to reach mutual understanding and a national peace-making process among the various groups in Israeli society.

Though the three museums were established by independent associations— the underground veterans' association for the 1947–48 Etzel Museum, the Haganah Veterans' Organization for the Haganah Museum, and the Yitzhak Rabin Center's association for the Israeli Museum, all three were recently adopted as official state institutions assigned for inculcating national heritage. The state thus tacitly recognized their respective descriptions and presentations of the war. This approval attributes further significance to the findings of this chapter and their conclusions.

Visitors to these museums can be divided into organized groups brought to the museum, such as students and soldiers, and voluntary visits by the general public (both Israelis and foreigners). Data regarding visitors to the museums in 2010 show that organized tours constituted the largest group going to the Haganah Museum and a small majority regarding the 1947–48 Etzel Museum.[8] Israeli Museum organized tours formed the smaller part of all visitors, apparently because the museum opened its doors to soldiers only in August 2010 and began receiving large groups of students only two months later. However, the partial data for these months indicate that the visitor population breakdown will soon be the same.[9] Thus, these museums effectively operate as educational institutions,

7. Udi Lebel, *The Road to the Pantheon: Etzel, Lehi and the Borders of the Israel National Memory* (Jerusalem, 2007); Amir Goldstein, "Acre Prison: Perpetuation, Memory, Politics," in *The Rebels: Etzel's Struggle against the British (1944–1948)*, ed., Yaakov Markovitzky (Jerusalem, 2008), 196–323 [both in Hebrew].

8. The 1947–48 Etzel Museum: 4,185 students, 4,981 soldiers, 7,726 general public; The Haganah Museum: 7,187 students, 16,675 soldiers, 7,826 general public; based on the Ministry of Defense Museum Unit Visitors Report for 2010.

9. The Israeli Museum at the Yitzhak Rabin Center: 9,200 students, 8,200 soldiers, 24,600 general public; based on a letter from Nurit Levinovsky, director of the Education Department,

reminiscent of Nora's "Les lieux de mémoire,"[10] in which varied collective memories are reproduced and instilled in the younger generation as national "heritage."

The chapter is structured so readers can virtually walk along the exhibition as regular visitors, allowing them a firsthand experience of visiting the museum and delving into the exhibition's contents, and letting them draw their own conclusions as well. I present my own translations from the exhibitions' Hebrew texts of the indented quotes below,[11] although the majority of captions and films at the museums also appear in English (at the Israeli Museum—in Arabic, as well). These translations to English are designed to be user-friendly for non-Israeli visitors by minimizing the use of terms unfamiliar to them at the cost of sometimes obscuring the original meaning of the display. I thus offer a more precise and complete translation from the Hebrew text to introduce the English readers as much as possible to the meaning of the display as planned by its curators.

The 1947–48 Etzel Museum

The 1947–48 Etzel Museum was opened in 1983 as a memorial: the Amichai Paglin ("Gidi") Etzel House in memory of the liberators of Jaffa—the Jaffa Liberation Museum. Established by an association of Etzel members, it was specifically established in order to memorialize the 41 Etzel fighters who fell in the battle for Jaffa in early May 1948. The association obtained the land from the Israel Land Administration. Construction was funded by donations and with the assistance of the Tel-Aviv Municipality and various government offices. The memorial was set up on the former battleground, in the erased Manshiyyah Quarter (part of Jaffa until the War of Independence), within a partially destroyed stone structure in which prominently visible dark steel and glass construction is integrated. The building is located in the southern part of the Tel-Aviv promenade (the Charles Clore Park) on the seashore, between grass, flora, and decorative paving. Subsequently, the association enlarged the exhibition within the memorial, converting it into a museum addressing the specific history of the Etzel battle for Jaffa and the general history of the organization.[12]

At the request of the Etzel association members, the memorial was transferred to the Ministry of Defense in 1987. The name was then changed to the 1947–48 Etzel Museum, and the Museum Unit of the Ministry of Defense together

---

10 April 2010. In 2013, approximately half of the 80,000 visitors were students and soldiers; based on a telephone interview with Nurit Levinovsky, 6 March 2013.

10. Pierre Nora, "Between Memory and History: Les lieux de mémoire," *Representations* 26 (1989): 7–25.

11. Edited by Batsheva Pomerantz.

12. Kavenshtok, "The Historical Museum," 112–13; Yossi Kister, director of the Etzel Museum and formerly director of the 1947–48 Etzel Museum, interviews: 16 March, 11 April 2011.

with the Etzel Soldiers Alliance began planning a new exhibit. The new exhibit, which presents Etzel activities following the 29 November 1947 UN Partition Resolution until the integration of Etzel into the IDF upon its establishment, was opened to the public in 1992. The Museum continued to be a memorial specifically to Etzel's members who fell in the battle for Jaffa as well as in the War of Independence. A computerized memorial station is located in the central space of the exhibit. There is a large screen next to it on which the names of the fallen soldiers are listed together with their pictures and biographies.[13]

A visit to the museum begins with a short lecture on the history of Etzel followed by a guided tour in selected parts of the War exhibit. These are tailored to the type of group and the time available. Most groups complete the tour listening to the personal testimony of a former Etzel member, a guide in the museum.

The museum exhibition opens with a display showing the borders of the UN Resolution accompanied by a contemporary condemnatory Etzel poster:

> The Jewish homeland, like the homeland of every nation, is complete historically! Dividing the homeland into pieces is illegal. Compliance of the Jewish institutions with this illegal action is also illegal and does not obligate our people who will continue to fight to liberate our entire homeland.

The objection to the Partition Plan and the dispute with the Zionist mainstream leadership are at the foundation of the entire display. Its main theme is the description of Etzel's fight against the Arabs and the British from December 1947 until June 1948 while being in conflict with the established Zionist institutions and military force, the Haganah.

After two displays that illustrate Etzel's fight, using historical photographs and a defense post setting, with sandbags and figures of fighters carrying guns, the exhibition proceeds. A signboard summarizes Etzel's part in the War and outlines the conflict with the Zionist leadership over "the partition of the homeland," and holds the Arabs responsible for the outbreak of the War and its escalation.

> On the morning after the UN decision, on 30 November 1947, Etzel headquarters issued a call to the Yishuv against partition of the homeland and an order of the day to the organization's commanders and soldiers "to prepare for a stormy period." Defensive and guard positions were immediately set up in the cities' suburbs and the settlements. After the call to the Arabs to stop the killing was ignored, Etzel went from a defensive to an offensive position against gangs centered in the three large cities. This was followed by conquest—sometimes acting independently and sometimes in cooperation with the Haganah.

---

13. *Visitors Guide: The 1947–48 Etzel Museum.* In addition to the 1947–48 Etzel Museum there is the Tel-Aviv Etzel Museum (1991), which presents the history of the organization and is also part of the Ministry of Defense.

The rest of the display is dedicated to presentations outlining the actions and operations in which Etzel took part during the War. One display is devoted to an Etzel operation, which although narrow in scope, has become a tragic event in the history of the Jewish-Arab conflict—the conquest of the village of Deir Yassin, initially by a combined force of Etzel and Lehi and, following the latter's failure, also by support of a Palmach unit.[14] Following the conquest of the village, Etzel was accused of conducting atrocities and massacring many of the village inhabitants. A signpost responds to this accusation with a detailed explanation for the large number of people killed during the village's conquest. At the same time, it states that the Haganah approved of this conquest (thus implying that the Haganah was also responsible):

> During the briefing before setting out, it was decided to forgo the element of surprise to ensure the safety of the citizens by using loudspeakers to warn the women, children, and elderly to leave the area. . . . The armored vehicle with the loudspeaker did not make it to the village's entrance because the Lehi unit in the armored vehicle ran into an Arab barricade . . . the armored vehicle overturned; the call to the inhabitants of Deir Yassin was drowned out by the sounds of shooting. . . . Almost every house in the village served as a resistance position, requiring the separate seizing of each house by throwing grenades and shooting by submachine guns. Many of the attackers [Lehi and Etzel fighters] and those in the houses were injured. . . . Five of our fighters fell in the battle for Deir Yassin, and the number of Arabs killed is disputed. The accepted version for many years was that 250 Arabs were killed. This astounding figure caused panic among the Arab population and indirectly influenced their flight from the Land of Israel during the battles of 1947–1948. Recent research raises doubts about the number of Arab dead. One of the versions holds that approximately 110 were killed. Beyond the controversy about the number of dead, all agree that the Deir Yassin battle was a key battle in the history of the War of Independence.[15]

The display adheres to the Etzel version, which has not changed since the War on the issue of responsibility for the battle and its outcome. The wording of the text on the signboard makes it clear that the authors expressed their opinion with extreme caution. However, they did not give up on presenting the full version of Etzel—that there were no mass killing or massacre at Deir Yassin, and that the

14. LEHI: Hebrew acronym of *Lohamei Herut Israel* (Fighters for the Freedom of Israel), a Jewish underground movement in Palestine, 1940–48.

15. See Benny Morris, "The Historiography of Deir Yassin," *The Journal of Israeli History* 24:1 (2005): 79–107; Walid Khalidi, *Deir Yassin, Friday 9 April 1948* (Jerusalem, 1999). I am grateful to Avraham Sela for referring me to this publication. See also Khalidi, *All That Remains: The Palestinian Villages Occupied and Depopulated by Israel in 1948* (Washington, DC, 1992), 289–92; Yoav Gelber, *Palestine 1948: War, Escape and the Emergence of the Palestinian Refugee Problem* (Brighton, 2001), 98–9.

battle's outcome in fact contributed to the victory of the Jewish side in this war. The display on Deir Yassin also refers to the subject of the refugees, albeit indirectly. The evacuation of Arab villages by their inhabitants is also mentioned in other displays in the same manner, with no reference to this subject other than the bare facts, representing a deliberate attempt to avoid political controversies over the charged issue of the Palestinian refugees.

Nonetheless, the display on Deir Yassin's conquest could not avoid reaffirmation of the Etzel's position regarding the dispute with the Haganah over the responsibility for the battle and its results. In Etzel's original declaration, entitled "To Denounce Hypocrisy," Etzel responds to the Haganah and Zionist leadership's condemnation of the "Dissident" organizations for their independent operation and massacre of defenseless villagers. The statement reiterates that "the truth about Deir Yassin" is that it was captured by Etzel and Lehi with the authorization of the Haganah Command in Jerusalem, which the latter denied after the conquest. The statement makes no attempt to hide its contempt toward the Haganah and Zionist leadership by reiterating the latter's official apology to King Abdallah of Jordan for the Deir Yassin massacre: "The fathomless hypocrisy of those who console Abdullah is denounced in the eyes of the entire nation."[16]

Another battle described here is the Battle for Yehud (Yahudiyyah) north of Lod (Lydda). The battle display is composed of two parts—the first part relates to the entire period of the battles on Yahudiyyah, while the second part focuses on the story of two female fighters. The panel of the first part describes how the village was captured by an Etzel force on May 4, 1948:

> The force attacked on three axes, and after fierce resistance the village fell into their hands. During the battle, all the inhabitants fled. At the end of May 1948, only a relatively small force remained, which also included about 20 girls who served both in guarding and in lookout duties. . . . On 11 June 1948, a large unit of the Arab Legion, reinforced by irregular Arab forces, attacked Yehudia under cover of armored vehicles.

The Etzel force was compelled to retreat. "At the same time, the enemy captured the mosque with a tower that was an observation point with two female soldiers—both were killed. . . . Twelve fighters fell on that day, including the two girls."

The second part of the display, entitled "The Legend of Ruth," is dedicated to the story of these two female soldiers, Ruth and Miriam. In the past, the display included audio recordings that were heard from a loudspeaker placed near the

16. On the Deir Yassin Haganah-Etzel controversy see David Niv, *The Irgun Zvai Leumi, in Open War 1947–1948*, Pt. 6 (Tel-Aviv, 1980), 86–92; Yehuda Slutzky, *History of The Hagana*, Vol. 3, Pt. 2 (Tel-Aviv, 1973), 1546–8 [Both in Hebrew]; Morris, "Deir Yassin," 80–4.

model of the village's houses and the mosque. Today, after the recordings stopped working properly, only the model remains. The Legend of Ruth is narrated by the guides as a substitute for the recordings.

The guide who leads a group of soldiers, opens by saying that, "[This is] a unique story in my opinion." Afterward she presents the story in a laconic form:

> Etzel captured Yehud. In the mosque, [there was] an observation point. The observation point was manned by Etzel [female] fighters. . . . The Jordanian Legion attacked. The order to retreat was received. Miriam . . . did not hear the retreat order. Suddenly, her voice was heard from the radio. Ruth, . . . her commander, took a Bren submachine gun and ran to the mosque. Her comrades called her to come back, [but she] did not answer them. [She] went up [to the tower of the mosque] and met her soldier. [They] decided to fight. When there was no more ammunition, [they] jumped to their deaths.

After finishing, the guide asked the soldiers: "Why do you think [they jumped to their deaths]?" One of the soldiers answered, "They would be tortured." The guide agreed with the answer and added: "They would be tortured to give information and then they would be killed. . . . Ruth knew that she did not want to provide information that would hurt the Etzel. . . . We see this as a courageous act. . . . She chose first of all to save her soldier. . . . [She] has the character of a leader."[17]

In an interview after the guided tour, another guide said: "We do not tell how they were found, beheaded, because they [the Jordanians] paraded with their heads. It is a difficult story for children and it is also difficult for soldiers. [It is difficult] for all ages who are guided here. It just creates an unnecessary violent [character]. . . . I focus on the story of Etzel."[18]

The museum's main display is the Battle for the Conquest of Jaffa, adjacent to the previous display at the center of the museum, as befits a site commemorating the fallen of the battle for Jaffa. It stresses the importance of Etzel's attack, focuses on describing the battle, while continuing the historical debate with the Haganah. The refugee issue is mentioned only as part of the description of the fighting, as a result of the bombardment of Jaffa by Etzel mortars.[19]

> On 25 April 1948 . . . Etzel soldiers were on their way to conquer Jaffa . . . and remove the danger it presented to Tel-Aviv and its residents. The goal of the conquest was to remove the threat of Jaffa becoming a naval base and military base for the Arab armies. On 28 April 1948, after three days of fierce fighting, the large Manshiyyah neighborhood was captured including its Hassan Beck

17. 1947–1948 Etzel Museum, guided tour, 8 May 2011.

18. B., guide in the 1947–48 Etzel Museum, interview, 11 April 2011.

19. According to the 1947 UN Partition Plan, Jaffa was to be part of the Arab State, constituting an enclave within the area allotted to the Jewish State.

Mosque, which threatened Tel-Aviv. Other parts of the city continued fighting with the help of 4,500 British soldiers. However, Etzel mortars continued their endless bombardment on the center of Jaffa causing its inhabitants to escape en masse. The attack on Manshiyyah had started before the wording of the operative sections of the agreement with the Haganah. The agreement took effect on 24 April—the Etzel was to act in coordination and at the consent of the Haganah high command. This was also the reason (in addition to the British factor [its military intervention]) that [finally] impelled the Etzel to sign the agreement [with the Haganah] and hand over Manshiyyah to the Haganah.[20]

The display consists of original weapons, historical photographs, the map of the battle, and clone figures of the fighters in their natural size. A computer screen next to it shows photographs of those who fell in this battle.

Another display nearby shows Etzel's activities in non-combat areas: acquisition of weapons and training in the country, alongside political and military activity overseas. This is how the founders of the display completed the picture of Etzel's fight against the Arabs and the British.

Toward the end of the display, a wide space is dedicated to another loaded issue—the story of the *Altalena*—the Etzel ship that carried significant amounts of weapons and over 900 passengers and arrived on Israel's shores on 20 June 1948, in the middle of the first four-week long truce after the proclamation of the State and the establishment of the IDF as its exclusive military force. Disagreement between Etzel's leadership and the Israel government over the designation of the ship's weaponry escalated into an exchange of fire that culminated in the sinking of the ship by IDF cannons on the Tel-Aviv coastline (near the current location of the museum). The *Altalena* display describes the series of events from Etzel's point of view, which claims that there was no justification to shell the ship that brought weapons and fighters to Israel, so desperately in need of them. The display does not include direct criticism of the IDF. The captions end with the presentation of the number of fallen fighters: "Many Jewish fighters were killed in the exchange of fire in Kfar Vitkin and Tel-Aviv: sixteen Etzel fighters and three IDF soldiers."

In an attempt to present this topic objectively, the sign is accompanied by two documents presenting the two contrasting perspectives regarding the *Altalena* affair, both prevalent at the time: the announcement by the Herut Movement and the bulletin of the IDF Brigade Commander on the Event.[21] The subjective perception of former Etzel members is presented nearby through a poem written

20. Alon Kadish, "The British Army in Manshiya," in Markovitzky, *The Rebels*, 253–67; Zahava Ostfeld, *An Army is Born* (Tel-Aviv, 1994), II, 628–30 [both in Hebrew].

21. On the perspectives of the Etzel, the Palmach, and Ben-Gurion, respectively, see Shlomo Nakdimon, *Altalena* (Jerusalem, 1978); Uri Brenner, *Altalena: Political and Military Study* (Tel-Aviv, 1978); Ostfeld, *An Army is Born*, 634–49 [all in Hebrew].

by one of the *Altalena*'s people. He views the people who caused the ship to sink as the biblical Cain who killed his brother Abel:

> Long years in Europe
> We toiled without pause
> The fruit of our effort, *Altalena*,
> We brought for you, O State.
> And if you ask from where
> We got these weapons,
> Then know you, Cain,
> That Etzel was and will be.[22]

The museum exhibit ends with the display Integration of Etzel into the IDF, which presents an unequivocal message—despite the terrible injury done to them, Etzel's members chose to integrate into the IDF and the State. It seems that the creators of the display tried to convey a non-partisan message, focusing less on the disputes of the past, especially at a time when the Likud, Etzel's political heir, had become a leading political power in Israel.

The Haganah Museum

The Haganah Museum is located in a historic building in the heart of Tel-Aviv on Rothschild Boulevard, a busy area of financial and entertainment activities. It is located in the house of Eliyahu Golomb, the "uncrowned commander of the Haganah," where he lived and operated secretly in the pre-state era.

The museum's establishment was initiated by an association organized to purchase the house and establish a museum of the history of the Haganah. Its head was then Foreign Minister Golda Meir and all its members were prominent public figures. After the purchase of the building the main part was preserved and another five-story structure was built next to it. The planning of the museum began in the mid-1950s. Its original display was inaugurated in 1961 in the presence of the Israel's president, the prime minister, and minister of defense, and the IDF Chief of Staff. Immediately upon its opening, the association transferred the museum to the Ministry of Defense, the first museum that the Ministry acquired and managed.

Most of the displays have been changed since its opening. Planning the current display on the history of the 1948 War began in 1997 and it was opened to the public in 2001.[23] The content of the War display (like all the other displays)

---

22. Rafael Kirsh, *"Song of the Altalena."* Kirsh joined the IDF and fell in the Negev during the War of Independence.

23. Gal, "The Contribution," 32–3; Kavenshtok, "The Historical Museum," 65–9; Haganah Museum Director Tali Shilo interview, 6 April 2011.

was defined by a steering committee comprised of representatives of the Ministry of Defense's Museums Unit and of the Organization of Haganah Veterans.[24]

The historical display extends over the three main floors of the building. The third floor is all dedicated to displays about the 1948 War. The panel opening the 1948 War display carries the heading "In Struggle" and reads:

> In the years 1946 and 1947, the struggle of the Yishuv against the British in the Land of Israel continued. At the beginning of 1947, the British government decided to present the question of Land of Israel to the UN. The Jewish Yishuv and the Haganah prepared for an emergency situation, including war against the Arabs of the Land of Israel and neighboring countries.[25] From the founding of the Haganah until this stage, approximately 1,000 members of the Haganah fell in the struggle to establish the State.[26]

Here and throughout the display, the founders chose to ignore the dissident groups of Etzel and Lehi and refrained from mentioning their salient role in the struggle against the British. The display founders also chose to note the period prior to the outbreak of hostilities by stating the number of the fallen of the Haganah during their service. The centrality of the fallen continues throughout the display, but in the entire exhibit there is almost no mention of the horrors of the war.

After going up a number of steps, the visitor encounters a display window in which there is one photograph: crowds celebrating in the streets of Tel-Aviv on the evening of the decision of the UN Partition Plan. The nearby panel states:

> On 29 November, the UN General Assembly decided to partition the Land of Israel into a Jewish state and an Arab state. The Jewish newspapers in the land and in the Diaspora described the joy of the Jewish people at the magnitude of the event. The Arabs were angry and opposed the decision. Already the following morning, the Arabs attacked the Jewish Yishuv. The War of Independence broke out.

Arab opposition to the partition is presented as the only reason for the outbreak of war—attacks by Arabs on Jews in order to prevent the partition of Palestine and the establishment of a Jewish state in part of it. Intra-Jewish debates on the

24. Ze'ev Lakhish, former Haganah Museum director, interview, 11 April 2011.

25. The display employs the terms "Arabs" or "Arabs of the Land of Israel" except for the panel dealing with the Haganah acquiring arms outside of the country, which ends with the words "in the war against the Palestinian Arabs and the Arab armies." Sometimes the question is raised concerning the use of both "Palestinians" and "Arabs"; N., Haganah Museum guide, interview.

26. A memorial at the museum's entrance shows the names of all the Haganah's fallen from its founding until the end of the War of Independence.

acceptance of Partition Plan (held by the Zionist Executive) or its rejection (as Etzel and other groups maintained) are not mentioned at all. Demonstrating the Haganah's responsible and timely reaction to the UN resolution, posters of enlistment to the Haganah are displayed in the same area. One, dated May 7, 1948, calls for mobilization of married men and fathers of children. The guide explains that this poster testifies to the great distress of the Yishuv after five months of fighting, reaching the point that it now became necessary to even mobilize men with families, who had been previously exempted.[27]

After climbing a few more steps visitors encounter a Haganah wall newspaper of December 9, 1947, just a few days after the UN Resolution. Regarding the Arabs and the British, the following is written: "The outbreaks are still local. The Mufti [Haj Amin al-Husseini] has still not succeeded in sweeping the mass of the Arab public into the cycle of rioting, but the attacks continue and are disturbing. Jews are injured and the government is silent." There is no explanation of why the Arabs attack and Jews are injured or how violence began, who the Mufti was, and why he attempted to sweep the "mass of the Arab public" to "the cycle of rioting." The British are presented as passive partners of the Arabs without providing any explanation for the British policy in that period.

The wall newspaper also refers to the "Porshim" (dissidents—Etzel and Lehi): "To the Porshim—stop. Do not disturb. Don't make it difficult for the Haganah. Don't give the British an excuse. . . . The Yishuv is united and on guard. Stop your deceptions now. Are you also willing to endanger the security of the people?"

According to the former director of the museum who was involved in the display's planning, the wall newspaper was integrated into the display primarily because of this final statement, as a response to his requirement that the 1948 War display also refer to Etzel and Lehi, despite the opposition of some members in the steering committee.[28] In previous parts of the display that relate to the period before the War, there are some references to those organizations and their activities. Nevertheless, their overall representation in the museum is minute, indicating the current struggle for shaping the Israeli collective memory of the War. This also reflects the lack of respect toward these movements by some of the Haganah members since the pre-State years.

At the head of the stairway, an old-fashioned radio announces Haganah headquarters' notices. In his messages, the announcer summarizes the organization's activities from the day of the UN Resolution to the day that the IDF was established. The content of the announcements was written specifically for the

---

27. Haganah Museum, guided tour, 6 April 2011. See Ostfeld, *An Army Is Born*, 52–5; Amitzur Ilan, *The Origin of the Arab-Israeli Arms Race: Arms, Embargo, Military Power and Decision in the 1948 Palestine War* (New York, 1996).

28. Ze'ev Lakhish, interview, 11 April 2011.

aims of the display. The first broadcast: "The Jewish Yishuv is preparing to ward off the Arab attacks. In the first stage, our forces have approximately 3,000 fighters, mostly from the Palmach, and other forces from the Hish, from the territorial defense, and the Notrim."[29]

The Arabs are organizing to attack, and the Jews are organizing to defend. The writers of the announcement are careful to mention all the Haganah's sections that took part in the war effort. In this way, they communicate with the memory keepers among Haganah veterans, making sure that all get credit.

The second broadcast: "At the end of two months of battles, it is now clear that the Arabs of the Land of Israel attack with irregular forces and are assisted by the Arab nations with equipment and personnel." The theme of self-defense against Arab attacks continues in the third broadcast: "Our slogan in the war is 'the entire land is a front, the entire people is an army.' Our secret weapon is 'there is no choice, we must win, no settlement will be abandoned, we are all for victory.'" There is no explanation why "there is no choice" and "we must win," apparently because it was obvious to those who designed the display, just as it is perfectly clear to current Israeli visitors.

The fourth broadcast presents the core Israeli narrative about the invasion of Palestine by a strong and aggressive Arab regular force fighting against a weak and peace-seeking Jewish Yishuv: "This morning, 15 May 1948, the first day of the State of Israel, the armies of Egypt, Transjordan, Syria, Lebanon, and Iraq invaded with a force of 30,000 soldiers, armed with artillery, armor, and planes. The forces of the Haganah are prepared to stop the enemy." It is only in the next announcement that the Jewish force is presented: "This morning, 1 July 1948, the Haganah becomes the Israel Defense Forces. The Haganah transfers to the IDF twelve infantry brigades,[30] an air force, a navy, an artillery corps, engineering and signal corps, and auxiliary corps. A total of 50,000 soldiers." This brief message is in fact aimed to the Israeli society, announcing the establishment of the IDF as a direct continuation of the Haganah. The former museum director explains: "We spoke [in the steering committee] about the centrality of the Haganah in building the IDF. This is the central message. . . . The central idea was the . . . fact that the Haganah was the army of the state-to-be that became the IDF."[31]

Immediately afterwards the visitor is led to a room designed as a war room—a table with a map of the Land of Israel. Red blinking lights indicate the places

29. Hish: Hebrew acronym of *Heil Sadeh* (field corps) was the Haganah's main surface corps; watchmen was a Jewish Police Force set up in 1936 by the British in Palestine to help defend Jewish settlements.

30. Nine brigades were under the direct command of the Haganah, and three additional brigades were under the command of the Palmach, a unit of the Haganah.

31. Ze'ev Lakhish interview. See Ostfeld, *An Army Is Born*, "Introduction."

where battles are taking place. According to the guide, when she stands here before a group, she points out the red lights on the map and directs the students to search for the focal points of the battles. She maintains that her purpose is to show that the Jewish border during the War was in every settlement, and this was the difficulty and uniqueness of the War of Independence. Afterward, she presents a map of the Partition Plan and explains that "If there had been no war, it is reasonable to assume that they would have settled for the partition borders. But since there was a war, [the Jewish forces] breached the UN partition borders."[32]

The tour in this room ends opposite a map of the 12 Haganah brigades—spread across the country, from the Galilee to the Negev—that became the main formations of the IDF upon its establishment. According to the guide, the visitors generally ask at this point, "'What about the other underground groups? What about the ship [the *Altalena*]?' Here I say a word about the IDF being established by uniting all the organizations. They actually entered the framework of the Haganah and established the IDF together. . . . This force was not easily established but in the end it came along."[33] In other words, the guiding also supports the display's theme that the role of the Etzel and Lehi in the struggle for the establishment of the State of Israel and the IDF was marginal. Even the visitors' demand to relate to the *Altalena* Affair, which included a confrontation within the IDF between former Haganah/Palmach members and former Etzel members, was met with an answer that the issue is not really worth consideration.

From here, visitors enter an auditorium set up like a war zone where a film is screened. They sit on "sand bags" representing "shooting positions," with original weapons from that period deposited before them and aimed at the screen. They watch a brief film of the War—the highlight of the exhibition. The film focuses on the image of a young fighter, Yitzik. Visitors would have already met him in previous displays as a young Holocaust survivor who reaches the Land of Israel as part of the illegal immigration, joins the Haganah, and takes part in the resistance to the British. Now he participates in the battle to capture the Castel—an Arab village dominating the road to Jerusalem which, for months, blocked the passage of supply convoys to the besieged Jewish neighborhoods in the city. During the movie, Yitzik is killed but the battle ends with the victory of the Haganah forces.

According to the former museum director, "There was no big debate about the story . . . only about the intensity with which he was supposed to die. It was clear that someone had to die at the end . . . but no one was able to predict the final

32. N., guide in the Haganah Museum.
33. Ibid.

outcome. I think it is somewhat exaggerated. . . . Here you actually see him get hit and die."[34]

At the end of the film, the narrator reads the poem "Here Our Bodies Lie," written after a platoon of 35 young Haganah fighters sent to reinforce the besieged Gush Etzion was entirely liquidated in a desperate battle with Arab villagers in the Judean Hills in December 1947. Beyond its tragic fate, that battle became, also due to the poem, a primary mythical story of the War of Independence in Israel.[35] The following is a translation from Hebrew of the poem's last passage:

> Here our bodies lie in a long line and we do not breathe.
> But the wind is strong in the mountains . . . and breathes.
> And the morning is born, and the dewdrops' dawn is rejoicing.
> We shall return, we shall meet again, we shall return as red flowers.
> You will recognize us immediately, the silent "mountain platoon."
> Then we will blossom, once in the mountains the last shot's outcry is quiet down.[36]

Together with the poem's narration, a representative list of the first names of some fallen Haganah members appears on the screen accompanied by quiet music.

At the end of the presentation, the guide turns to the group of soldiers in the auditorium and asks what the names were. The soldiers answered that they were of the Palmach members. The guide says that the answer was correct,[37] adding that the number of those killed in the war was 6,000, or 1 percent of the 600,000 Jews then living in the country.[38]

In front of the exit door of the movie auditorium, the group passed by a panel entitled "The Losses," which shows the data of the fallen in a precise and detailed form:

> From the establishment of the Haganah in 1920 until April 1949, 5,151 members of the Haganah fell. In the War of Independence, 4,790 fighters fell, of whom 3,952 were Haganah members. Many were injured and became disabled. An entire generation of youth fell on the battlefields of 1947–1949, and they were, in the words of the poet, "the silver platter upon which the Jewish state was given."

---

34. Ze'ev Lakhish, interview. On the myth that Holocaust survivors were sent to their death in the context of Latrun, see Anita Shapira, "Historiography and Memory: Latrun, 1948," *Jewish Social Studies* 3.1 (1996): 20–61.

35. Motti Zeira, "Beginning of the Myth of the 35," *Yahadut Zemanenu* 10 (1996): 41–71.

36. Haim Guri, "Here Our Bodies Lie," in *The Songs* (Jerusalem, 1998).

37. The guide ignored the fact that the answer related to the Palmach. Such is the confusion between the Palmach and the Haganah; many Israelis consider the Palmach as a fourth organization, along with the Haganah, Etzel, and Lehi.

38. Haganah Museum, guided tour. It is estimated that the Jewish population numbered 600,000 in November 1947.

The last sentence is taken from the poem by Nathan Alterman, "The Silver Platter," published in the first days of the war.[39] Today it is a central component in all memorial ceremonies for the fallen of the wars of Israel and it appears in its entirety in the museum entrance.[40]

In the movie, as well as in the entire war display, there is no mention of the enemy losses or the subject of refugees. According to the former director, "The subject of refugees simply did not come up. . . . I don't remember if it was even brought up and rejected."[41] The story of the Palmach Museum construction (established by Palmach veterans in 1999), as described by the curator, helps us to understand what is behind this oversight: "In the association that established the Palmach Museum, they did not want to include the subject of the refugees. . . . They opposed by arguing that the subject of the refugees is a political decision and they did not make the decision. . . . The perspective of the war in the museum is our suffering, our fallen."[42]

Behind the exit door near the movie auditorium, a caption stands out on the opposite wall—words of David Ben-Gurion, taken from the "Order of Establishment of the IDF" on 31 May 1948:

> Upon the establishment of the State of Israel, the Haganah evolved from an underground to become a regular army. The Yishuv and the Jewish People owe a great debt to the Haganah in all stages of its existence and development . . . In the chronicles of the State of Israel, the part about the Haganah will shine with pride and glory—never to be obscured.[43]

At this point, the guide leaves the group saying: "The IDF did not come from nowhere. The Haganah was the infrastructure for the IDF created on Ben-Gurion's command."[44]

Israeli Museum at the Yitzhak Rabin Center

The Israeli Museum is part of the Yitzhak Rabin Center, which is

> dedicated to commemorating the activities and memory of Prime Minister Yitzhak Rabin, and to strengthen Israeli democracy by learning the lessons that can be learned from the assassination of the prime minister. The Center combines

---

39. *Natan Alterman,* "The Silver Platter," *Davar,* 19 December 1947.

40. See Ilana Shamir, *Commemoration and Remembrance: Israel Way of Shaping the Patterns of its Collective Memory* (Tel-Aviv, 1996) [Hebrew].

41. Ze'ev Lakhish, interview.

42. Orit Shaham Gover, curator of *The Palmach Journey in the Palmach Museum,* interview, 27 April 2011.

43. This also appears at the entrance to the museum.

44. Haganah Museum, guided tour.

educational activities, museum commemorations and documentation, and is active in all sectors of Israeli society.[45]

The Rabin Center was established by order of The Yitzhak Rabin Center for commemorating the memory of Yitzhak Rabin Law, 1996. The law determines that the State will provide the required land for the Center. Construction of the Center will be funded by contributions, and ongoing activities will be funded by the State in addition to donations and independent income.[46] Planning the Center and the Museum began shortly after Rabin's assassination in November 1995. Historians and designers took part in the planning. They were given a free hand by the Rabin family. The museum was opened to the public in January 2010.[47] The Center building stands on a hill overlooking the central park of Tel-Aviv, near three other museums and Tel-Aviv University.

The Museum presents the biography of Yitzhak Rabin—prime minister and minister of defense, who was murdered at a peace rally in Tel-Aviv on 4 November 1995—parallel with the history of the pre-state Jewish community in Palestine, and the State of Israel during his lifetime (1922–95). The visitor passes through signboards of the deceased leader's life displayed in a spiral corridor. There are openings in this corridor that lead to additional display spaces that display the history of Israel throughout its various periods and constitute in their entirety "the Israeli Museum." In this way, the visitor repeatedly goes between the personal story of Yitzhak Rabin and the national story of Israel.[48]

The 1948 War display opens with a photograph of the UN General Assembly on the day of the vote for partition. With earphones, the visitor can hear the famous broadcast of the voting besides a panel with the following text:

> A United Nations Special Committee on Palestine (UNSCOP) recommended the partition of the Land of Israel and the establishment of two states, Jewish and Arab. On 29 November 1947, the UN General Assembly adopted the partition recommendation. Although many Jews, from the right-wing and left-wing groups, opposed the partition, on that night all were united in joy. The Arabs[49] completely rejected the UN decision. Riots broke out deteriorating into war

45. Israeli Museum, visitor brochure.

46. The Yitzhak Rabin Center for commemorating the memory of the Yitzhak Rabin Law, 1996, http://www.knesset.gov.il/laws/special/heb/rabinlaws.htm.

47. http://www.rabincenter.org.il/museum/pages/default.aspx; Nurit Levinovsky, interviews 4 April and 5 May 2011; Credits panel of the museum.

48. The Rabin Center, *Content and Planning Concept*, June 1999; The Israeli Museum, visitor brochure.

49. The museum also uses the term "Arabs" or "the Arabs of the Land of Israel" in the parts of the exhibition relating to prior to the War of Independence. The term "Palestinians" appears for the first time in the display of 1967–77.

between the Jews and Arabs for control of the roads and the cities with a mixed population. In April 1948, Haganah forces initiated counterattacks to ensure control over the areas that the UN had designated for the Jewish State.

This statement is noteworthy for acknowledging that opposition to the Partition Plan came from both right- and left-wing. This, however, is partly balanced by the immediately following emphasis on the unifying joy that swept the Jewish community as a whole on the night of the voting, while the Arabs, presented as a monolithic group, all opposed the partition. The caption does not explicitly say who is responsible for the deterioration of the riots into an Arab-Jewish war, though by mentioning the Haganah's initiation of counterattacks it clearly leaves the impression that the Arabs attacked the Jews first.

A guide leading a group of English speakers says at this point that the war that began on the morrow of the UN decision on partition was a "civil war," which, by the end of the British Mandate on 15 May, turned into the "invasion of Arab nations." He then stated that during the entire war that lasted one and a half years, there were 6,000 Jews killed, constituting 1 percent of the Jewish population in the country at that time.[50]

A short film is then shown that opens with pictures of the UN General Assembly, shifts to celebrations of the Yishuv, following the partition decision, and ends with pictures of the onset of the War. The Jewish community is depicted as being attacked by the Arabs and defending itself to the best of its ability. The film is accompanied by rhythmic music and includes many segments showing mobs of Arabs running with rifles in their hands. Included is an interview with Ben-Gurion, prime minister and minister of defense during the war, who relates that when the UN made its decision on partition, it was clear to him that war would break out and therefore he did not celebrate that night. The film leaves the viewer with the feeling of the existential danger sensed by the Yishuv.

Further on, a map of the invasion routes of the Arab armies is presented. The partition lines are also shown on the map. Then there is a panel entitled "A State Named Israel":

> Shortly before the British forces evacuated the country, the moment of the long-awaited proclamation of independence arrived. On 5 Iyar 5708 [14 May 1948], the members of The People's Council (Mo'etzet Ha'am) gathered in the Tel-Aviv Museum. David Ben-Gurion, the chairman of the Jewish Agency Executive, read the Declaration of Independence. A State named Israel was founded. After more than two thousand years, Jewish sovereignty was renewed in the Land of Israel.

The display, "One Army or Many Armies—the *Altalena* Incident," appears next to the Proclamation of Independence. It includes a film that focuses on Etzel's ship of

50. The Israeli Museum, guided tour, 31 March 2011.

munitions and fighters that reached the shores of Israel after the founding of the State. It opens with newspaper headlines from the period describing the course of events until the ship was sunk, followed by a quotation from a letter by Ben-Gurion: "This time there can be no compromises. Either they accept the orders or we fire. This time I am opposed to any negotiations with them and to any agreement. Force must be used without hesitation and immediately." Additionally, an interview with Rabin is shown, where he says: "There was a long battle of an hour to an hour and a half. Then a cry began 'Begin is on the ship.'[51] Some of the Palmach people heard 'Begin is on the ship' and they began a heavy bombardment. This was one of the most difficult incidents that I remember." A special display is dedicated to the *Altalena* incident (a short and insignificant episode in the context of the War itself, but a defining incident in the collective Israeli memory to this day) that is almost the same size as that devoted to the long months of war with the Arabs. Rabin himself played a relatively minor role in the *Altalena* Affair. But over the years, when he became a leading political figure and prime minister who led the Oslo agreements, there were those who tried to exaggerate his role in this incident, aiming to weaken his public influence. Apparently, this is the explanation of the expanded exhibit—the connection between the struggle for the collective memory of the 1948 War and the struggle for the collective memory of Rabin's legacy.[52]

The title of the next panel is "The War of Independence."

> On 15 May 1948, Arab armies invaded the western part of the Land of Israel. In the first month of fighting, the IDF had difficulty standing against the regular armies, but in June, it shifted to the offensive, which continued until March 1949. During this time, Israel succeeded in taking control of a larger area than that allocated to it in the Partition Plan—in the center of the country, the Galilee, and the Negev. Jerusalem was divided: the western part to the Jews, the eastern part to the Arabs under Jordanian sovereignty.

The panel is accompanied by a large photograph of soldiers riding open field cars carrying machine guns, racing in the open desert, "Shimshon Foxes heading south," and a film on IDF combat. The film opens with a description of the great danger hovering over Israel due to the Arab military invasion and ends with Israel's victory culminating in reaching the south tip of the Negev at the Gulf of Aqaba (Eilat). The film ends with the words: "The War of Independence ended, leaving behind 6,000 killed and one new state." The statement is heard against a background of photographs of a temporary military cemetery in which bereaved parents mourn on the graves of their children. The end of the War is thus presented by emphasizing its heavy toll.

---

51. Menachem Begin (1913–93), Etzel leader.
52. Anita Shapira, *Yigal Allon, Spring of His Life* (Tel-Aviv, 2004), 344–9.

An additional short film is shown in this location on a small screen, "The Arab Refugees 1948." Segments of documentary films from that period are shown repeatedly presenting people getting on trucks, barefoot men stuck in mud, barbed-wire fences, tents, and children standing in line for food distribution. Quiet music accompanies the movie, in which there are no words. During the tour, the guide points in the direction of the movie and says to his group that the discussion about refugees who ran away to Arab lands had been renewed and much attention is given to their "right of return," which is part of the negotiations with the Palestinians. He also adds that the refugees hold onto the keys to their original houses to this very day.[53] According to the director of the Education Department, the team that established the museum did not dispute the need to include the film about the refugees in the display. After opening the museum, however, it turned into a bone of contention among visitors with some demanding that the film be removed from the display. The management of the museum insists that it remain in place: "I feel that the film about the Arab refugees is very powerful. It does not leave you indifferent. Most of the visitors have never seen anything like this before. Although the film is part of the general presentation, it is of significant influence."[54]

The last panel to complete the exhibit is called "Little Israel."[55]

> The borders of the State of Israel (the Green Line) were fixed in armistice agreements with Egypt, Jordan, Syria, and Lebanon. The Israeli victory in the War of Independence was at great cost; approximately 6,000 civilians and fighters, one percent of the population, were killed. Eleven Jewish settlements were captured and their inhabitants killed or evicted from their homes. The Arabs of the Land of Israel were the losing side in the War. Approximately 650,000 went into exile.[56] Israel did not allow the Arab refugees to return to their homes at the end of the fighting. 146,000 Arabs remained in Israel.

The summarized results of the War include repeated and detailed references to the heavy price that the Jewish side paid, but there is also an attempt to refer to the cost for the other side. Despite their marginal place in the 1948 War exhibit, the few sentences devoted here to describe the refugees are very significant, especially when combined with the short film shown before, "The Arab Refugees 1948." The number of Arabs who were killed is not mentioned, but compared to the 1947–48

---

53. The Israeli Museum, guided tour.

54. Nurit Levinovsky, interviews.

55. "Little Israel" is a nostalgic term used after the 1967 War in which Israel occupied large territories beyond its 1949 Armistice lines, reflecting a longing for "the days of innocence" at the beginning of the State, a time that will never return.

56. Most Israeli scholars refer to 650–700,000 refugees. Among Arab scholars it is 750–800,000.

Etzel Museum, which relates to the refugee issue only casually, and the Haganah Museum which ignores the entire issue, the Israeli Museum displays the number of refugees in order to illustrate the extent of their disaster, mentioning that the State of Israel refused to allow them to return to their homes. The director of the museum's Education Department explains that:

> The concept of "the righteousness of our cause" is an essential part of the museum. The team that planned and designed the exhibits felt that there is not enough justification to tell a separate narrative for "the other side"—the Arabs. However, it can be mentioned in the framework of our narrative. One of the objectives is to present the Zionist enterprise as a successful one—there are problems and difficulties, but let us look back with a certain pride.[57]

The exhibit ends with a map of the armistice lines (the Green Line), including a detailed map of the divided city of Jerusalem. There is a large photograph of the raising of the Ink Flag (an improvised Israeli flag) on the shore of the Bay of Eilat along with a caption, "Eilat is in our hands."[58]

Conclusion

The narratives in the exhibits of the 1947–48 Etzel Museum and the Haganah Museum represent the typical narrative of the 1948 generation as formulated during and shortly after the War. The narrative in the Israeli Museum, which was established 20 and 10 years after the Etzel and Haganah Museums' displays, respectively, represents a slightly different perception of the 1948 events, especially in its informative reference to the Arab refugees.

On the whole, however, this museum adheres to the same creeds and uses almost the same terminology as the two other museums about the righteousness of the Zionist enterprise, the Arabs' negative policies, and the consequent Jewish-Arab relations before and during the 1948 War.

The 1947–48 Etzel Museum and the Haganah Museum present the history of the 1948 War from the narrow point of view of the organizations they represent. The exhibits in both museums follow the agenda of their founders—the veterans of these organizations. In both museums, the exhibit is limited to describing the War operations rather than to its impact later on. Etzel veterans focus on two

57. Nurit Levinovsky, interviews. "The museum projects a picture of the Zionist enterprise as a success story—not without patches, difficulties and failures, but because of these difficulties, the success story is even more prominent." See http://www.rabincenter.org.il/museum/pages/default.aspx.

58. The Ink Flag on 10 March 1949 is marked in Israel's collective memory as a symbol of the end of the War and Israel's victory. It is also associated with Rabin who served as deputy commander of the Southern Front at the time.

major topics: presenting their contribution to the victory in the war, and legitimatizing their activities during this period. In contrast, Haganah veterans focus on one major topic: presenting the IDF as a direct and natural continuation of the Haganah. Most of the exhibit ignores the Etzel story during the War as well as the role of other groups that contributed to the victory. In contrast, the Israeli Museum, which is not committed to the story of any particular organization, attempts to present the War from an independent and more broadly consensual point of view. Despite its name, the Israeli Museum also makes almost no mention of the contribution of Etzel and Lehi to the war effort, and limits itself to the description of the military operations and the War's immediate results.

The displays at the Etzel and Haganah Museums focus on events that took place on the Jewish side, while events on the other side are described only as an illustration or a motive for the war operations of the Jewish side. On the other hand, the display at the Israeli Museum presents some exception in this issue. Indeed, it also focuses on the Jewish side and, while most of it also ignores the Arab side, it nevertheless presents the issue of Palestinian refugees in a short film and a few sentences, in contrast to the Haganah Museum that does not address the refugee issue at all, and the Etzel Museum that mentions it only indirectly, in the context of the Haganah-Etzel controversy over Deir Yassin.

All three museums share the blame of the Arabs as the aggressive party, but none of the museums gloat on the harsh defeat suffered by the Arab enemy and there is no attempt to dehumanize the enemy. They dedicate significant space and effort to commemorate the fallen in the war. The 1947–48 Etzel Museum, originally established as commemoration sites, clearly adheres to this mission, which is the epicenter of its display. At the Haganah Museum, the display starts and ends by commemorating the fallen on top of mentioning them throughout the display. The Israeli Museum does not address the commemoration but like the other two museums, it emphasizes the large number of fallen soldiers on the Jewish side. The concluding film presents photographs from military cemeteries.

The three displays are dedicated to a tough and vicious war in which the Jewish side won an overwhelming victory following a period of existential fear. However, it is impossible to find any celebration of the victory. The price of the victory is presented more prominently than the actual victory, leaving visitors of all three museums deeply aware of the staggering cost of life—both soldiers and citizens—the Jewish side paid for its survival and secured sovereignty.[59]

These museums are museums of history, attempting to provide the visitors with historical facts through documents, historical photographs, films, and detailed captions. However, they differ significantly from one another in their

---

59. Such reference to victory and its price is also common in Israel regarding subsequent wars in the Jewish-Arab conflict.

design. The design of the 1947–48 Etzel Museum is the oldest (1992). In today's terms, it can be called "outdated." The display in this museum consists mainly of still photographs, captions, and original items. The design of the Haganah Museum display, opened about a decade later (2001), includes photographs, items, and captions as well, but the main part of the exhibit is a film. The exhibit at the Israeli Museum combines films that were edited from films produced during the War as well as captions and photographs. Of the cases examined, the Haganah Museum speaks to the emotions in the most direct manner. The style used in the 1947–48 Etzel Museum is mostly factual and documentary, but it addresses the emotional aspect as well, especially in the "The Legend of Ruth" and *Altalena* displays. The historiographical element is more prominent at the Israeli Museum with the emotional aspect downplayed, but it still exists throughout the exhibit.

I found a discernible amount of silence about unpleasant past events in all three museums. This is the case with regard to the intra-Jewish conflicts, which are largely narrowed and understated, as well as regarding the tragedy that befell the Palestinian-Arabs in the War,[60] despite the disparity found in the Israeli Museum.

The partial and minor presentation of the Haganah-Etzel internal conflict, especially their military competition during the inter-communal war and violent clash after the proclamation of the state over the *Altalena* in which a broader confrontation was avoided in the last moment; The avoidance of presenting multiple opinions of the Jewish side regarding the War, its operations and results; The Israelis' traumatic memory of the War and the continuous mourning of the fallen, as well as the minimal presentation of the Arab side and the impact of War on the fate of the Palestinians and the neighboring Arab states—all indicate that the three museums aim at intra-Israeli commemoration of the War. As such, despite some differences, the three museums contribute to preserve a national memory mostly concerned with conformity and unity rather than functioning as educational centers offering the public a profound understanding of the complex history of the War and especially of its causal connection and relevance to the ongoing struggle between rival political parties in Israel, as well as to the continuous Israeli-Palestinian conflict.

The 1947–48 Etzel Museum and the Haganah Museum were established by public bodies who wished to legitimize their narrative, generated under the influence of the disputes between rival political factions and pre-State underground movements over the nature of commemoration, during Israel's first two decades.

---

60. For a similar case of silence of Israeli museums about the history of Jewish agricultural settlement in Palestine, and comparison with British exhibition of history of the industrial revolution and the class struggle it triggered, see Tamar Katriel, "Telling the Story of Eretz Israel: The Ethnography of a Museum of the History of the Jewish Settlement," *Dvarim Ahadim* 2 (1997): 65–6.

These issues, however, had largely ceased to play any conspicuous role, and in fact almost disappeared from the public discourse already before these museums were established. In this respect, they retain a degree of anachronism. Although apparently the founders of the Israeli Museum did not have the limitations that affected their predecessors, they chose to introduce the difficulties created by the 1948 War, with its effects felt until today, in a minimalistic way. Therefore, we can say that the Israeli Museum is also characterized by some anachronism. Despite the anachronism, these museums continue to exist as they are. This perhaps indicates the stability of the Israeli narrative, presented in each of the three museums in its own way—with a distinctive tone and emphasis.

OFER BOORD is the curator of the Ministry of Defense museums. He is author of *"Take the Stolen Money from the Hands of the Killer!": The Kibbutz Movement and the Reparations Agreement, the Personal Compensations and the Restitutions from Germany.*

Part 2: The Politics of Space Memory

4　Contested Urban Memoryscape Strategies and Tactics in Post-1948 Haifa

Ziva Kolodney

Introduction

Haifa's Memorial Garden (Gan ha-Zikkaron) was the subject of an architectural competition immediately after the 1948 War. It was a main urban open space, situated at the heart of the city's current municipal center along the confrontation seam between the pre-1948 Arab quarter of Haifa's downtown area and the Jewish neighborhood of Hadar ha-Carmel. Today, the garden overlooks the long-gone Old City area of Haifa, which was demolished during the Shikmona Operation in 1948–49. Along with concrete and imagery landscape memory production practices (memoryscape) of street re-naming, war monuments and memorials construction in the urban fabric in the early 1950s, and the Haifa Municipality's yearly organized school students walking the footsteps of 1948 worriers' trail, the Memorial Garden design and layout attempt to reconstruct a collective commemoration of the local/national Israel War of Independence 1948 and tell its official story.[1] Similarly, the traces of the old urban fabric on new paving along Haifa's newly developed Government Center's sidewalks and the adjacent Treasury Garden (Gan HaOtzar), built during the 1990s, are an official urban construction of memory building. However, inspired by the 1993 Oslo Accords, its plan and details conceal the chronicle of the long-gone Old City Arab-Palestinian inhabitants.

Against these memoryscape strategies of architectural production, competing practices of commemoration take place in the city space: Zochrot ([women] remembering) organization re-posts pre-1948 street names and organizes walks

---

1. On memoryscape concepts and practices see Lisa Yoneyama, "Taming the Memoryscape: Hiroshima's Urban Renewal," in *Remapping Memory: The Politics of TimeSpace*, ed. Jonathan Boyarin (Minneapolis, 1994), 136–99; Sannon Davis and Jacky Bowring, "The Right to Remember: The Memorials to Genocide in Cambodia and Rwanda," in *The Right to Landscape: Contesting landscape and Human Rights*, ed. Shelley Egoz, Jala Makhzoumi, and Gloria Pungetti (Burlington, 2011), 211–26.

The War of 1948 (2016); 101–120, DOI: 10.2979/warof1948.0.0.06

in former Arab city quarters telling the Palestinian narrative; individual scholars and activists lead urban walks, including artists such as Ilana Salama Ortar, whose experiments in urban memory signify another sort of such tactics.[2] These actions are another way to gauge the cityscape contested history of the mixed Jewish-Arab city of Haifa and share its memories. Following Christine Boyer's proposition to discover the basis of the public realm for a fractured society, one that allows "the play of oppositions the existence of randomness, disturbances, dispersions and accidents,"[3] such examination reveals the story of Haifa's 1948 events in the urban public realm, suggesting a non-binary approach to the different Jewish and Arab historical narratives, where 1948 marks the break.[4] Despite their differences, both memoryscape strategies and tactics bear witness to the history of 1948 War events and share its memories publicly. It raises questions about the power of the urban landscapes as expressions of identity[5] and a means of shaping the relationships between those who inhabit them, especially in the mixed city of Haifa that is praised as a model of Jewish-Arab coexistence.[6] Their different ways of reframing and reinterpreting a sense of belonging through physical forms of buildings, street layouts, monumental structures, and informal acts, reveals conflicts between interests and powers and raises an understanding of diachronic processes of history and synchronic processes of memory as on-going urban practices.

2. Ilana Salama Ortar was born in Alexandria, living in Tel-Aviv and Berlin. The information presented here was gained through many talks with her over 1995–2012, her archival material, and based on her work book *The Camp of the Jews: Uprooting, Refugeeism and Immigration* (Tel-Aviv, 2005) [Hebrew].

3. Christine M. Boyer, *The City of Collective Identity: Its Historical Imagery and Architectural Entertainments* (Cambridge, 1994), 68.

4. Against the Israeli myth of rebirth and independence, Palestinian time is defined by the events of the 1948 war and the cataclysm of the Nakba. See Tamir Sorek, "Cautious Commemoration: Localism, Communalism, and Nationalism in Palestinian Memorial Monuments in Israel," *Comparative Studies in Society and History* 50.2 (2008): 337–68.

5. On urban landscape production of memory building processes see Ziva Kolodney and Rachel Kallus, "'Big' and 'Small' Cityscapes: Dilemmas of Mnemonic Landscapes," in *The Right to Landscape: Contesting Landscape and Human Rights*, ed. Shelley Egoz, Jala Makhzoumi, and Gloria Pungetti (Burlington, 2011), 197–210; Rose-Redwood Reuben, Derek H. Alderman, and Maoz Azaryahu, "Collective Memory and the Politics of Urban Space: An Introduction," *GeoJournal* 73.3 (2008): 160–3: and articles in Mark Crison, ed., *Urban Memory: History and Amnesia in the Modern City* (London and New York, 2005).

6. On the connection between urban space practices and coexistence in Haifa, see Joseph Leibovitz, "Faultline Citizenship: Ethnonational Politics, Minority Mobilisation, and Governance in the Israeli 'Mixed Cities' of Haifa and Tel-Aviv-Jaffa," *Ethnopolitics* 6.2 (2007): 235–63; Rachel Kallus and Ziva Kolodney, "Rethinking Urban Space: between Localism, Nationalism, and Globalization," *Journal of Urban Design* 15.3 (2010): 403–22.

Drawing on Michel de Certeau's distinction between the meta-level practices of the city and the intimacy of the individual's relationship with place, and by Haim Hazan's perception of the Israeli society's mythical and diachronic time dialog, these urban sites and actions are examined here on both official and civic levels: as calculated strategies and processes of landscape memory design and tactics of everyday experience of landscape memory production.[7] Such exploration presents a dialectic tension between landscape perception as a collective production and as familiar phenomena that may lead to strengthen dominant powers, or to invent an everyday public realm that will help its occupants to be open to counter memory discourse. Following Andreas Huyssen's study of urban memory-building practices, I examine the landscape's unique role as a concrete influential public instrument of memory, and stress its significance as a political and cultural construct in the making of the cityscape.[8] Due to its temporality notion and the constant changing of our social, cultural, and national identities, says Huyssen, we need the footprint of our past to hold on to in the city fabric.

As a place of memory, I argue that the cityscape is both a site for symbolic control and symbolic resistance. Further to this argument, the practice of urban memory, enacted by the Israeli-Palestinian conflict, is deeply embedded in Haifa's cityscape. Accepting the cityscape as a palimpsest that traces both collective and personal history, in what follows I explore not only how Haifa's memoryscape sites and actions define official and everyday landscapes, but also how they negotiate the memory and amnesia of Haifa's 1948 events for the last decades. The growing scholarships of urban memory at large and about 1948 memory and amnesia, poses a number of questions: Why are we obsessed with the sense of belonging? Why are new frames of belonging invented in different eras? How is the urban fabric being used for this task?

Urban Landscape Memory and Loss

Urban landscapes are both expressions of identity and a means of shaping individual and communal memory, reinterpreted as changing expressions of power relations.[9] The city, claims Christine Boyer, is not just a metaphor for individual

---

7. Michel de Certeau, *The Practice of Everyday Life* (Berkeley, 1984); Haim Hazan, "Between Times: The Essence of Israelism," *Zemanim* 68–69 (1999–2000): 156–246 [Hebrew].

8. Andreas Huyssen, *Present Pasts: Urban Palimpsests and the Politics of Memory* (Palo Alto, CA, 2003).

9. On landscape and memory see John Gillis, "Memory and Identity: The History of a Relationship," in *Commemorations: The Politics of National Identity*, ed. John Gillis (Princeton, 1994), 3–24; Denis Cosgrove, *Social Formation and Symbolic Landscape* (Madison, WI, 1998); John Wylie, *Landscape* (London-New York, 2007).

recollection but also a giant device for shaping collective memory.[10] It is constructed to cultivate identification through narratives and myths, strongly linked to concrete sites and specific landscapes, often seeking to unite people in a symbolic narrative of "imagined community" as argued by Benedict Anderson.[11]

The landscape's duality as a concrete site and an imagery symbolic naturalized meaning is significant in the making of the urban memory.[12] As an actual place where traumatic war and terror acts had happened, urban sites constantly engage with the physical, marking an image of history. Thus, urban landscapes are a silent witness to historical actions that accumulate critical landscape knowledge in layers of political and cultural contexts. It is a fertile ground through which political agendas are constructed and the politics of memory is rooted. Moreover, as a natural phenomenon of everyday routines, the urban landscape gives a concrete form to political and social ideas, simultaneously shaping the image and identities of its users. In this way, Dianne Harris asserts that landscapes are an efficient tool for reinforcing formal and informal strategies of national identity and of memory construction.[13] Lionella Scazzosi regards landscape as a source of collective meaning—an artifact, a document, and an archive of the past, claiming that reading landscapes as a palimpsest unites the concrete site with the idea of the past.[14]

The dynamic of the time-space memory building of cityscapes emphasizes memory production as a negotiable entity. Boyer views cityscapes as a generative power of national identity, in which one monolithic memory of a specific past or a particular ideology is choreographed and promoted over the other.[15] In this battleground of memory construction, the urban landscape wields symbolic powers. Dianne Harris argues that its natural-like phenomenon of everyday routines gives a concrete form to political and social ideas, simultaneously shaping the image and identities of its users.[16] While Simon Schama discusses landscape as

---

10. Boyer, *The City of Collective Identity*, 3.

11. Benedict Anderson, *Imagined Communities: Reflections on the Origin and Spread of Nationalism* (London, 1991).

12. On the politics of landscape memory productions see Dianne Harris, *The Nature of Authority: Villa Culture, Landscape and Representation in 18th Century Lombardy* (Philadelphia, 2003); Carol Burns and Andrea Kahn, eds., *Site Matters* (London-New York, 2005); Kolodney and Kallus, "From Colonial to National Landscape: Producing Haifa's Cityscape," *Planning Perspectives* 23.3 (2008): 323–48.

13. Harris, *The Nature of Authority*, 12.

14. Lionella Scazzosi, "Reading and Assessing the Landscape as Cultural and Historical Heritage," *Landscape Research* 29.4 (2004): 335–55.

15. Ibid., 3.

16. Harris, *The Nature of Authority*, 12.

the surface of selective myth and memory of national identity, W. J. T. Mitchell explores landscape as arena of amnesia and erasure while studying the Israeli-Palestinian conflict.[17] Both perceptions are mandatory to understanding the landscape dynamic as an eternally changing nature representing memory or its loss, a source of personal and collective meaning.

Such collective heterogeneous memory experience is questioned in mixed city societies like Haifa. Yet, only a few studies have been devoted to identity building production of the city urban fabric. The geographer Maoz Azaryahu dedicated several articles to Haifa's cityscape, focusing mainly on the Israeli official collective identity building formalities of street naming and memorial construction in the urban fabric in tribute to the war events and heroes.[18] From an historical point of view, Yfaat Weiss investigates the amnesia of the pre-1948 Arab residents of Wadi Salib in favor of its memory emergence as an Israeli site, assisted by interviews she conducted with former citizens of the neighborhood.[19]

This study is based on architectural archive sources—drawings, plans, reports, and memoranda of meetings since the British Mandate via Israel's nascent years to the present. It indicates the historical and current significant urban presence of the 1948 confrontation seam and the few significant public memory sites and actions scattered along, as the Memorial Garden, the memorial slabs, and sequel footsteps of the 1948 events. It also indicates the Treasury Garden built during the 1990s in the prior Old City area. This was followed by the various sites' specific historical insights of visual material such as maps, aerial photographs, and drawings, and on fieldwork at the sites themselves. The research is augmented by joining Zochrot walks and Jane Walks that are held in Haifa, the various urban walks led by scholars and activists, and witnessing Ortar's art displays and interviewing her, all located along the 1948 confrontation seam sites and their surroundings.

Producing Memoryscape Strategies

During the Ottoman era, Haifa was a small walled fishermen's village along the seashore, later called the Old City. Under the British Mandate, Haifa developed

17. Simon Schama, *Landscape and Memory* (New York, 1996); William J. T. Mitchell, "Holy Landscape: Israel, Palestine, and the American Wilderness," *Critical Inquiry* 26.2 (2000): 193–223.

18. Maoz Azaryahu, "War Memorials and the Commemoration of the Israeli War of Independence, 1948–1956," *Studies in Zionism* 13.1 (1992): 57–77; "The Power of Commemorative Street Names," *Environment and Planning D: Society and Space* 14 (1996): 311–30; Maoz Azaryahu and Rebecca Kook, "Mapping the Nation: Street Names and Arab-Palestinian Identity: Three Case Studies," *Nations and Nationalism* 8.2 (2002): 195–213.

19. Yfaat Weiss, *A Confiscated Memory: Wadi Salib and Haifa's Lost Heritage* (New York, 2011).

into a modern imperial port and an economic and strategic asset for British interests in the Middle East as a whole. By 1935, the city harbor became a terminal of the oil pipeline from Iraq with storage and refineries, a railroad center for trains from Syria and Lebanon, and new downtown commercial centers.[20] Haifa's population in 1895 was estimated at 9,908 (mostly Arabs), and by 1944 this number soared to about 128,000 (52 percent Jews), making it a multicultural city. This rapid population growth was followed by the development of new residential quarters and a socio-geographic pattern of community division. By and large, Arabs settled in the downtown area along the strip between the waterfront and the foot of Mount Carmel, while Jews moved to the new neighborhoods built up Mount Carmel slopes and in the Bay area. With its large and fast growing Jewish labor force, Haifa soon became the Zionist workers' city, nicknamed "Red Haifa." Facing such massive shifts in its demographic balance, and embroiled in political and economic power struggles, Haifa soon faced ethno-national tensions between Arabs and Jews.

The "mixed city" in Mandatory terms, came to an end in the course of the 1948 War when on April 21–22 the Jewish Haganah forces took control over the city.[21] Between 35,000 and 40,000 of Haifa's Arab residents left the city before the city's conquest by the Jewish forces and about a further 30,000 left during and immediately after, assisted by British ships waiting in the port, and headed north toward Acre and Lebanon. Altogether, hostilities before and during the war drove some 65,000 Arab residents out of the city, leaving downtown Haifa, including the Old City area, practically deserted. The remaining 3,566 Arab residents, Christians and Muslims alike, were confined by the Israeli authorities to the Wadi Nisnas neighborhood. These circumstances encouraged Israel to demolish the vacant Old City area in the military Shikmona Operation, apart from the

20. On Ottoman Haifa see Mahmoud Yazbak, *Haifa in the Late Ottoman Period, 1864–1914: A Muslim Town in Transition* (Leiden, 1998). On Haifa during the Mandate see May Seikaly, *Haifa: Transformation of an Arab Society 1918–1939* (London-New York, 1995); Tamir Goren, *The Fall of Arab Haifa in 1948* (Sede Boker, 2006); Gilbert Herbert and Silvina Sosnovsky, *Bauhaus on the Carmel and the Crossroads of Empire* (Jerusalem-Haifa, 1993) [both in Hebrew]; Benjamin Hyman, "British Planners in Palestine, 1918–1936" (PhD diss., London School of Economics and Political Science, 1994); Robert K. Home, *Of Planning and Planning the Making of British Colonial Cities* (London, 1997); Kolodney and Kallus, "The Politics of Landscape (Re)Production: Haifa Between Colonialism and Nation Building," *Landscape Journal* 27.2 (2008): 173–89.

21. On the war events in Haifa see Walid Khalidi, "The Fall of Haifa," *Middle East Forum* 35.10 (1959): 22–32; Alon Kadish, "The British Military during the Evacuation of Haifa," in *Haifa in 1948, Compilation of Articles, 60th Anniversary of the State of Israel*, ed. Y. Safran (Haifa, 1998), 54–60 [Hebrew]; Benny Morris, *The Birth of the Palestinian Refugee Problem Revisited* (Cambridge, 2004); Goren, *The Fall of Arab Haifa*, 20.

religious buildings, leaving a large portion of the area abandoned and in ruins, still evident to this day. Israel's early years witnessed massive Jewish immigration and settlement of many newcomers in Haifa's formerly abandoned Arab quarters. In 1951 the city's population was estimated at 149,917 inhabitants, 95 percent Jewish.[22]

Immediately after the war (1949) the Haifa city council, advised by the municipal commemoration committee and Haganah local leaders, decided to commemorate the spirit, sacrifice, and commitment of Haifa's fallen soldiers and Jewish citizens in actual urban war sites.[23] In a sense, urban monuments were metaphorical troops indicating the identification with Israeli statehood and a sense of local identity. Accordingly, 13 war memorial landmark slabs were placed on the facades of buildings that were associated with the War events. Among them were memorials located along the main route of Stanton-El-Burj road that connected specifically the Old City and downtown area up the topography of Mt. Carmel slopes with the neighborhoods of Hadar ha-Carmel. This narrow and winding route was the venue of bloody events before and during the 1948 War and marked the confrontation line, separating the Arab quarters located in the lower city of the downtown area along the seashore from the Jewish area located upward on Mount Carmel.

During the war this route was a main thoroughfare of the Jewish forces that took over the Arab frontline. Physically and symbolically, setting the serial memory objects along the road turned it into what I call the 1948 Memorial Route. The iron cast memorials included a short description of the war events and artifacts of a soldier's helmet and a torch, as a conceptual and personalized memory reflection of space, time, and identity. Later on they were included in the War Memorials National Plan, approved in 1982, that aimed to protect local War Memorials during future urban redevelopments, since some of them were situated on privately owned buildings' facades.[24] This act intended to express the accumulation of national memories locally, through physical and associative imagery traces left by interweaving collective memory patterns with everyday experience.

Along with war memorial practice, during the mayoralty election of Aba Houshy in 1951, the commemorate committee recommended to replace street and neighborhood names that negated the current Israeli national narrative, most of them in the former Arab area and the former British infrastructures. Hence,

---

22. Israel Bureau of Statistics, 1951.

23. On the Haifa Memorial Garden see Azaryahu, "War Memorials and the Commemoration," 18. He claims that war memorials and monumental commemoration practice of the 1948 War and its heroes aimed at permanently combining the Israeli national narrative of glory and sacrifices with the land and the cityscape.

24. Haifa City Engineer Archive (1982), *Memorials National Plan (No. 21)*, approved on 14 November 1982.

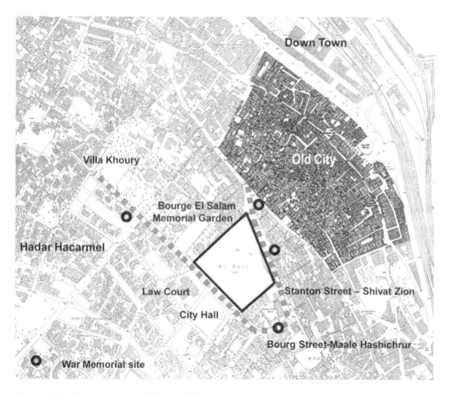

Fig. 1. The "1948 Memorial Route"
(Ziva Kolodney)

along the 1948 Memorial Route, El-Burj St. turned into Ma'ale HaShichrur (Liberation Heights), and Stanton St. (named after British Colonel Edward Alexander Stanton, Haifa's first British military governor (1918–20) turned into Shivat Zion (return to Zion). Yet, Hassan Shukri St., named after the first mayor of modern Haifa (1914–20, 1927–40) and known for his conciliatory attitude toward the Jewish community, was not changed. These various urban practices meant to instill the new Israeli state's triumph and sacrifice in everyday urban public life. Imbued with feelings of belonging the new names were essential in inscribing the Israeli collective memory of the War into the cityscape banal routines, becoming a local knowledge that narrated a specific sense of time and place.[25]

25. On "local knowledge," see Venda Louise Pollock and Joanne P. Sharp, "Constellations of Identity: Place-ma(r)king Beyond Heritage," *Environment and Planning D: Society and Space* 25.6 (2007): 1061–78.

Fig. 2. War Memorials along the "1948 Memorial Route" building's facades
(Courtesy of Haifa City Engineer Archive)

The Memorial Garden

Designing the city Memorial Garden was another hegemonic memoryscape strategy. Immediately after the war, the City Council assembly proposed establishing a central Memorial Garden site in the heart of the emerging Haifa new civil center in the Hadar HaCarmel neighborhood, facing the historically notable buildings of Haifa City Hall and the City Court to the south along Hassan Shukri St. To the north, it faced the downtown, the Old City remains, and Haifa Bay area. The new center, located at the intermediary plateau between the lower and the upper city, connected Hassan Shukri road downward to the 1948 Memorial Route and the downtown area. Geographically and symbolically, the Memorial Garden was located on the remnants of Burj El-Salam and its surroundings, the high watchtower that was constructed by the Galilee's Arab ruler Dahir al-'Umar in the late eighteenth century, guarding the Old City and Haifa Bay from above.

Similarly, the garden was located at a key strategic site, overlooking the remains of the Old City that was demolished during Shikmona Operation, suggesting that the garden's location symbolized the territorial victory over the Arab enemy and the elimination of the mixed nature of the Jewish-Arab city at that time. On May 14, 1948, the city celebrated Israel's birth at the Memorial Garden site across the Municipality Hall, coordinating with the central ceremony held in Tel-Aviv where Israel's independence was proclaimed, Israel's flag was raised, and the declaration text was read.

A planning competition initiated by Haifa Municipality in 1950 aimed at marking the profound bonding between the garden and its national-local ceremonial role. During the first city council meeting after independence on 28 December 1950, Mayor Shabtay Levi announced an architectural competition for a Memorial Garden and a Memorial Monument "in the memory of those who fell fighting for our freedom in the war of independence."

The competition's guidelines included the construction of a garden, a central memorial monument to commemorate the more than 400 fallen soldiers and Haifa's citizens in the defense of Israel and the city altogether, a museum that would be devoted to the victorious story of the war, and a governmental office building. An imagery axis was to be designed to visually connect between the rows of trees located in front of the main entrance to the Technion historical building in the upper Hadar HaCarmel area, aligned with the adjacent City Hall, and ending in the proposed monument to be located at the edge of the Memorial Garden.

Haifa-based architect Yehuda Unger won first prize.[26] The plan's design and layout suggested the garden as Haifa's new civic center to be located in the heart of the Jewish neighborhood of Hadar HaCarmel, adjacent to the already existing City Hall and the nearby Law Court Hall building. Unger suggested a formal garden layout and a wide piazza with a row of formal trees to emphasize an open corridor toward a suggested tall obelisk and the open view toward the downtown and Haifa Bay as its backdrop. He claimed that his project was influenced by the large pedestrian piazzas, urban monuments, and focal point methods of Italian formal garden design. The tall obelisk, designed by the artist Jo Davidson, stands on the apex of the piazza toward the sea. The nearby museum dedicated to the fallen soldiers had one hall with wide glass building panels to allow a view to the downtown area and the sea.

Eventually, the garden was designed by the municipality gardener Zvi Miller as a vast open park with meandering trails and a pergola overlooking Haifa Bay. A modest memorial stone wall was placed in the garden's west wing indicating "Memorial Garden: A sacred memory of the sons and daughters who fell in the War of Independence"; the names of troops, military formations, and

---

26. Of the 21 entries to the competition proposals only two were found: Yehuda Unger's drawing, see Haifa City Engineer Archive (1952), *Yehuda Unger Plan (Haifa Plan No. 850)*; Isaac Kutner's proposal, Issac Kutner, *Man, Garden and Landscape* (family and friends edition, 1969) [Hebrew].

organizations were carved in stones along the garden's natural setting trails (Haganah, Etzel, Lehi, The Liberators of Haifa, breaking the way to Jerusalem, Battalions 22, 23, and 24); and a central water fountain was designed to symbolize the spring of life. The Memorial Garden was opened in 1953 in the presence of IDF Chief of Staff Mordechai Maklef who commanded the Haganah forces during the decisive battle for the city in April 1948.

In 1979 a Memorial Monument called "Liberation of Haifa 1948" was placed at the garden's entrance to tell the story of the War for the city. Designed by the municipality worker at that time the artist Gershon Knispel, and assisted by Amy Atias, the object includes a relief map of Haifa neighborhoods and war battle in particular sites, and a sculpted soldier and an angel on both sides. Once a year, on the eve of Israel's Memorial Day, the city central ceremony is held at the garden, coordinated with the official national memorial ceremony at the Western Wall in the Old City of Jerusalem. This ceremony is attended by the Mayor of Haifa, bereaved family members, war veterans, and the municipality's distinguished guest list members. This act of memoryscape association of memory and history has taken place at the Memorial Garden every year since Haifa's ceremonial declaration of independence in 1948.

Fig. 3. The "Liberation of Haifa 1948" Memorial Monument
(*Ziva Kolodney*)

During the week of Israel's Commemoration and Independence Days, Haifa's intermediate school students walk the "Footsteps of 1948 Warriors" trail, joined by veterans who tell the story first hand.[27] "We are confident that you'll take with you impressions of the various routes," states Zvi Rak the former Municipal Director of Education, Culture and Social Welfare. "It will serve you in establishing and strengthening the bond between yourself and the city, between the physical space—city, neighborhood, street, house—and the spiritual place knowing where you come from and where you are going to."[28] The trail starts next to the Municipality at the Memorial Garden and passes among others along the 1948 Memorial Route—the war memorial landmarks slabs, and other 1948 war event sites—and concludes in a tribute ceremony to Haifa's old veterans of 1948.

Along with street re-naming, war memorials, and the yearly ritual of the footsteps of 1948 warriors trail, the Memorial Garden is an official landscape production construct, an outcome of local politics working hand in hand with architectural practitioners, army forces, and civil organizations. I consider the garden as a representation of memoryscape strategy, a formal Jewish ceremonial myth of urban memory. Although located in the heart of a mixed city that officially praises its Jewish-Arab co-existence, these, or any other acts of commemoration, give no room for remembrance of the city's Arab community members who once lived in the city and died or were displaced as a result of the Nakba.[29] Arab victims of 1948 in Haifa do not constitute a memory community rallied around the city's Muslim and Christian cemeteries nor in any other public commemoration.

The Treasury Garden

Similar to the Memorial Garden, the Treasury Garden, located in the heart of Haifa's new Government Center in the downtown area, is an official memoryscape construct. Designed in the early 1990s, when private and global investments

27. On Israeli memorial ceremonies see Eviatar Zerubavel, "Social Memories: Steps to a Sociology of the Past," *Qualitative Sociology* 19.3 (1996): 283–99; Edna Lomsky-Feder, "The Bounded Female Voice in Memorial Ceremonies," *Qualitative Sociology* 28.3 (2005): 293–314. On walking and memory see Jackie Feldman, "Between Yad Vashem and Mount Herzl: Changing Inscriptions of Sacrifice on Jerusalem's 'Mountain of Memory,'" *Anthropological Quarterly* 80.4 (2007): 1145–72.

28. Jacky Youngman, ed. *In the Footsteps of Fighters: The Battle for the Liberation, Department of Education, Culture and Social Welfare* (Haifa, 2003), 3 [Hebrew].

29. After 1948 Israel encouraged movement of displaced Arabs from the Galilee (mainly Nazareth) into Haifa due to employment considerations.

changed the local market economy, it is an urban plaza situated above a parking lot at the foot of the new Treasury Building and the Government Building. Like the rest of the Government Center, the garden's site includes erasures, modifications, and re-building since it is located in what used to be the Old City area. According to British serial plans of the Old City area, in the Haifa City Plan of 1920 drawn up by the renowned urban planner Patrick Geddes and local planner Asaph Ciffrin, and in the later Haifa Skeleton Plan approved in 1934, part of the area was to be demolished to construct the broad King George the 5th Avenue in the center of the Old City urban fabric. In the 1947 plan the site was designated for demolition as part of the entire Old City, and for later rebuilding of the area and its surroundings anew.[30] None of these plans was executed mainly due to economic reasons, although they were approved as official city planning policies for the area.

Similar to the entire Old City, characterized by narrow winding alleys with random buildings and no consistent geometric order, the Treasury Garden site contradicted the British planners' vision for Haifa, seen as an obstacle to the strategic connection between the new harbor and the industrial infrastructure in the Bay Area. Hence, the British City Engineer Lionel Watson saw the Old City, inhabited mostly by Arabs, as a typical Middle Eastern urban agglomeration, unsuitable for modern living. "Although the old city [has] an oriental romantic heritage, it poses a serious problem for modern city-planning development, and a serious sanitary and transportation problem," he reported to the British planning authorities.[31]

During the 1948 War and the Shikmona Operation, the Treasury Garden site together with large parts of the Old City area was demolished and remained in ruins. In the mid-1950s the site became the main public garden within the vacated downtown area, planted with rows of trees. Among the remains of the Old City and a few new office buildings built in the 1970s, it formed a surrealistic oasis of greenery. The actual construction of the new Government Center and the garden site took place only in the 1990s, and attempted, once again, to transform the area by imposing on it a modern economic and cultural reality.

Following the optimism aroused by the Oslo Accords, the idea for the open spaces between the new government buildings was to reconstruct the memory of the Old City, integrating the Treasury Garden to tell its story architecturally. The intention was to integrate the Old City's urban fabric into the layout of the new public open spaces located between the new governmental buildings. It was

30. On British planning and architecture of the Old City see: Kolodney and Kallus, "From Colonial to National Landscape."

31 Haifa City Archive (1941–42), *City Engineer's Annual Report*, 26.

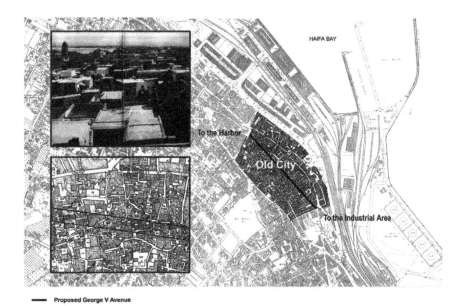

Proposed George V Avenue

Fig. 4. Haifa Old City scheme, including King George the 5th Avenue proposal in the center. Outlined—a view of a typical street in the Old City (1939), and a detail of the Old City Survey (1939)
(Ziva Kolodney)

proposed by the city planners and the architectural firm of Man-Shenar, which had prepared a master plan for part of the area, superimposing traces of the old urban fabric on new paving, thereby creating a juxtaposition of old and new. This was implemented by the landscape-architecture firm of Miller-Blum, who prepared the master plan for the whole area, and later by the firm of Greenstein-Har-Gil, the landscape architects of the Treasury Garden site. Stone has been used to recall the Old City's materiality, and mosaic images of Haifa's history have been integrated along a central axis shaded by steel garden arches and the geometrical layout of the Old City urban fabric of former houses was traced in the new paving and the garden planters.

Although the Treasury Garden is intended to approximate the Old City both ritually and symbolically, these embellishments turn its story into a mere diagrammatic scheme of shapes and materials. A mini-display of the city's history is conveyed via an official construct of public remembrance, of which the municipality is both curator and executor of an attempt to domesticate the memory of the urban "other." However, despite these attempts, along with the Memorial Garden, the Treasury Garden gives no room for personal recollections, nor does it encourage any alternative personal rituals of remembrance. Yet, unintentionally, the postmodernist

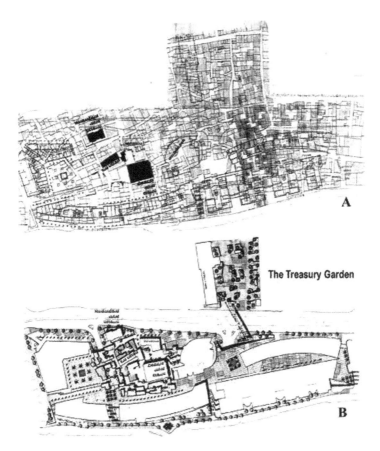

The Treasury Garden

A

B

Fig. 5. A—Superposition layout of Haifa new Governmental Center on the Old City urban fabric. B—Superimposing traces of the Old City urban fabric on Haifa new Governmental Center
(Courtesy of Haifa City Engineer Archive)

new Government Center, located within the demolished Old City boundaries, the remaining churches, mosques, and the scattered ruins, is itself a "presence of absence," becoming an urban memory matrix of the long-gone Old City.

Producing Memoryscape Tactics

Haifa's municipal efforts since 1948 to shape the urban memory space in accordance with Jewish narratives and experiences has recently been challenged by grass root groups and individuals, most saliently by Zochrot, an Israeli-based association established in 2002, aiming "to promote Israeli Jewish society's acknowledgement of and accountability for the ongoing injustices of the Nakba and the reconceptualization of Return as the imperative redress of the Nakba and a chance for a better life for all the country's inhabitants."[32]

In November 2004, the Zochrot association hosted an educational tour on the Palestinian *Nakba* in the city of Haifa. Among the tour's participants were Jewish and Palestinian local activists. Haifa's program began with a walking tour of Arab Haifa, guided by Dr. Johnny Mansour, who spoke about the pre-*Nakba* history of Arab Haifa, and specifically about the vanished landmarks of the town, as well as the changes that have occurred since then. During the tour, signs were posted bearing the pre-1948 street names in Arabic and Hebrew, including Ummiyya St, El-Iraq St., El-Rahibat St. (Madregot Hanevi'im (Stairs of the Prophets), and El-Burj St. (Ma'ale Hashihrur).

The December 15, 2004 headline of the *Maariv* daily newspaper asked— "Who moved my street? Who is trying to change the names of Haifa streets to the street names in the period prior to the War of Independence?"[33] These questions preoccupied many city residents, who turned to Mayor Yona Yahav to investigate the affair. National Religious Party Councilor Yaffa Peretz hastily submitted a proposal to discuss the matter at the City Council. She could not believe that the Arab city residents were behind the initiative since they "behave in an exemplary manner, and we live in an excellent co-existence with them." The municipality confirmed that a few such signs were found on the city streets but that they had been immediately removed.

Walking in the city and telling its story, especially along disputed areas of pre-1948 Arab neighborhoods, became a common practice of individuals and scholars in Haifa. During Jane's Walks,[34] for example, organized yearly by the Haifa Museum of Art, individuals led walks around the city and told stories of their neighborhoods, streets, houses, gardens, or trees, and of the people who lived or still live in and around them. During the second Jane Walks, on May 3–4, 2012, Dr. Johnny Mansour led a walk in the Wadi Nisnas neighborhood, giving voice to three Arab poets who had lived in the neighborhood; the photographer and architecture student Gil Bar led a walk between Wadi Salib's vacant houses, shedding light on their architectural qualities; using personal photographs and records, the art and craft collector Toni Ashkar articulated stories of Arab private

32. Zochrot website: http://www.zochrot.org/en Accessed 21 May 2014.

33. http://www.nrg.co.il/online/1/ART/838/017.html; http://www.zochrot.org/en/content/who-moved-my-street.

34. Jane's Walk is a worldwide movement of locally led walking tours inspired by the late urban activist and writer Jane Jacobs. The walks get people to explore personal and collective narratives of their cities and to promote a community-based approach to urban planning. See Haifa Museum of Art in 2012: http://hms.org.il/Museum/Templates/showpage.asp?DBID=1&LNGID=2&TMID=84&FID=2601&PID=0.

stories; the artist Abed Abdi gave a voice to his late mother who used to live in the city; the anthropologist Roli Rosen enlightened Arab women's memories of pre-1948 downtown Haifa. These stories and many others are both collective and individual memoryscape practices, they tell the tales of Arab Haifa as it has never been recorded in the annals of history.

Ortar's series of art sites, displays, and performances (1995–97) is another memoryscape tactic. Similarly to Zochrot practices and Haifa's Jane Walks, it expresses the accumulation of personal memories through physical and associative urban traces left by interweaving patterns of everyday life.[35] Ortar based her art sites in the historical civic center along Hassan Shukri St. that links downward to the 1948 Memorial Route. Developed into an administrative and commercial center, along the years it became an interstitial zone and a meeting point between different populations that live in Wadi Nisnas, Lower Hadar, and the Downtown neighborhoods. It was there, in the midst of the social and cultural divides that Ortar choose to test her "Urban Traces" project of Arab and Jewish communities' memory and exile.

The first site was the Migdal HaNevi'im (Prophets Tower) shopping mall, built in 1986, where previously stood Villa Khoury. Traces of the demolished Khoury building were installed in the new urban matrix as a commodity objects display inside the building and its shops' frontage windows.[36] The exhibition inside the shopping mall included a scale model of Villa Khury, archival documentary exhibits of maps, urban plans, ground and aerial photographs of the Villa and its surroundings, and a video in which various residents narrated their living experiences in Haifa. According to the artist, the site's specific art installation meant to carve disturbing historical memory insinuates on the customer's banal everyday window-shopping experience.

Another installation in 1996 was the "Memorial Park as a Living Picture (Tableau Vivant)," placed in Haifa's Memorial Garden across the street and in front of the City Hall. During the week of Memorial Day and Day of Independence, Ortar installed a wooden structured mini kiosk in the garden, walled with aerial views, maps, and images of the city fabric and particular sites of pre- and post-1948 city history.[37] Passers-by were invited to the kiosk to tell

35. Pollock and Sharp claim that along with the urban vocabulary of architectural remembrance sites, variants of new genre public art, urban public art tends to serve an active commemorative function of contemporary urban landscapes, "Constellations of Identity," 25.

36. Due to the building's geographical strategic site overlooking the downtown and bay area, Villa Khury was the location of a crucial battle during the 1948 War with both Jewish and Arab sides trying to capture this key site in order to dominate the city.

37. According to Ortar, because her installation demanded a half-hour personal interview, fewer than 20 people could participate in her act, but passers-by stopped at the kiosk to look at the maps and pictures (yet no record or data of the passers-by is available).

Fig. 6. Ilana Ortar art installation "Memorial Park as a living picture (Tableau Vivant)," located in Haifa's Memorial Garden across the street and in front of the City Hall (1996)
(Courtesy of Ilana Ortar Archive)

their personal story and reflections over the city's history, assisted by a small card game format questionnaire and information about various historical buildings. "Haifa? Nobody can tell me what was here 40 or 50 years ago" was the reflection of a forty-five-year-old local photographer:

> I walk my dog and I see countless destroyed buildings; mere walls are all that remained. I wanted to know who lived there and I was told it had been an Arab village. They all fled because of the war. Where are they now? Those people who during their whole life thought they would live here, with their children are gone, just like that. It is like the situation now; we think that we are at home, in our own land. But I do not know what will be here fifty years from now, who knows what there will be for my son in this country.

Amir Khalil, an Israeli-Palestinian teenager who responded to an image of the Memorial Garden that appeared on some of the questionnaires wrote:

> My name is Amir Khalil. I am one of those exiled from the Biram village. I study at the St. John School near Hassan Shukri St. In my class I have friends from Haifa, from the Galilee, from 'Usfiyya, and from Dalyiat al-Carmel. In 1948 we had a beautiful village, Biram. One day soldiers of the Zionist army came and took us out of there. Our land has not been returned [to us] to this day. We pray that you give it back, and I hope that we will return there.

Addressing the same site, Zvi Miller, the original landscape designer who planned the Memorial Garden, wrote: "The local municipality and the government were in dispute about the designated use of this land. When Haifa's mayor at the time Aba Houshy heard about the government's plan to build offices on this plot, he asked me to draw plans for a sort of a 'Central Park' for this highly populated area. At the time thousands of new immigrants were living in this area in very poor conditions and this park was meant to better their living conditions—to serve as a place in which to relax and breathe some fresh air."

Once a year on the Day of Commemoration of the Fallen at precisely 11:00, a siren sounds throughout the country and the flow of life stops for two minutes during which citizens stand to respect and remembrance of the fallen in Israel's wars. During the evening before, a memorial ceremony takes place in Haifa's Memorial Garden opening the city's events. Ortar's choice of time and space for displaying her installation in the Memorial Garden and during the week of Israel's Memorial Day and the immediately following Independence Day can be seen as a memoryscape tactic. Parallel to the institutional memory ritual that has been held in the garden since 1948, she performs a temporary public event that challenges urban memory strategies and creates an opportunity for an alternative memoryscape.

Conclusion

The chapter has addressed the interweaving relationships between competing advocates of history and memory in Haifa since 1948. Its findings underline the intertwined nature of memory-building shaped by official and unofficial agencies and everyday life practices. The findings on Haifa raise questions about the ability of official efforts to reconstruct the urban—and for that matter, also rural—landscape in a way that entirely obliterates the marks of what stood there before—houses, buildings, neighborhoods, and their names—and bury the "other's" visible past. Especially in a mixed city like Haifa and for that matter, Israel as a whole, the past remains alive not only in remnants of physical ruins and trees. It claims the attention, memorization, and reconstruction by people who live in these spaces and wish to give meaning to what remains. Regardless of the scope of public attendance, and consent to the efforts of grass-root groups and individuals in making the other's past visible to the city dwellers, the significance of their work is that it breaks the silence imposed by the official agencies about the city's past that was cut off by the 1948 War.

Street re-naming, memorial sites, the Memorial Garden, the Treasury Garden urban memory plan, and Zochrot and Ortar's urban memoryscape practices are not mere physical territories and actions. They are complementary symbolic entities, identified by their founders, planners, designers, artists, executors, and users. Both are attempts to materialize Haifa's memory of 1948 events, give it meaning and build a collective and personal identity through it. However, while memoryscape strategies merely represent the victorious party of the 1948 War, memoryscape tactics gives room to the defeated as well.

Zochrot's efforts to bring "justice" to the streets of Haifa by renaming them, telling personal recollections during Haifa's Jane Walks of pre-1948 Arab cityscape, and Ilana Ortar's art practices, all contest the formal urban memory construction. Ortar's card game reflects the intimacy of the individual's relationship with the urban history and challenges the institutional routines. In its intuitive reflection, the visitors attending the art installation and card game of urban traces practice evoke a powerful urban remembrance; it is an activation of memoryscape. Memoryscape strategy acts cannot invoke that. By addressing the site-specific physical and mnemonic traces in the current urban matrix, Ortar provokes the city's Palestinian residents to raise their personal insights of urban memory and in raising the Nakba to the awareness of Haifa's Jewish residents and increasing their acknowledgement of the city's different pasts.

ZIVA KOLODNEY is a practicing landscape architect and a lecturer. Her recent publications include "Landscape Production" in *The Planners: Concepts in Urban Planning in Israel*; "Between Landscape Production and Representation," *The Journal of Architecture*; "Rethinking Urban Space: Between Localism, Nationalism, and Globalization," *Journal of Urban Design* (with Rachel Kallus); and "Between Colonial and National Landscapes," *Planning Perspectives* (with Rachel Kallus).

5 The Making of a Myth

The Story of Kfar Etzion in Religious Zionism 1948–1967

Dror Greenblum

Introduction

Between 1948 and 1967 the story of Kfar Etzion, one of the best-known cases of heroism in Israel's War of Independence, became the defining myth in religious Zionism. No other story or single event in the history of religious Zionism has attained such mythical proportions and had so much influence on religious Zionists. The essence of religious-Zionist belief, how to live a life of purity and holiness and how to die a hero's death, all for the sanctification of God's name (*kiddush ha-shem*) is an integral part of this story.

Kfar Etzion was one of the four kibbutzim (the others were Massuot Yitzhak, Ein Tzurim, and Revadim) of Gush Etzion (the Etzion Bloc) in the Judean Mountains, on the Bethlehem-Hebron road. Three were affiliated with the Religious-Zionist Movement, but the story of the Bloc, as it has been carved in the national consciousness and especially that of religious Zionism, is primarily that of the life and death of Kfar Etzion's members.

The chapter traces the origins and development of the myth and explains its central status in the ethos of religious-Zionist heroism. It explains the construction of the myth and its inculcated in the religious-Zionist Movement and shows the close link between myth-making, memory, and the politics of the commemoration and historiography of the War of Independence [henceforth, the War].

The heroic nature of Gush Etzion's persistence as an isolated stronghold in a purely Arab region and of its tragic fall after a long and desperate struggle was repeatedly noted by Israeli political and military leaders, such as Prime Minister David Ben-Gurion and IDF Chief of Operations Yigael Yadin as soon as the War

This chapter is based on my unpublished doctoral dissertation, "From the Heroism of the Spirit to the Sanctification of Might—Might and Heroism in Religious Zionism between 1948 and 1967" (University of Haifa, July 2009) [Hebrew].

The War of 1948 (2016): 121–144, DOI: 10.2979/warof1948.0.0.07

came to an end. However, this praise represented an attempt to appropriate the bravery of Gush Etzion's defenders as part of the Israeli national memory along the lines of the Mapai ruling party, and was a source of frustration for the religious Zionists. In eulogizing the fallen in 1950, Ben-Gurion emphasized the nation's gratitude to Gush Etzion's defenders for saving Jerusalem by their steadfastness and desperate battle.[1] The tenacious holding of the Bloc as an exemplary act of dedication to the defense of Jerusalem's southern flank became a primary factor in fostering the Kfar Etzion story as an exclusive religious-Zionist myth of heroism in the war and especially in the eventual preservation of Jewish Jerusalem.[2]

For many years after 1948, however, the story of Gush Etzion remained marginal in Israel's pantheon of national memory. The key factors that elevated it to a national myth of heroism were primarily activist figures of the national-religious movement and even more so, the reestablishment of Kfar Etzion by the defenders' children in the wake of the 1967 war. The heroic story made further headway into Israeli collective consciousness thanks to the publication, almost four decades later, of a book documenting interviews with the children of Kfar Etzion during the 1948 War. Some of them dismissed the glorification of Kfar Etzion as a new "Masada" myth, pointing to its story as traumatic and blaming the Yishuv's leadership, especially Ben-Gurion, for abandoning Kfar Etzion and for its unnecessary sacrifices.[3] However, most of the children of its defenders who were evacuated from the kibbutz during the War of Independence and returned to it after the Six-Day War expressed deep longing for the place between 1948 and 1967, elevating it to the status of a symbol in a narrative analogous to that of the Jewish people's 2,000 years of exile and redemption upon the return to the Land of Israel.[4] These children grew up on the myth and deeply identify with it; they perceive it as their defining life story and played an active role in fostering it. Their published personal stories aroused great interest and excitement in religious-Zionist circles and heightened the sense of the continuing significance of the myth in religious-Zionist life. The fostering of this myth should be understood within the context of the "religious meaning of the state of Israel as perceived by religious Zionism," which "transforms the patriotism of the

---

1. Cited by Mordechai Naor, *Gush Etzion from its Beginning to the War of Independence* (Jerusalem, 1996), 123 [Hebrew].

2. Shaul Raz, *Memories of Etzion* (Tel-Aviv, 1973), 30. See a poem in this vein, *Hatzofe*, 2 May 1949 [Hebrew].

3. Amia Lieblich, *The Children of Kfar Etzion* (Haifa, 2006), 456; Shilo Gal, *Was Gush Etzion Abandoned in the War of Independence?* (Ramat Gan, 2007) [Hebrew].

4. Hanan Porat's interview in Lieblich, *The Children of Kfar Etzion*, 452.

movement into religious patriotism,"[5] a modern-day version of the *akeda*, the sacrifice of Isaac.

Though "a close look at the story immediately brings forth its mythic foundations, both in Jewish terms and in universal terms,"[6] apart from Amia Lieblich's book, which focuses on the personal stories of the children of Kfar Etzion, and David Ohana's work on the "myth of return" of Kfar Etzion and its significance in the messianic view of Gush Emunim (Bloc of the Faithful),[7] no scholarly attention has been paid to the origins and development of the Kfar Etzion myth. I address the development and internalization of the myth of Kfar Etzion as a religious-Zionist myth of heroism from its beginning to its elevation to the status of a central myth of heroism in the collective consciousness of religious Zionism.

In presenting the elements of the Kfar Etzion myth within the religious value system, I show that it is not only a story of Zionist heroism, but primarily one that seeks to be a link in the historical chain of Jewish heroism and a core story in religious-Zionist history.

The Historical Backdrop[8]

The Jews first who settled in the area between Bethlehem and Hebron in 1927 were ultra-Orthodox from Jerusalem who founded a settlement Migdal Eder. In the 1929 Arab riots, the settlement was destroyed and its residents fled to Jerusalem. In 1935, Shmuel Zvi Holzman founded the El Hahar Society, and its members settled in the same spot. The settlement was abandoned again in 1936 during the Arab Revolt. In 1943, the Avraham Group established Kibbutz Kfar Etzion on the hill. Its members had belonged to the religious-Zionist youth movements of Bnei Akiva and Hashomer Hadati in Poland, had fled the Nazi conquest, immigrated to Palestine, and founded a temporary kibbutz near Kfar Pines, from which they went to settle in the Hebron Mountains. The main economic resources of the new kibbutz were agriculture and a resort where many religious-Zionist leaders stayed. It had a lively religious and social life and by late 1947 included some 160 residents,

<hr>

5. Asher Cohen, "Religion and Patriotism – Completion or Contradiction: Visions and their Frustration in Religious Zionism," in *Patriotism*, ed. Avner Ben-Amos and Daniel Bartal (Tel-Aviv, 2004), 455 [Hebrew].

6. Lieblich, *The Children of Kfar Etzion*, 81.

7. A post-1967 messianic and political movement committed to the wholeness of the Land of Israel and establishment of Jewish settlements, mainly in the occupied West Bank. See David Ohana, "Kfar Etzion: The Community of Memory and the Myth of Return," *Israel Studies* 7.2 (2002): 175–94.

8. Unless otherwise mentioned, this section draws on Lieblich, *The Children of Kfar Etzion*, 30–6; Naor, *Gush Etzion*; Yohanan Ben-Yaacov, *The History of Gush Etzion* (Kfar Etzion, 1979) [Hebrew].

60 of them children. In 1945, another religious settlement, Massuot Yitzhak, was established nearby. A year later, Ein Tzurim was founded, and in 1947, Kibbutz Revadim, of the nonreligious Hashomer Hatzair Movement, joined the Bloc.

According to the 1947 UN Partition Resolution on Palestine, Gush Etzion was not to be included in the Jewish state. The hostilities between Arabs and Jews that erupted on the day following the Resolution put Gush Etzion under effective siege, and the military clashes between its residents and the surrounding Arab population continued until the Bloc's final fall in mid-May 1948. The Haganah Command of Jerusalem made repeated efforts to help the besieged Bloc by sending combatants and arms, but Gush Etzion's situation kept deteriorating. The reinforcements were insufficient or failed to break through the Arab siege.[9] In January 1948, the children, mothers, and elderly were evacuated to Jerusalem.

Gush Etzion, particularly Kfar Etzion, constituted a constant obstacle to the movement of the Arab Legion's convoys along the Hebron-Bethlehem road and was thus ceaselessly attacked by Jordanian soldiers and local irregulars. The last battle for Kfar Etzion began on May 12. That night, a small group of women and wounded men was evacuated to Massuot Yitzhak after all the outposts of the kibbutz had fallen. The next day, Arab Legion armored vehicles burst into the kibbutz. The combatants' attempt to arrange a surrender by raising a white flag failed and they were all killed, except for three men and a woman who survived and managed to reach the other settlements by a circuitous route.

The fall of Kfar Etzion was followed by the surrender of the other three kibbutzim, and their inhabitants who were taken captive by the Arab Legion. Six weeks later, the women were released; the men remained in prison for another nine months. Kfar Etzion's survivors included 17 men, 32 or 33 widows, and 46 orphans. Only 10 families remained intact. The fallen combatants were interred in a mass grave in Jerusalem on November 17, 1949.

The Struggle for the National Memory of the War of Independence

The struggle for shaping the national memory was so fierce and ideologically charged that it became one of the primary issues in the first general elections to the Knesset. The question of "who built the state" was at the heart of the election campaigns waged by the political parties.[10] The historiography of 1948 was one of many ideological and political controversies that occupied the politics during the first decade. It is within this ideologically charged environment of the struggle

9. The most notable attempts were the Convoy of the 10 (December 1947); the Platoon of the 35, which perished in battle before reaching the Bloc; and the Nebi Daniel Convoy (March 1948), ambushed by Arabs near Bethlehem.

10. Ze'ev Tzahor, "Mapai, Mapam, and the Formation of the First Israel Government in 1949," *Iyunim Bitkumat Israel* 4 (1994): 383 [Hebrew].

over the collective consciousness and the nature of the state that the religious-Zionist Movement endeavored to leave its own imprint.[11]

The struggle for the "true" historiography of the War began even before the guns fell silent. Like Churchill during WWII, Ben-Gurion, whose cognizance of the role of historiography and national memory was a major factor in his political conduct,[12] led the effort to make his own version of the War its official history. Yet the War generated competing narratives, many of which were a response to feelings of deprivation and deliberate forgetfulness. The most salient of these struggles were conducted within the Labor Movement between Ben-Gurion's loyalists and the Palmach, represented by Mapam, and the right-wing opposition Herut, which represented the dissenting groups of Etzel and Lehi.[13]

Within this struggle for the national memory, the heroic story of Kfar Etzion was subjected to competing attempts of appropriation and interpretation in the context desired by each political leader. At the first memorial service for the fallen of Gush Etzion, Ben-Gurion said,

> I know of no battle in all the brave struggles of the Haganah and the Israel Defense Forces that was more glorious, tragic, and heroic than the battle in Gush Etzion. Their sacrifice, more than any other war effort, saved Jerusalem . . . The supreme bravery of the defenders of Gush Etzion will shine in a special light of honor . . . and each one who was privileged to take part in this marvelous undertaking is promised a place in the world to come and the perpetuity of the Jewish people.[14]

Conversely, the tenacious holding of the Bloc and its crucial role in saving Jerusalem became the primary elements in the fostering of the Kfar Etzion story as the sole and exclusive religious-Zionist myth of heroism in the War. One of the few survivors noted, "For . . . Jerusalem we kept guard at an isolated outpost . . . Who but us in the war for Jerusalem was chained to the front line and shown no mercy?"[15]

11. Yehiam Weitz, *Israel in the First Decade* (Tel-Aviv, 2001), 83–6 [Hebrew].

12. Ze'ev Tzahor, "Ben-Gurion as a Creator of Myths," in *Myth and Memory,* ed. David Ohana and Robert Wistrich (Jerusalem, 1997), 131–52 [Hebrew].

13. Mordechai Bar-On, *Memory in the Book* (Tel-Aviv, 2001), 141–66; on the sense of deprivation and efforts of self-commemoration by the dissident movements see Udi Lebel, "'Beyond the Pantheon': Bereavement, Memory, and the Strategy of De-Legitimization against Herut," *Israel Studies* (2005) 10.3: 104–26. On Hakibbutz Hameuhad's struggle for an appropriate place in the national narrative see Efrat Kantor, *The Shaping of the Collective Memory in Hakibbutz Hameuhad* (Sede Boker and Ramat Efal, 2007), 38–122 [Hebrew].

14. Quoted by Dov Knohl, *Gush Etzion and Its War* (Jerusalem, 1954), 543; in Ben-Yaacov, *The History of Gush Etzion,* 303–4; and in 1950, cited by Naor, *Gush Etzion from its Beginning,* 123; Yigael Yadin, "Introduction," in *The Fortress of Etzion* (Tel-Aviv, 1949), 7 [Hebrew].

15. Raz, *Memories of Etzion,* 30; *Hatzofe,* 2 May 1949, published a poem later included in a textbook for religious-national schools. See Yehoshua Tversky and Alexander Malkiel, *Customs of Israel for the Seventh Grade* (Tel-Aviv, 1952) [Hebrew].

The decision, partly conscious and partly intuitive, to turn the story of Kfar Etzion into a myth of glorified heroism with clear trappings of sanctity was already made during the battles for Gush Etzion, and it was renewed with vigor immediately after the Bloc's fall. This decision was closely linked to the struggle for national memory and the writing of the history of the War, a struggle already in full swing while the battles were still being fought and immediately after the War.[16]

During the War, Moshe Arieh Kurtz, a prominent member and activist of Hapoel Hamizrahi, a socialist-Orthodox movement, was its representative on the Haganah's staff and in charge of religious settlements and the conscription of religious men. In the introduction to Lieblich's book she refers to documents she found by her father, Arie Kurtz, one of which consists of four densely written pages recording his words at a Hapoel Hamizrahi security committee meeting in August 1948. The text was also submitted as an opinion piece to the religious-Zionist daily *Hatzofe*, but was rejected by the censor.[17]

Kurtz writes, inter alia, "We, the soldiers of religious Jewry, are deemed fit to be sent on the most dangerous missions . . . in any dangerous place, but only as simple soldiers and as low-level commanders, nothing more." The religious soldier feels that he is merely "cannon fodder." He inveighs against the IDF's Culture Department, which started publishing battle histories of the War. The first three booklets were about Mishmar Haemek, Yad Mordechai, and Nahshonim (non-religious settlements). Kurtz complains of discrimination. How could it be, that in the material published thus far nothing has been said about Tirat Tzvi and Sde Eliyahu, Beerot Yitzhak and Gush Etzion, or Kfar Darom, which could serve as

> wondrous examples of total devotion, perseverance, heroism, and steadfastness, than which one can imagine none more sublime? . . . Were there any shining points brighter than the heroic courage with which Gush Etzion fought? For generations to come the light of the flame lit with the revival of the new kingdom of Israel shall continue to shine . . . All these have been doomed to silence and silencing by the Culture Department.

The historical documentation Kurtz concludes, constitutes "obstructive discrimination and distortion of the historical facts . . . obliterating the truth."[18] Even during the War the religious Zionists claimed that they had not been given their due in the written history.

---

16. Bar-On, *Memory in the Book*, 39–41, 44–6, 143–7; Kantor, *The Shaping of the Collective Memory*, 41–2.

17. Lieblich, *The Children of Kfar Etzion*, 19.

18. Ibid., 20–1. In 1949, the IDF Culture Department published the booklet *Kfar Darom –A Village of Heroism*, by Nehemia Aminoah, a member of a religious kibbutz. A similar argument was made in 1954 by Dov Knohl, the chronicler of the story of Gush Etzion.

This grievance apparently drew on the negative experience of religious-Zionist soldiers in the Haganah and Palmach units even prior to 1948, whose special needs were not heeded or were treated with contempt.[19] The sense of deprivation was openly and repeatedly expressed in the course of the 1950s. Thus, an opinion piece by *Hatzofe* editor, Shabtai Don Yehiya, entitled "Those Who Were Not Mentioned," stated that

> Modern Jewish history knows of no greater heroism than that of the lives and deaths of the people of Etzion. In that place were the choicest of the choice, thanks to whom the nation was granted liberty. If not for the political climate today, we would turn Mt. Etzion into an education center for young people. The state was founded by the light of the flames of Etzion.[20]

A decade later, Hakibbutz Hadati (the Religious Kibbutz Movement) and Bnei Akiva published *Shalom Karniel, His Life and Teachings*. Karniel, one of the leaders of Kfar Etzion, became a mythic figure in his own right. In the introduction Rabbi Moshe Tzvi Neriyah, a leading figure of the religious-Zionist movement, recounts an exchange between the delegates to the 7th Hapoel Hamizrahi convention, held in 1935, and Ben-Gurion, chairman of the Jewish Agency's executive. The delegates complained of discrimination in allocations of aliya, labor, and settlement. According to Neriyah, Ben-Gurion replied, "You are also deprived in the cemeteries. Where are your sacrifices for building the country?"[21] Since then, Neriyah writes, many rivers of blood have flowed, and not only are religious Zionists not deprived in the cemeteries, they have a most substantial place there. However, the stories of these fallen are not being told.

> We do not misremember, but others come and maliciously obliterate. They obliterate the sacrifice of the people of Kfar Etzion, they obliterate the campaign for Beerot Yitzhak and the wondrous steadfastness of Kfar Darom, and therefore it is incumbent upon us to bear witness to the blood of our martyrs and not allow their sacrifice to be consigned to oblivion.[22]

Grievances regarding discrimination and deliberate obliteration from the national memory thus remained deeply embedded in the religious-Zionist community between 1948 and 1967. By 1966, despite many acts of commemoration and documentation, primarily with regard to Kfar Etzion, the grievances remained unrelieved. Religious Zionists' efforts to integrate their story into the official

19. Mordechai Friedman, *The Religious Units in the Haganah and the Palmach* (Ramat Gan, 2005), 11–15, 36–63 [Hebrew].

20. *Hatzofe*, 18 April 1956. See also 23 April 1950; 18 April 1953; 23 April 1958; and Michael Hazani, *Religious Settlement on National Land* (Jerusalem, 1951), 8 [Hebrew].

21. Shaul Raz, ed., *Shalom Karniel: His Life and Teachings* (Tel-Aviv, 1966), 10 [Hebrew].

22. Ibid.

historiography of the War represented a struggle for acknowledgement of their role in the War and a place in the Israeli pantheon of national memory. The religious-Zionist leadership was not interested in rigorous historical research regarding any particular battle but rather in the inclusion of its religious-national narrative about the War in the national memory and consciousness.[23]

Even as the religious Zionists demanded that a "true" history be written and created the myth of Kfar Etzion, they were not seeking an "alternative national memory," as Daniel Gutwein notes.[24] Rather, they demanded that what had been marginalized be introduced into the national narrative that the national memory be filled out with their story, and that the heroism of the religious Zionists be granted legitimacy and a respectful place in the national narrative.[25] Beyond the eagerness to reshape Israeli national consciousness, there was an urgent need to rewrite the story of religious Zionism in the War for "internal" purposes. The movement needed its own myths of heroism to foster pride and confidence in itself.

Religious Zionism fervently desired the establishment of the State of Israel, and for most of its followers the advent of the state symbolized the beginning of redemption. Thus it was inconceivable that the role of religious Zionists should be missing from the history of the struggle that led to this great creation. This is important for understanding the motivation behind the creation of a unique religious-Zionist myth of heroism. Despite these needs and the feeling of being marginalized in the national memory of 1948, apart from the Gush Etzion saga, they did not generate much to historical or literary writing. The protagonists of the Kfar Etzion myth were aware of the story's power and its ability to influence the national memory, thus they deliberately decided to devote most of their efforts to fostering and enhancing this particular case and showed little interest in other aspects of the War.

The Making of the Kfar Etzion Myth

Jewish Memory, Myth, and the Case of Kfar Etzion

"Myth and memory collaborate,"[26] but only in Israel "was the commandment to remember perceived as a religious obligation for the entire people."[27] In national

---

23. On the experience of war as a corner stone in national consciousness and memory, see George L. Mosse, *Fallen Soldiers: Reshaping the Memory of the World Wars* (New York, 1990), 6–7.

24. Daniel Gutwein, "New Historiography or Privatization of Memory," in *Between Vision and Revision*, ed. Yechiam Weitz (Jerusalem, 1997), 311–41 [Hebrew].

25. Bar-On, *Memory in the Book*, 161.

26. Ohana and Wistrich, *Myth and Memory*.

27. Yosef H. Yerushalmi, *Zachor: Jewish History and Jewish Memory* (Seattle, WA, 1996), 9.

memory, however, it is "not the history, as is usually assumed, but rather the mythical time that keeps recurring."[28] The Jewish people keep returning to the unique event of the giving of the Torah at Mt. Sinai. Jewish memory is a collective memory, and the commemoration of individuals and their deeds, as is customary in most commemorations of the fallen, is a new phenomenon in Jewish history.[29] Where is the place of the new myth in the chain of core myths in Jewish history? Will a myth of heroism like that of Kfar Etzion be included in the chain of defining events, such as the binding of Isaac and the conquest of Eretz Israel, or will it remain a local myth, true only for the immediately following generations? Similarly, will the myth of Kfar Etzion enter the new national memory? Will it become part of the Zionist myths of heroism that have just been created, alongside the Hasmoneans, Bar Kochba, Masada, Tel Hai, the ghetto fighters? It seems that the attempt by religious Zionists to create a unique myth of heroism was aimed more at being added to the list of Jewish myths than to the Zionist list.

The scholarly approach to myths is very broad and beyond the scope of this chapter; thus, I confine myself to the definitions in several studies of the development of myths in the Zionist movement and in Israeli society. I show that a significant number of the components that appear in their definitions can be found in the story of Kfar Etzion.

Sacrifice for one's homeland is a supreme value in national movements, and the Zionist Movement is no exception. It incorporates both the use of force and sacrifice on the battlefield.[30] Consequently, to the fundamental Zionist myths "about the connection to the land and the project of settlement there, a story was added . . . the birth of the country in blood and fire."[31] The function of the many myths that grew around this story was to interpret reality and to give meaning to the sacrifice. For religious Zionists, Kfar Etzion is the story of the birth of the country in blood and fire, a story that indeed provides an interpretation of reality and gives meaning to the sacrifice.

"Myth is an ideal story that does not raise questions and by which a society tells about itself—where it came from and where it is going."[32] This definition matches the needs of religious Zionists in the beginning of the 1950s. They had an urgent need to create for themselves an ideal story of their own, and the story of Kfar Etzion was that story. Moreover, "myth provides an interpretation of reality,

---

28. Ibid., 10.

29. David Roskis, "Memory," in *Lexicon of Contemporary Jewish Culture*, ed. David Roskis, Arthur H. Cohen, and Paul Mendes-Flohr (Tel-Aviv, 1993), 179 [Hebrew].

30. Dan Bitan, "Exalted Might Blossoms," in Ohana and Wistrich, *Myth and Memory*, 169.

31. Emmanuel Sivan, *The Founding Generation: Myth, Portrait, and Memory* (Tel-Aviv, 1991), 11 [Hebrew].

32. Ohana and Wistrich, *Myth and Memory*, 12.

proposes a message, shapes the consciousness of individuals and collectives, mobilizes the emotions, guides the way and directs to action without any connection to its historical preciseness."[33] Another important definition of myth is "a story that describes events of exceptional importance to the community, which often gives the story the special status of sanctity . . . The truth of the myth . . . exists within the myth itself and in the social truth it represents and transmits. The reality to which the myth relates is the reality as seen by the consumers of the myth."[34] Myths of heroic events in the past carry a message for the future: "Does the myth burst into our lives only from the past or also from the future? Does it tell us only where we have come from, or does it also tell us where we are going?"[35]

Kfar Etzion is an ideal social model to be remembered and emulated by Jewish society as a whole. An echo of this belief is found in the writings on Kfar Etzion by quite a few authors. Thus, its story simultaneously meets two urgent needs of the religious Zionists. It serves in the struggle for the collective memory and for inclusion in the national narrative, and at the same time it constitutes a unique internal story of religious Zionism. As such, it is integrated in the messianic yearnings and vision of imminent redemption that are at the core of the religious-Zionist ideology.

Ohana argued that the story of Kfar Etzion was shifted from the "secular time" of the founding of the state to the post-1967 "messianic time" of Gush Emunim, and to a biblical place, which gave rise to the nation and the Messiah.[36] However, there is no shift here, and "messianic time" does not originate with the Gush Emunim worldview. True, it gathers force in this period, but it existed long before and was very much alive in religious Zionism during the War and throughout the 1950s and 1960s. The activist messianic stream at the core of religious Zionism in the first decade following the establishment of the state was a convenient incubator for the development of the Kfar Etzion myth and its dissemination among religious Zionists.[37]

33. Bitan, "Exalted Might Blossoms," 169. See also Ehud Luz, "On the Maccabees' Myth of Resurrection," *Hauma* 16 (1979): 44 [Hebrew].

34. Maoz Azaryahu, *State Rituals: Independence Day Celebrations and Commemoration of the Fallen in Israel 1948–1956* (Sede Boker, 1998), 4, 113 [Hebrew].

35. Avi Ravitzky, "Messianic Myth and Historical Drama," in Ohana and Wistrich, *Myth and Memory*, 92.

36 David Ohana, *The Origins of Israeli Mythology: Neither Canaanites Nor Crusaders* (New York, 2012), 101–2.

37. See Yaacov Rimon's poem in *Hatzofe*, 23 April 1948, 3: "I saw the splendor of the crown of kings rolling among the blood . . . sparks of the messianic longing carried in lead bullets, a divine miracle in the sanctified battle for life." See Greenblum, "From the Heroism of the Spirit to the Sanctification of Might," 29–30, 72–126.

The repeated portrayal of Kfar Etzion's story in lofty traditional Jewish concepts of '*kiddush ha-Shem*' and '*akeda*' aimed to engrave the myth in Jewish memory as a whole, and not only in religious-Zionist memory.[38] This connotes not only that the Kfar Etzion fighters went to their deaths willingly for the sake of the highest religious principles, but also that the war for establishing the State of Israel was a religious war and hence calls for conducting a religious way of life. "Sanctification of God's name" in the context of Kfar Etzion takes on a complex of meanings: the sanctity of life, a holy way of life, willingness to risk one's life, and total dedication.[39]

With regard to self-sacrifice, the use of the *akeda* story stands out. The *akeda* is part of the Israeli secular culture of memory and appears often in stories of wartime heroism, but over the years it has come under increasing criticism. The demand that young men die for the sake of their homeland raises the moral question of the right of the parents' generation to sacrifice their children. The critical interpretation of the act of sacrifice began to appear mainly after the Six-Day War.[40] Prior to that, sacrifice was essential in the Zionist ethos of heroism and referred to the sacrifice of the fallen who had given their utmost for the sake of the homeland, not for God. The Zionist ethos thus rejects the Jewish concept of sacrifice only in its religious context.[41] In the Kfar Etzion story, the *akeda* is the religious foundation of the myth. In addition to the "secular" connotations of sacrifice on the altar of the homeland and sacrifice for the sake of statehood and independence, there is also an emphatic religious meaning of sacrifice as the most exalted example of sanctification of God's name. Whereas one of the essential changes that Zionism made in the traditional myth is "the transfer of the center of gravity . . . from the relationship between Avraham and his God . . . to the relationship between Avraham and Isaac"[42] (emphasizing the unity and shared will of pioneer fathers and their Sabra sons regarding the sacrifice), in the religious-Zionist ethos the *akeda* combines both motifs, emphasizing the Jewish religious

38. As maintained by Ohana, *Origins*.

39. Yeshayahu Gafni and Avi Ravitzky, eds., *The Sanctity of Life and Risk of Life* (Jerusalem, 1993). The first issue of religious-Zionist periodical *Mahanayim* (Hanukkah, 1960), was devoted to the sanctification of God's name in Judaism.

40. Azaryahu, *State Rituals*, 123–4, note 24; Sivan, *The Founding Generation*, 201–4; Yael Zerubavel, "Battle, Self-Sacrifice, Sacrifice," in Ben-Amos and Bartal, *Patriotism*, 75–85; Moti Zeira, "The Emergence of the Lamed Heh Myth," *Contemporary Judaism* 10 (1995–96), 57–62; Dan Horovitz, *Blue and Dust* (Jerusalem, 1993), 85 [Hebrew].

41. Uri S. Cohen, "Bereavement and Sacrifice," in *Peace and War in Jewish Culture*, ed. Avriel Bar Levav (Jerusalem, 2006), 285 [Hebrew].

42. Oz Almog, *The Sabra: The Creation of the New Jew* (Berkeley, 2000), 40–1; Zerubavel, "Battle, Self-Sacrifice," 67. On the *akeda* motif in the Kfar Etzion story, see Ohana, *The Origins of Israeli Mythology*, 117–22.

interpretation over the secular Zionist one. Hence, "on the ruins of Kfar Etzion *the heavenly Kfar Etzion has risen* [emphasis added, D. G.], and the legend of its defenders will be woven into the age-old legends of our people's heroism."[43] Kfar Etzion is thus praised like no other case of heroism of religious Zionists in the War.

The Elements of the Myth

A rare combination of heroic combat and a tragic fall enshrined the Kfar Etzion story in the nation's consciousness even while the war was still being fought. The Kfar Etzion myth emerged even before the fall of the Bloc and had already attained a hue of sanctity by the eve of the declaration of independence.

Gush Etzion's story was linked to two of the War's greatest stories of heroism and painful failure, namely those of the Lamed Heh platoon and the Nebi Daniel convoy. These events made the fall of the Bloc one of the severest blows to the Yishuv, which anxiously observed the events in Gush Etzion. Over 50,000 attended the collective burial of the fallen in Jerusalem in November 1949, and Israeli leaders in the early 1950s repeatedly glorified their heroism and bravery.

The transformation of the Kfar Etzion story into a myth was possible because it contained an unusually powerful set of elements, almost everything a story needs to be transformed into a myth:[44]

> A. Gush Etzion, in the heart of the Hebron Mountains, was the historical cradle of the nation.[45] Although the religious Kibbutz movement was initially opposed to settling this area because of its unsuitability for agriculture, after the fall of the Bloc's settlements their location endowed them with unique significance for religious Zionists, beyond the general ideal of settlement in the Land of Israel.
>
> B. Prior to the War, and even more so while it was taking place, the Zionist institutions saw the settlements bloc as protecting Jerusalem, the heart of the nation. Ben-Gurion's statement that the steadfastness of Gush Etzion saved Jerusalem became fixed in the minds of that generation. As fighters, the settlers saw themselves as fulfilling the same mission as that of the fighters at Tel Hai. Just as Tel Hai saved the Galilee, so Kfar Etzion would ensure that Mt. Hebron would be part of the State of Israel.[46]
>
> C. The repeated attempts to strike roots in the area in the course of 40 years the fourth of which was after the Six-Day War was seen as a typical reflection

---

43. *Fortress: The Faithful of Israel in the War of Independence* (Jerusalem, 1959), 9 [Hebrew].

44. Lieblich, *The Children of Kfar Etzion*, 484–5.

45. Ben-Yaacov, *The History of Gush Etzion*, 11–18.

46. Ibid., 15. Many such statements repeatedly appeared in *Hatzofe* during the war and throughout the following decade.

of the "fall and revival," a core idea in Jewish visions of redemption. The third attempt, in 1943, was already considered a Zionist model of courage, of pioneers who insisted on returning to claim this part of the homeland. The third fall of Kfar Etzion, in 1948, heightened the glory and the tragic nature of the story and contributed greatly to its becoming a myth. The fourth return to Gush Etzion after the Six-Day War further charged the myth with symbolism. The return was perceived by many religious Zionists as a divine act of redemption, strengthening the messianic vision concerning resettlement of Judea and Samaria.

D. The community of Kfar Etzion, that the Avraham Group settled in 1943, was the ideal utopian community of the religious-Zionist vision, a typical "Torah and Labor" community, pure and holy.[47] The lives and deaths of its members were dedicated to the sanctification of God's name, the loftiest value for religious Zionists, and thus became a modern-day version of the *akeda*, the sacrifice of Isaac. Thus, the community was portrayed as a role model and an object of veneration even before its fall.

E. The proximity of the fall of the Bloc, and especially the Kfar Etzion massacre, to the declaration of the State of Israel the following day, perceived as the beginning of the invasion of the Arab armies, contributed greatly to heightening Kfar Etzion's symbolism in the context of "fall and revival." This was expressed in statements such as, "The founding of the State of Israel was lit by the torch of the burning Gush Etzion!"[48] and "The flames of the sacrifice of Etzion . . . lit the revival of the state."[49]

F. That some of the settlers of Kfar Etzion were Holocaust survivors, a number of whom fell in the battle, added further symbolism to the story, turning it into a typical example of the Jewish story of destruction and redemption. Not only did these survivors live for the sanctification of God's name, "in Kfar Etzion they stood and fought God's war against the enemy . . . until the fate of the entire kibbutz was sealed, even though the kibbutz was the most magnificent of all the kibbutzim both spiritually and materially."[50]

G. After the Bloc's fall, most of the survivors of Kfar Etzion, widows, orphans, and a handful of men—remained together, assisted by the Religious Kibbutz Movement. They met annually and, together with other survivors of Gush Etzion, took an active role in commemoration, publishing books and pamphlets and

47. Yaacov Edelstein, *Hatzofe*, 29 March 1948.

48. Ben-Yaacov, *The History of Gush Etzion*, 298. Similar quotations appeared after the fall of the Bloc in the press, literature, and textbooks, e.g., *Hatzofe*, 19 April 1953, 2, and a Bnei Akiva youth movement booklet (Jerusalem, 1957).

49. Ben-Yaacov, *The History of Gush Etzion*, 298.

50. Gal, *Was Gush Etzion Abandoned in the War of Independence?*, i.

holding summer camps for their children. The Sons of Gush Etzion Society disseminated the myth among the general public, and each year the survivors met in growing numbers at Mt. Herzl on Memorial Day for Israel's fallen. After the service they went to the Judean Hills in the hope of seeing Gush Etzion from afar and identifying the lone oak tree that for 19 years had symbolized the location of Gush Etzion. The means of commemoration and the story of the oak tree were well known to religious Zionists and contributed to the transformation of the story into a mythic narrative with all the trappings of sanctity.[51]

Shaping the Myth: Discourse, Documentation, Literature, and Education

This section shows how, from May 1948, the story of Kfar Etzion was shaped and inculcated through the press, poetry, prose, textbooks, and the youth movement's training programs, and how it became the defining religious-Zionist myth of heroism. The elaboration demonstrates the extent to which the myth imbued every aspect of life and the great extent to which it was used in every means of communication in that period. Unlike any other story of the War, the saga of Kfar Etzion inspired, from the very beginning, a broad variety of written documentation, memoirs, prose, poetry, and scholarship.[52] The following examples discussed at length are the most significant representations of the process of construction and inculcation of this mythical story.

Hatzofe Daily

Hatzofe played a central role in fostering and elevating the story of Kfar Etzion to the level of myth. Two days after the fall, editor-in-chief Shabtai Don Yehiya elucidated the myth, which henceforth was identified with religious Zionism:

> At the moment that Israel has become independent, a fortress in the Judean hills has collapsed and fallen, a fortress of the best of men in the entire creation. . . . Every man and woman in Etzion is a magnificent crown, the crème de la crème, Jewish purity realized collectively. The entire village is the peak of peaks. This is a war of life and death of an ancient, proud people, long-suffering and girded with might. The flames of Kfar Etzion shed light on the deep reason for the war.[53]

---

51. Ben-Yaacov, *The History of Gush Etzion*, 311–19; *Hatzofe*, 5 June 1958, describes the Gush Etzion exhibition in Petah Tikva that drew 30,000 visitors. On the oak and its mystical symbolism, see Ohana, *Origins*, 110–17.

52. For a comprehensive bibliography on Gush Etzion, see Greenblum, "From the Heroism of the Spirit," 260.

53. *Hatzofe*, 16 May, 2. See Izhak Ben-Zvi, ibid., and Rabbi Alter Meir, 17 May 1948, 2.

Anyone who visited Kfar Etzion, he wrote, saw "A magnificent view . . . The spirit of the place wrought an act of creation, the spirit of the place is the sanctification of heaven." And, "In the mountains of Hebron walked the emissaries of the creator of the earth and of its fruit, and they carried out his mission, the mission of creation." The people of Mt. Etzion were thus participants in God's act of creation: "Above these mountains they bore the vision of the Lord's prophets. *Here in the temple of creation, where a man sees his creator with no screen [between them] and the hand reaches out to touch the very margins of heaven* [emphasis added, D. G.] . . . there lives and exists forever the sanctity of the reality we live in, its full realization as required by divine prophecy . . . The people of Mt. Etzion were from among the few in Israel, the chosen, from among millions of Jews," who by enormous effort rose and fell and climbed up "to the peak of realized Judaism." They charged at the wilderness, the evil, the ruination, and destruction. "Their charge was motivated by the enormous concentration of the essence of goodness and mercy, the essence of yearning of the Jewish elite for a holy and pure life of work."[54] A year later he wrote, "All the battles of the War of Independence are holy, and the Scroll of Etzion is the holy of holies. It stands on the pinnacle of the history of the world, . . . Etzion is the *akeda* of the nation's patriarch, it is the walk toward death with open eyes and clear consciousness, to save Jerusalem, the Yishuv, and the state from total destruction."[55]

It seems that the religious Zionists needed to draw up a theoretical model that would express powerfully and clearly their most sacred values; they could not have written a more sublime story than that of Kfar Etzion. The sights of destruction and redemption that were revealed to the members of that generation as they were taking place transformed Kfar Etzion into a myth of heroism of enormous proportions. A talented writer, like the editor of *Hatzofe*, defined the myth at the moment of its creation and in accord with the public mood at that time. The poet Haim Hamiel wrote about the valor of devotion to the land, the valor of war, and the valor of willingly going to the *akeda*, all of which were interpreted as preparing the way for the coming of the Messiah.[56]

The passing of years has not diminished the force of the emotions and their expression. Especially on Israel's Memorial and Independence days *Hatzofe* perpetuates the myth. On Memorial Day in 1953 it stated,

Before the flames of the terrible sacrifice on the mountain were extinguished, the state was born. The connection between the events became the deepest symbol of

54. Ibid., 16 May 1948.

55. Ibid., 2 May 1949, 2, and N. Aminoah in the same issue; also 18 April, 2, and 31 March 1950, 6.

56. Ibid., 31 March 1950, 6.

the campaign for liberty . . . The people of Etzion walked with open eyes toward their annihilation in order to give life to Jerusalem.[57]

Henceforth, the motifs of *akeda* and sanctification of God's name, longing for the mountain, and yearning for redemption annually enhanced the myth.[58]

Anthology, Literature, and Poetry

Two books of history and literature pertaining to the community of Kfar Etzion and its role in the War stand out for their contribution to the inculcation of the myth prior to 1967. Both were produced by its survivors. Combining fact and fiction, eyewitness accounts and literary creations, they create a blend of glorious and majestic myth for their generation.

The elements of the Kfar Etzion myth were first defined by a voluminous anthology edited by Dov Knohl in 1954 and followed by a revised edition three years later. It was the second volume of a series dedicated to the religious-Zionist record in the War.[59] This monumental commemoration and documentation is the most comprehensive project commemorating a single narrative of the War. In his preface to the second edition, he expressed his concerns about the impact of the first edition, especially in the context of commemoration and its contribution to "molding the spiritual character of the young generation."[60] These goals were attained fully, and within a few months the first edition was sold out. The book was received enthusiastically by the Bloc's survivors and, according to the editor, was useful to scholars and educators in schools and youth movements. His book was also published in English (1958) and in a second edition (1973) added an epilogue describing the return to the Etzion Bloc after the 1967 War.[61]

One cannot overestimate the significance of Knohl's book in creating and fostering the myth of Kfar Etzion. It remains the most important source about the Bloc and Kfar Etzion during the War. It focuses mainly on Kfar Etzion, explaining that it was the heart of Gush Etzion, the oldest of its settlements, and where "the last battle for the Bloc took place."[62] The following book's characteristics explain its foundational significance in the myth-making process.

First is its religious framework: the motif of the *akeda*. The first page is given over entirely to commentaries about the *akeda* for example, a midrash from *Pirkei*

---

57. Ibid., 19 April, 2. See entire page devoted to Kfar Etzion, 20 April 1953.

58. Ibid., 22, 23 April 1958; 1 May 1960; 28 April 1963; 5 May 1965; 24 April 1966.

59. *Misgav*, Vol. 1, was dedicated to all the settlements of the Religious Kibbutz Movement during the war, save Gush Etzion, and is only 184 pages long.

60. Knohl, *Gush Etzion and Its War*, 15.

61. Dov Knohl, *Siege in the Hills of Hebron: The Battle of the Etzion Block* (New York, 1973).

62. Knohl, *Gush Etzion and Its War*, 16.

Derabbi Eliezer, in which Avraham and God engage in a dialogue: "He said to him [to God], Ruler of the universe, on which mountain? He [God] said to him: In any place where you see me standing and waiting for you, and I will tell you, That is the altar." The story of Mt. Etzion is the story of the mount of the *akeda*. The parallels drawn between Mt. Moriah and Mt. Etzion and between Avraham, who sacrifices his son (who goes to his death willingly), and the members of Kfar Etzion, who are willing to give up their lives for the homeland and for the sanctification of God's name, are the theological underpinnings of the story of Kfar Etzion and of Knohl's book. While not directly drawing these parallels, the impression made by the opening page stays with the reader, who is aware of the story's conclusion, throughout the book.

Second, the book compiles a richness of primary sources: diaries, fighters' letters, financial reports, reports of committee meetings, descriptions of battles, and words of commemoration, all of which combine to create a human mosaic of Gush Etzion. The author's decision to show everyday life instead of going off on flowery tangents is an ideological one, and it makes the book unusually high drama. The introductory chapters and the historical summary are not the heart of the book. The descriptions of the War and the battles come entirely from the kibbutz members and the fighters. The decision to publish a commemorative book based on eye-witness reports, which compiles almost every accessible piece written about the Gush, aims to tell a human story and to constitute a perpetual memorial rather than to be a precise historical investigation and a chronological description of the battles.[63] The rich and diverse documentation of Gush Etzion includes stories and memoirs, prose, poetry, and philosophy by settlers, fighters, and outside commanders, official reports and documents and newspaper items, many of which had been collected in the Kfar Etzion Archive. This archive was destroyed in the War, but parts of it, including diaries and accounts written throughout the six months of fighting, had been copied and sent to Jerusalem, and some items were reconstructed.[64] This is the kind of book that educators and thinkers need and in which one can easily find quotable passages, an exemplary story, or a figure with whom to identify. This is how one fosters a myth.

Third, the book describe everyday life, routine episodes and battle stories told in plain, direct, and concrete language by the fighters themselves, all of which generate the exaltation and awe that readers are meant to feel. It is this "non-heroic" style, the absence of the mythic dimension in the writing that creates the myth. Stories of anti-combatants, anti-heroes, who found themselves in the midst of a sacred and fateful situation, ultimately underline the myth of the

63. Ibid., 14.
64. Ibid., 14–15; Lieblich, *The Children of Kfar Etzion*, 492–9.

heroism of Kfar Etzion. The role of personal heroism in the battle itself is minor in the overall story. The heroism is that of sacrifice, dedication, determination, holding on to the land, everyday life under siege; courage in battle is just one element of the whole. Not one story of personal heroism in the battles of Gush Etzion has become a shining example for future generations. Not one battle story from among the many of battles conducted by the Gush's defenders became a myth. The sanctification of God's name, the *akeda*, and the life of purity, these are the elements of the myth.

The volume's editor points to the grievance of the Bloc's members at being abandoned by the Yishuv without help. In an attempt to mitigate the complaint, however, he adds that there were other places and needs on other fronts "whose importance in deciding the war immediately was apparently considered to be greater."[65] Many of the Bloc's members understood that their fight was doomed to fail. Word came that Haganah commanders had warned that the Bloc would not hold out, and even the British repeatedly uttered similar warnings. Knohl recounts it thus:

> The defenders of Gush Etzion saw their isolation and the absence of a clear decision about their future as a sign that the Bloc's campaign was not important in itself; instead, its purpose was to aid the war effort as a whole. There was nothing to do but to bear their fate with restraint and to hope for divine miracles.[66]

The restrained, yet critical manner in which Knohl's questions were raised might seem incomprehensible, especially against the backdrop of the common argument that the Bloc's fighting saved Jerusalem. If the campaign was not important and did not contribute to the defense of Jerusalem, why was it necessary? It may be that framing the Bloc's battle in the conscious hopelessness of its defenders attempted to further elevate the self-sacrificial nature of the battle.

Shaul Raz and Yaacov Even-Chen recounted the story of Gush Etzion and Kfar Etzion in prose and poetry, respectively, immediately after the fall of the Bloc. Both were from Kfar Etzion and remained there throughout the siege. They published a total of eight volumes of poetry, fiction, and factual accounts about Gush Etzion, which clearly mark its story as their life project. Many of the stories and poems were first published in *Hatzofe* and in periodicals later compiled into books.

---

65. Knohl, *Gush Etzion and Its War*, 12.

66. Ibid., 12; Shaul Raz, *Mountains Song: Chapters of Ambiance and Valor* (Tel-Aviv, 1958), 85, quotes his own writing on 6 February 1948, about the inability of the Yishuv to secure the Bloc's defense; Gal, *Was Gush Etzion Abandoned in the War of Independence?*, 489–544, adds first-hand accounts to this effect; Uri Milstein, *History of the War of Independence*, IV (Tel-Aviv, 1993), 97–100 [Hebrew].

Their writings are similar to each other in character and style and are brimming with infinite love for Kfar Etzion, longing for the place and its people, and intense love of its landscape. Combining historical truth with fiction, the poems and stories both describe and document. Thus, Raz "interviews" the refugee from the last battle, in a story that is essentially historical though parts of it are apparently ambiance fictional.[67] Similarly, Even-Chen wrote a great poem, "The Last Battle,"[68] and compiled personal stories of the people of Kfar Etzion in his book *Oaks in the Rock*. The stories are narratives of destruction and redemption, salvation and revival, immigrating to the Land of Israel and leaving loved ones behind, cleaving to the land and cultivating the soil, the Holocaust, and battles and the fall of heroes in the war. They deal with individuals but reflect the story of the nation. Raz writes in his poems about the real people who were his friends and companions, mixing eyewitness accounts and real people with mythical elements.

In *The Scroll of Etzion*, he writes, "O, your everlasting spirit that soars like the sun; the spirit of grandfather Avraham in the furnace; the spirit of Rabbi Avraham, author of *The Lights of Sanctity*; . . . the spirit of the Avrahams who were burned at the stake of Etzion, in the chain of valor."[69] The *akeda*, the sanctification of God's name, the defense of Jerusalem, all these appear in his poems and stories, in addition to expressions of rage and calls for wreaking vengeance on the enemy.[70]

Raz and Even-Chen's poems and stories are found in all the religious-Zionist publications: newspapers, periodicals, and textbooks, and in training programs of the Bnei Akiva and Ezra youth movements. Although their stories and poems are central in fostering the myth and imparting it to future generations they rarely address battlefield valor. Rather, the myth's power lies in the heroism of the collective, its determination and ability to stand and fight while knowing full well that the worst is expected.

A Personal Myth: Shalom Karniel

Only one individual became a symbol and a mythic figure in the story of Kfar Etzion, Shalom Karniel, who fell in the battle fought by the Convoy of 10 on its way from Jerusalem to the Bloc on 11 December 1947. Fostering the image of Karniel as a role model reveals the values of the shapers of the myth and the

---

67. Raz, *Mountains Song*, 92–6.

68. Yaacov Even-Chen, *Beyond the Mountains* (Jerusalem, 1958), 12–28 [Hebrew].

69. Raz, *Memories of Etzion*, 50. The quotation refers to Rabbi Avraham Kook, after whom the Avraham Group was named.

70. Ibid., 13.

image of heroism they wanted to impart to the coming generations. It was not his exceptional fighting record or falling in battle that underpinned his valor. Rather, it was his role as an exemplary model, as an individual whose life best represents the Kfar Etzion community as an ideal of the Torah-and-Labor society, adding luster to the entire community. Karniel embodied everything this society aspired to: broadly learned in Jewish studies, a pioneer who immigrated to the Land of Israel in order to live as a laborer in a kibbutz, a respected leader of Hashomer Hadati in Poland, and a core member of Bnei Akiva in the Land of Israel, a leader who dealt with everyday matters and contributed greatly to the development of the kibbutz, a poet, a philosopher, and a humanist. He is described as modest and truthful, of moral integrity and utter seriousness, and yet with the character of a Hasid, ecstatic in prayer, singing with infectious devotion.

As one of the first casualties of Kfar Etzion it added to the aura his holiness:

> He was all pioneer, all dedication . . . who gave everything to the idea and the move-
> ment . . . The first among the first . . . with open eyes he walked up the path to the
> *akeda* . . . Our brother Shalom in the mountains of Etzion, you were like Trumpeldor
> in the Upper Galilee. You were pure in your life and saintly in your death.[71] He lived in
> public and died in public, lived in the leadership of the youth movement, the kibbutz,
> the adult movement, and died in a *minyan* [a prayer quorum of ten] of saintly and
> pure men.[72]

Though a book about his life and rich literary remains was only published in 1966, already on the 30-day memorial of the Convoy of 10, the kibbutz bulletin, *Bemahanenu*, devoted much space to his memory.[73] Karniel is an unusual mythic figure in religious Zionism: the first among the first yet not superior to them, or unusual in his way of life. He stands out as a mirror of the entire community, a symbol and representative of the kibbutz and a role model for the Bnei Akiva.[74]

Karniel's image was fostered and absorbed exclusively by the Religious-Zionist Movement as part of mythologizing the story of Kfar Etzion and in accordance with its particular values and need for uniqueness and self-esteem. He, however, remains unknown to the Israeli-Jewish public and, unlike other mythical heroes of the 1948 War, was not adopted as such by the entire nation.

---

71. Ibid., 8–9.

72. Rabbi Zvi Neriyah, "Preface," in Raz, *Shalom Karniel*, n.p.

73. Ibid., 300.

74. For example, *Zraim*, April–May 1949, 7.

The Myth in Youth Education

In the 1950s and 1960s the myth of Kfar Etzion was systematically inculcated in the religious-Zionist youth movement and education system, both formal and informal. In 1954 *Zraim*, the bulletin of Bnei Akiva, noted:

> On Memorial Day we think especially of the people of Mt. Etzion who went up to heaven in flames on the eve of the recognition of the State of Israel and with their deaths saved Jerusalem the capital and the entire state . . . Their daily lives, filled with honesty and justice, Torah and commandments, were a wondrous preface to their settlement on the sacred peak, among the most exalted and awe-inspiring in Israel's history . . . They are the best of boys who brought liberation and redemption . . . Their simple and great lives, their sacrifice for the salvation of all Israel, are an everlasting model.[75]

In its training program on heroism, in 1954, the valor of the religious settlements in the war is defined as the supreme expression of heroism.[76] Even-Chen and Raz's stories appeared in the movement's bulletins for many years.[77] A teacher's guide for schools summarizes in a question the importance of the story of Kfar Etzion for religious Zionists: "In what way were the people of Kfar Etzion unique in their lives and considered holy by all? Or, in other words, what made Kfar Etzion sacred and the symbol of heroism in our day?"[78]

Youth movement members and schoolchildren in the 1950s and 1960s were brought up on the myth of Kfar Etzion and internalized its main messages: the eternity of Jerusalem, the *akeda*/sacrifice, the sanctification of God's name, the pure life, the life of Torah, and labor. The basic tenets of religious Zionism, which it sought to inculcate in its children, are all found in the story of Kfar Etzion. The return home of the children after the Six-Day War was an extraordinary event that many religious Zionists saw as "the light of the Messiah."[79]

Conclusion

The Kfar Etzion myth encompasses the most powerful values, symbols, and beliefs of religious Zionism: destruction and redemption, Holocaust and revival, a life of purity and labor, and a martyr's death in a heroic battle for the sanctification of God's name. The life and death of the people of Kfar Etzion thus perfectly reflect the *akeda* in its traditional religious meaning and constitute an integral part of the historic chain of Jewish martyrdom.

75. *Zraim*, May 1954, 8; ibid., April 1950, 5; April–May 1952, 12–20.

76. The Trainer's Expression (Jerusalem, October 1956) [Hebrew].

77. *Zraim*, January 1952, 2, and April 1956, 6.

78. Even-Chen, ed., *Rise, Etzion* (Jerusalem, 1974), 95.

79. *Hatzofe*, 9 June 1967, 4.

The story of Kfar Etzion became a defining story of religious Zionism soon after the settlement's fall and, like many other myths, grew more powerful in the course of time. The enhancement of the myth by the press, prose, poetry, textbooks, and formal and informal education systems shows the significance of a focused and systematic construction and differentiation of the story and its mythic dimensions, which shunts aside all the other religious-Zionist stories of heroism.

The fourth return to Kfar Etzion, in 1967, an extraordinary phenomenon in itself by any historical measure, gave the story additional power and had a great influence on the turn religious Zionism has taken since then toward a messianic vision of redemption. In the worldview of many religious Zionists there was no clearer or more tangible harbinger of the imminent redemption than the moment of return of the children of Kfar Etzion to their homes to carry on in the place where their fathers' lives were cut off. One of the returnees was Hanan Porat, a prominent Gush Emunim leader and an ardent proponent of the messianic vision.

That the Kfar Etzion myth became a model of emulation among religious Zionists, especially in times of crisis, is evident in the way in which the settlers of Gush Katif (a bloc of settlements in the Gaza Strip that Israel dismantled as part of its unilateral withdrawal in 2005) relate to the myth, as they document and commemorate their own story. The methods with which the Kfar Etzion story was documented and commemorated, including a meeting with the "children of Kfar Etzion," have been copied almost precisely in the construction of the new religious-Zionist myth, the myth of Gush Katif.[80]

Precisely because of its saturation with religious, and after 1967, also messianic connotations, the myth of Kfar Etzion remained identified with the religious Zionists. Though the story had occupied a central place in the public's attention at the time of its occurrence and shortly after, it had little or no success in permeating the Israeli national memory, which remained essentially secular. The fading of Kfar Etzion's story in the memory of the Israeli general public is even more salient when compared with the persistence of the memory of the Lamed Heh, another story of heroism of that war. The historical link between these stories, the shared mythical elements of heroism, sacrifice, and dedication to the task up to the last bullet, and the view of the fallen as "the elite who served the nation" all led some to perceive them as permanently intertwined and a single unit of memory.[81] But in retrospect, although during the war the Gush Etzion settlers saw the fall of the Lamed Heh as part of their own campaign, over the years the Israeli national memory increasingly adopted the Lamed Heh story as "one of the most authentic

80. Gush Katif Commemoration, http://www.yadkatif.com/index.htm (accessed 12 June 2009).

81. Zeira, "The Emergence of the Lamed Heh Myth," 68, 71.

expressions of the founding generation,"[82] while the religious Zionists fostered the myth of Kfar Etzion as their exclusive case and shunted aside the Lamed Heh story. Hence, in all the Memorial Day and Independence Day issues of *Hatzofe* between 1948 and 1967, Gush Etzion is mentioned almost exclusively and there is no trace of the Lamed Heh. Precisely because a combined commemoration of the two stories overshadowed religious-Zionist heroism, the link was broken and the Kfar Etzion myth assumed a life of its own, though it remained largely an internal religious-Zionist story.

DROR GREENBLUM is CEO of Kiryat Tivon community centers. He is author of "The Attitude toward Military Heroism and Physical Force in the Bnei Akiva Youth Movement," *The Kipa and the Beret-Image and Reality: The Public Discourse on Religious Zionism and Military Service.*

82. Almog, *The Sabra*, 207–8.

Part 3: Palestinian Traumatic Memory

6 Descending the *Khazooq*

"Working Through" The Trauma of the Nakba *in Emile Habibi's Oeuvre*

Assaf Peled

Introduction

Many Palestinian intellectuals have written about the harsh realities of their people following the *Nakba*, but only a few of them have critically dealt with the traumatic facets of the event and their present repercussions. Literature on the *Nakba* represents a salient effort to serve the Palestinian people's struggle for their natural rights. While this focus on the injustices perpetrated against the Palestinians and the need for restitution is tempting, it leaves little room for critical reflection on the experience itself. As its point of reference is external, it dooms the writer to act out[1] the past.[2] In recent years several researchers have explored the traumatic dimensions of the Nakba and its impact on those who have remained in the homeland that became the State of Israel,[3] but no systematic effort has been made to critically take on these traumas.

Against this background, the literary works of Emile Habibi, a prominent Palestinian-Israeli writer, journalist, and politician stand out as a unique voice worthy of a separate investigation. In his work, Habibi draws a connection

---

1. La Capra defines "acting out" as the performative reliving of the past as if it was fully present rather than represented in memory. Dominick La Capra, *Writing History, Writing Trauma* (Baltimore, 2001), 70.

2. Avraham Sela, "Arab Historiography of the 1948 War: The Quest for Legitimacy," in *Perspectives of Israeli History*, ed. Laurence J Silberstein (New York and London, 1991), 140–3; Rashid Khalidi, "The Palestinians and 1948: The Underlying Causes of Failure," in *The War for Palestine: Rewriting the History of 1948*, ed. Eugene L. Rogan and Avi Shlaim (Cambridge, 2001); Mustafa Kabha, "Introduction," in *Toward Formulating an Historic Narrative for the Nakba: Problems and Challenges*, ed. Mustafa Kabha (Haifa, 2006), 1–5 [Arabic]; Honaida Ghanim, *Reinventing the Nation: Palestinian Intellectuals in Israel* (Jerusalem, 2009), 81–2; Gideon Shilo, *Israeli Arabs in the Eyes of the Arab States and the PLO* (Jerusalem, 1992), 33; Mahmud 'Abbasi, "The Evolvement of the Novel and the Short Story in the Arab Literature in Israel Between the Years 1948–1976" (PhD diss., Hebrew University of Jerusalem, 1983), 114, 137–8 [all in Hebrew].

3. Ghanem, *Reinventing the Nation*

The War of 1948 (2016); 147–170, DOI: 10.2979/warof1948.0.0.08

between the Palestinians' inability to extricate themselves from their present plight and their suppression of the trauma they suffered from the *Nakba* with which he seeks to critically deal in his writings. In his play *Luka Son of Luka*, Habibi expresses this belief through one of his main protagonists, Budur, who wonders: "What brought our defeat? What chased us away? What did and didn't we do?" To this replies the host of the play "The hearts of those men refuse to set the secret free. The great shock, the fire from the sky, the volcanos . . . covered the memory and cast a coat of self-pity on the wounds."[4]

The chapter examines the ways in which Habibi deals in his literature with the collective trauma of the *Nakba* as it was experienced by the Palestinians who became citizens of the state of Israel. The term *Nakba* refers to the Palestinian catastrophe in the 1948 War, one facet of which was the dissection of the Palestinian society into distinct social and geographical sub-groups: refugees in the neighboring Arab countries, the West Bank, the Gaza Strip, and Israel, and the steady residents within historic Palestine. While they all share an understanding of the disastrous meaning of the *Nakba*, these groups are varied in their war and post-war experiences. I focus on the experience of the Palestinian citizens of Israel. I contend that through his writings, Habibi seeks to translate his personal experiences into collective knowledge that might help the Palestinian society in Israel work through its traumas. The process he sought to instigate involved encouraging an acknowledgment of the reality of the trauma and the new situation it created, and mending the rift in individual and collective identity.

The chapter sheds light on a significant aspect of the *Nakba* and of Habibi's work that has received little if any attention. The attitude of Arab critics toward Habibi's writing has been diverse, albeit shaped primarily by the framework of "Resistance Literature," as outlined by Kanafani. According to Kanafani, Habibi and other writers among Israel's Arab citizens defied Israeli attempts to erase the national identity of the Palestinians in Israel,[5] and constituted part of a larger body of Palestinian "Resistance Literature," which assisted in generating an armed resistance consciousness.[6] While many observed Habibi's political activities and individual experience as separate from his literary oeuvre,[7] some rejected his work completely.[8]

---

4. Emile Habibi, *Luka Son of Luka* (Haifa, 2006 [1980]), 175–6 [Arabic].

5. For a survey of this literature, see Ghassan Kanafani, *The Palestinian Resistance Literature under the Occupation 1948–1967* (Beirut, 1987), 38 [Arabic].

6. Ibid., 13–14.

7. Shimon Ballas, *Arab Literature in the Shadow of the War* (Tel-Aviv, 1978), 81 [Hebrew]. See also Sabri Hafiz, "Emile Habibi and the Narration of the Palestinian Collective Memory," *Majallat al-Dirasat al-Filastiniyya* 27 (1996): 110–33 [Arabic].

8. Such as the Egyptian critic Ghali Shukri; Shilo, *Israeli Arabs in the Eyes of the Arab States*, 39–40.

Like their Arab counterparts, Israeli writers tended to differentiate between Habibi the author and Habibi the political dissident. They praised his artistic achievements as universalistic, while obscuring his constant criticism of the state's oppressive attitude toward its Palestinian citizens.[9] Specific review of his work is rare, as literary critics have usually treated his oeuvre as part of broader reviews of the Palestinian literature in Israel.[10]

The chapter will briefly address the theoretical aspects of psychic traumatization and its relevance to the collective; illustrate the impact of the *Nakba* as a collective trauma; provide a background on the life and work of Habibi, who meant not only to depict the realities of Palestinian life in Israel, but also to bring about social change using his experiences as an individual and a member of the Palestinian collective.[11] It then examines the circumstances that enabled him to turn these experiences into collective knowledge and elaborates on the ways and means by which Habibi endeavored to instigate a "working through" process. It explains the impact of the specific conditions experienced by Palestinian-Israeli citizens and their responses, and discusses the uniqueness of Habibi's work regarding his therapeutic endeavors.

Psychic Traumatization

Theoretically, the chapter draws mainly from the concept of collective trauma. To understand this complex concept, I will first introduce the concept of individual psychic trauma, on which the collective trauma is based, and explain the mechanisms by which this extrapolation is possible.

Psychic traumatization is a psychological impairment that stems from an overwhelming experience. The experience involves a threatening event that leads to a cognitive failure, resulting in extreme emotional distress and in an ineffective response. Traumatization cannot be identified with a specific event, as interpretations and responses to a particular occurrence may vary between individuals and societies.[12] As prior schemas fail to explain the occurrence and to suggest an adequate response to counter the threat, the individual is seized by an intense

---

9. Hanan Hever, "The Refugees for the Refugees: Emile Habibi and the Canon of Hebrew Literature," *Hamizrah Hahdash* 35 (1993): 106–7 [Hebrew].

10. See Ballas, *Arab Literature in the Shadow of the War.*

11. Seraje characterized Habibi's use of personal and collective experience to tell the Palestinian past as "collective autobiography." Seraje Assi, "Memory, Myth and the Military Government: Emile Habibi's Collective Autobiography," *Jerusalem Quarterly* 52 (2013): 87–97.

12. Rolf J. Kleber and Danny Brom (with Peter B. Defares), *Coping with Trauma: Theory, Prevention and Treatment* (Amsterdam, 1992), 129–30.

sense of helplessness and horror.[13] Lifton observes, "One comes to feel the self-disintegrating at moments when one's inner forms and images become inadequate representations of the self-world relationship and inadequate bases for action."[14] This observation helps us understand trauma not only as a response to direct threats to the body but also as a threat to the self, which is more noticeable in cases of vicarious traumatization.

The memory of the traumatic experience is persistently and unwillingly re-lived in nightmares, flashbacks, and daily behavior.[15] In this confusing and dis-tressing situation, the individual's sense of reality is often undermined.[16] He may never totally transcend the trauma, but neither is he doomed to continuously relive the past.[17] While he spends much of his time and energy on avoiding stimuli associated with the event,[18] he is also in constant search of new, more adequate formulations of the self-world relationship that might help produce meaning for that event, and finally place it in his past.[19] Although personal schemas may be shattered, the individual can still recruit for the reformulation process the images and forms that are made available through interaction with others, culture, and history.[20]

La Capra argues that the totalizing nature of trauma is countervailed by people's capacity to "work through" the experience. "Working through" involves thought or action that helps attain a certain critical distance from the trauma or, in other words, reconstruct the borders of self and time as to enable moral agency. For example, he mentions mourning as an important modality of working through as it "brings the possibility of engaging trauma and achieving a reinvest-ment in, or recathexis of, life which allows one to begin again."[21] Awareness of one's feelings and acknowledgment of their legitimate existence helps people cope

13. Ibid., 144; American Psychiatric Association [APA], *Diagnostic and Statistical Manual of Mental Disorders* (Arlington, VA, 2000), 463.

14. Robert Jay Lifton, *The Life of the Self: Toward a New Psychology* (New York, 1976), 38.

15. Ibid., 5; APA, *Diagnostic and Statistical Manual,* 468. Symptoms usually begin within the first three months after the trauma, although there may be a delay of months, or even years, before they appear, ibid., 466.

16. Robert Jay Lifton, *Death in Life: Survivors of Hiroshima* (New York, 1967), 486; Cathy Caruth, "Introduction," in *Trauma: Explorations in Memory,* ed. Cathy Caruth (Baltimore and London, 1995), 6.

17. La Capra, *Writing History Writing Trauma,* 22.

18. APA, *Diagnostic and Statistical Manual,* 468.

19. Lifton, *Death in Life,* 526; *The Life of the Self,* 39.

20. E. Ann Kaplan and Ban Wang, "From Traumatic Paralysis to the Force Field of Modernity," in *Trauma and Cinema: Cross Cultural Explorations,* ed. E. Ann Kaplan and Ban Wang (Hong Kong, 2004), 1–23.

21. La Capra, *Writing History, Writing Trauma,* 66.

with them, and reduce the use of defense mechanisms such as projection and dissociation. This is an important step toward rebuilding the defense mechanisms that were overwhelmed by the trauma.[22]

The concept of individual trauma has recently been extrapolated to the level of the collective. I focus on the mechanisms by which this extrapolation, usually taken for granted in the literature on trauma, is possible. Collective trauma might be defined as an experience, shared by a substantial number of group members that stems from the group's failure to protect its members from a disastrous event and thus harms its collective identity. McFarlane and Van Der Kolk observe that "One core function of human societies is to provide their members with traditions, institutions, and value systems that protect them against becoming overwhelmed by stressful experiences."[23] The failure of these structures may deeply undermine members' confidence in the collective body and, as people's sense of continuity is involved with that of the community, their related death imagery is reactivated.[24]

Collective trauma does not refer to a single coherent memory held by an organic collective body but to a memory embodied in group members. Collective traumas contain a variety of experiences, and individual bearers of traumatic memories come to understand that they share common meanings with others through societal interaction. Trauma can thus serve as a source of inspiration for communality.[25] Trauma may even be transferred to others who did not experience it directly,[26] for example, through family dynamics.[27]

The *Nakba* as a Collective Trauma

The 1948 War profoundly and violently unsettled the Palestinians' world—the familiar and normal disappeared and was replaced by a reality of unrelieved suffering, all too difficult to tolerate.[28] A major difficulty of coping with the

22. Alexander C McFarlane and Bessel A. Van Der Kolk, "Trauma and Its Challenge to Society," in *Traumatic Stress: The Effects of Overwhelming Experience on Mind, Body and Society,* ed. Bessel A.van der Kolk, Alexander C, McFarlane, and Lars Weisaeth (New York, 1996), 426–8.

23. Ibid., 25.

24. Lifton, *The Life of the Self,* 32; Maurice Eisenbruch, "From Post-Traumatic Stress Disorder to Cultural Bereavement: Diagnosis of Southeast Asian Refugees," *Social Science and Medicine* 33.6 (1991): 673–80.

25. Kai Erikson, *A New Species of Trouble* (New York and London, 1994), 231; Aleida Assman, "Transformations between History and Memory," *Social Research,* 75.1 (2008): 50.

26. APA, *Diagnostic and Statistical Manual,* 467.

27. Marianne Hirsch, "The Generation of Post Memory," *Poetics Today* 29.1 (2008): 103–28.

28. Ahmad H. Sa'di, "Catastrophe, Memory and Identity: Al-Nakbah as a Component of Palestinian Identity," *Israel Studies* 7.2 (2002) 175–198.

war's events, and later on with the trauma itself, was the element of surprise. Palestinians had foreseen the violent confrontation, but had not imagined they would suffer a defeat on such a scale. While the Yishuv was preparing for the war that was expected to break out with the declaration of the state of Israel, the Palestinians suffered from profound weakness—social and political fragmentation, and lack of effective leadership and institutions—all of which underlined their reaction to the unfolding events as unhurried and complacent.[29] Rabinowitz and Abu-Baker ascribe the Palestinians' disregard for the surrounding geo-political struggle to their unrelenting belief in their natural rights to their homeland.[30] This complacence relied immensely on their faith in the Arab solidarity, a state Avraham Sela characterizes as psychological dependency. The Palestinians felt that they were an integral part of the Arab-Muslim peoples, and counted on their public and political support for their cause.[31]

This state of affairs manifested itself in the rapid disintegration of the Palestinian society following the eruption of the civil war in late 1947 and the gradual British withdrawal from the country. The combination of the early exodus of the social and political elite, low morale, a sense of abandonment and intense fear largely facilitated the Jewish offensive that began in April 1948. Palestinian and foreign volunteer forces were quickly defeated, morale broke down, and a panicked exodus from rural and urban areas commenced.[32]

By the end of the war, 650,000–700,000 Palestinians had fled or been driven out of the territory that came under Israeli sovereignty and more than 400 urban and rural communities had been destroyed. Only 156,000 remained in the State of Israel, less than one-fifth of the original population in that territory on the eve of the inter-communal war. The backbone of society, the middle urban class, had almost entirely disappeared while most of the remaining Palestinians were poorly educated villagers. About a fifth of these were internal refugees who found

29. Dani Rabinovitz and Khawla Abu-Baker, *The Stand Tall Generation: The Palestinian Citizens of Today* (Jerusalem, 2002), 27 [Hebrew]; Constantine Zureik, *The Meaning of the Nakba* (Beirut, 1948), 9 [Arabic]; Honaida Ghanim, "Poetics of Disaster: Nationalism, Gender, and Social Change Among Palestinian Poets in Israel After Nakba," *International Journal of Politics, Culture and Society* 22 (2009): 23–39.

30. Rabinowitz and Abu-Baker, ibid., 27. For a first-hand testimony as to this belief in historical justice and sense of security, see Hadara Lazar, *In and Out of Palestine, 1940–1948* (Jerusalem, 1990), 216 [Hebrew].

31. Avraham Sela, "Arab and Jewish Civilians in the 1948 Palestine War," in *Caught in Crossfire: Civilians in Conflicts in the Middle East*, ed. P. R. Kumaraswamy (London, 2008), 15; Zureik, *The Meaning of the Nakba*, 5–6.

32. Benny Morris, "The Origins of the Palestinian Refugee Problem," in *Perspectives of Israeli History*, ed. Laurence J Silberstein (New York and London, 1991), 43–4.

themselves impoverished visitors in neighboring communities after their own villages had been destroyed.[33]

In addition to surprise, two more salient reactions to the war were the widespread feelings of terror and helplessness. Many Palestinians fled due to rumors deliberately spread by Jewish agents, atrocities (real and inflated) committed by the Jewish forces, especially after the Deir Yassin massacre, and due to prefixed expectations regarding the treatment of a vanquished enemy.[34] Some of the Arab villagers also fled for fear of having their women's honor violated by the Israeli soldiers.[35] The experience of helplessness was manifested in the term adopted to describe the war's results—"*Nakba*," which connotes "Sudden disasters which befall man while he stands helpless against them."[36] The term thus well reflects the psychological shock that many Palestinians experienced during and after the war.

The *Nakba* constituted a founding event for the Palestinians. It shattered their long-lived societal and political structures, rendering more than half of them penniless and denied their sources of living, most significantly their land. It undermined individual and collective identities, and created new sub-identities. Many Palestinians experienced a profound sense of guilt and shame for failing to prevent the loss of their homes and land, and the concomitant sense of dignity, security, and belonging. Their sense of self-efficacy as Arabs and Palestinians was damaged,[37] and despite their bitter criticism of the Arab governments for their failure in the war, their psychological dependency on them only intensified.[38] Many refugees explained the defeat largely as a result of Israeli terrorist tactics.[39] However, Kanafani's writings reveal feelings of private guilt and shame among the refugees. For example, in his story *The Land of Sad Oranges* he writes about a refugee who lost faith in God and the world and whose father, not being able to stand the loss of hope and dignity, tries to kill his children because they reminded him of his helplessness.[40]

33. Rabinowitz and Abu-Baker, *The Stand Tall Generation*, 29; Hillel Cohen, *The Present Absentees: The Palestinian Refugees in Israel since 1948* (Jerusalem, 2000), 21 [Hebrew].

34. Morris, "The Origins of the Palestinian Refugee Problem," 46. On the Haganah psychological warfare, see Benny Morris, "The Causes and Character of the Arab Exodus from Palestine: The Israel Defense Forces Intelligence Branch Analysis of June 1948," *Middle Eastern Studies* 22.1 (1986): 10.

35. Ghanim, *Reinventing the Nation*, 85.

36. Ibid., 48.

37. Zureik, *The Meaning of the Nakba*, 7.

38. Yehoshafat Harkabi, "The Present Absentees: The Palestinian Refugees inside Israel Since 1948," in *The Palestinians From Slumber to Awakening*, ed. Moshe Maoz and Buzz Kedar (Tel-Aviv, 1996), 252–3 [Hebrew].

39. Ibid., 246.

40. Ghassan Kanafani, *The Land of Sad Oranges* (Beirut, 2006 [1962]), 73–81. See also *Returning to Haifa* (Beirut, 2006 [1963]). See "Emile Habibi's Complete Notes Regarding the Debate around Luka Bin Luka," *al-Katebe* 1.2 (1981): 11–16 [All in Arabic].

As the *Nakba* was incompatible with prior Palestinian expectations of history, time was frozen at the moment of the loss and suspended until the inevitable restoration of the normal as perceived by the Palestinians.[41] Hence, although the *Nakba* has since the 1960s been a foundational experience in the narrative of Palestinian national revival, the latter's overwhelming political objectives precluded coping with the painful aspects the *Nakba* exposed, such as the Palestinians' helplessness, which kept burying its traumatic core in the Palestinian collective memory.[42]

Emile Habibi and his Literary Legacy: Coping with a Collective Trauma

Emile Habibi was born in Haifa in 1921 to a Protestant family originating from Shafa 'Amr. At the age of 19 he began his lifelong ideological and practical commitment to communism. He became a fervent advocate of a joint Jewish-Arab struggle against British colonialism, and a democratic resolution of the conflict over Palestine. As a member of the communist party, in 1943 he was one of the founders of the National Liberation League in Palestine, which adhered to an independent democratic Palestinian state in which the rights of Arabs and Jews would be preserved.[43]

In the aftermath of the 1948 War, Habibi joined the Israeli Communist Party (Maki) and became one of its most prominent leaders. From 1952 to 1972 he was a Maki member of the Knesset (and, after its split in 1965, of its successor, Rakah) and later resigned his position in order to devote his time to his literary work and to edit the party's Arabic language paper *al-Ittihad*.[44] In 1991 he left the Communist Party due to deep ideological disagreements with his colleagues.[45]

Habibi's literary oeuvre is relatively modest. During the forties he published several short stories in different literary journals, but neglected writing for the sake of his political creeds. He recommenced writing only twenty years later, publishing various novels, plays, and essays in the remainder of his lifetime. His works

41. Ghanim, *Reinventing the Nation*, 48; Salim Tamari, "Bourgeois Nostalgia and the Abandoned City," *Comparative Studies of South Asia, Africa and the Middle East* 23.1–2 (2003): 173–80; Yehoshafat Harkabi, "The Palestinians in the Fifties and their Awakening as Reflected in their Literature," in *Palestinian Arab Politics*, ed. Moshe Maoz (Jerusalem, 1975), 64–6.

42. Sela, "Arab Historiography of the 1948 War," 140–3; Khalidi, "The Palestinians and 1948," 16; Jenny Edkins, *Trauma and the Memory of Politics* (Cambridge, 2003), xv.

43. Anton Shalhat and Majid 'Alayyan, "Emile Habibi: the Biography," *al-Sharq*, 26 (1996): 2, 4; Maher al-Sharif, "Emile Habibi and the Suffering of the Political Intellectual," *Majallat al-Dirasat al-Filastiniyya* 27 (1996): 135 [both in Arabic]; Yehoshua Porath, "The National Liberation League 1943–1948," *Asian and African Studies* 4 (1968).

44. Shalhat and 'Alayyan, "Emile Habibi: The Biography," 4.

45. Al-Sharif, "Emile Habibi and the Suffering," 144.

gained worldwide acclaim, particularly his novel *The Secret Life of Sa'id, the Ill-fated Pessoptimist* (henceforth, *The Pessoptimist*), which established his reputation as a pioneer of modern Arabic literature.[46] He received a number of literary awards from Arab institutions and in 1992 won the Israel Prize. Habibi died from cancer on 2 May 1996, and was buried in the Protestant cemetery in Haifa. In his will he requested that his tombstone be engraved with the words "Emile Habibi: Remained in Haifa."[47]

Like most Palestinian intellectuals of his time, Habibi maintained that his intellectual work was inseparable from his political work.[48] In his books he championed the causes of communism and Palestinian nationalism but Habibi was certainly not a politically committed writer in the narrow sense of the term. In an article from 1981, he stated his unrestricted commitment to the truthful depiction of a contradictory and changing reality, but he expressed remorse for subordinating his literary work to his political activity.[49] He believed that associative writing enables the writer to express his true self and personal experience that in turn tells the story of the collective experience and dominates his oeuvre.[50] For Habibi, the private was also political and the political shaped the private.

The Palestinians who became Israeli citizens evolved into a sub-group. Though they had much in common with the rest of their people, they were markedly different in several aspects.[51] In Arab publications they were distinguished from the rest of Palestinian society by name: they were varyingly referred to as "Arabs of Israel," "Arabs of the Occupied Lands," The Inside [Israel] Palestinians, and other designations.[52] However, the differences between the Palestinian citizens of Israel and the rest of the Palestinian people were not reducible to the territorial and political superficialities implied in those designations; they originated largely from unique traumatic experiences.

Habibi maintained that the Palestinian tragedy affected all of those who left the homeland as well as those who stayed, but he also acknowledged the variation of traumatic experiences within the Palestinian society. For instance, he distinguished between the experiences of rural and urban Palestinians: while many villagers managed to maintain their original communal framework even in the refugee camps, the state of urban society was very different. The urban society, which before the war was in the process of rapid transformation, was shattered

---

46. Shalhat and 'Alayyan, "Emile Habibi: the Biography," 4–5.

47. Ibid., 5.

48. Ghanim, *Reinventing the Nation*, 28.

49. Emile Habibi, *Saraya, the Ogre's Daughter* (Haifa, 2006 [1996]).

50. Habibi, "Emile Habibi's Complete Notes," 12.

51. Ghanim, *Reinventing the Nation*, 97.

52. Shilo, *Israeli Arabs in the Eyes of the Arab States*, 67.

and scattered all over. The few who remained in cities were isolated, deprived of much needed networks of social support.[53]

In his works Habibi focuses on the collective trauma of the Palestinian citizens of Israel with allusions to broader circles of Palestinian and Arab identity. By his writings he attempted to help the Palestinians in Israel to cope with a traumatic reality that had not stopped since the *Nakba*. The process he sought involved encouraging an acknowledgment of that reality and its consequences, and mending the rift within both individual and collective identities.

A salient example of Habibi's use of his private experience to deal with a traumatic issue that troubled the Palestinian society in Israel is his writing about the Arab accusation of Palestinians in Israel as traitors. As early as 1947, Habibi was persecuted for his political activities, apparently due to his support of the partition of Palestine into Jewish and Arab states.[54] That year he received several death threats from the Palestinian national leadership and an attempt was made on his life, which could explain his flight to Lebanon.[55] In November 1959, *al-Fajr* published a series of articles in which Habibi was accused of helping Israel to import weapons from Czechoslovakia during the 1948 War. It was also claimed that Habibi's return to Haifa (by August 1948, at the latest) must have been permitted in return for spying on the Arab forces.[56] These allegations were repeated in 1988 by the editor of the Israeli-Arab weekly *al-Sinnara*, Lutfi Mash'our. Habibi later successfully sued *Mash'our* for slander.[57] Given his experience it is not surprising that a central motif in Habibi's works is the defense of Israel's Palestinian citizens' patriotic reputation.[58]

In view of the difficulty of trauma victims to organize their experiences in narrative form, how was Habibi able to work through his personal experiences and turn them into collective knowledge that could help others? Behavior during a traumatic event and character traits are key variables that affect an individual's ability to cope with resulting trauma.[59] His political activity in the Communist Party and the National Liberation League clearly indicate that he was not a passive

---

53. Habibi, *Saraya, the Ogre's Daughter*, 36–7.

54. Habibi was among the members of the National Liberation League who supported the partition in accordance with the official Soviet policy on this matter, which was first stated in the UN General Assembly in May 1947.

55. Yaira Ginossar, "The Escape and Weapon of Emile Habibi," *Iton 77*, 237 (1999): 19.

56. It belonged to the Mapam Party, a political rival of the Communist Party.

57. Ginossar, "The Escape and Weapon of Emile Habibi," 20–2.

58. See the story of Sa'id in: Emile Habibi, *The Secret Life of Sa'id, the Ill-fated Pessoptimist* (Haifa, 2006 [1974]) [Arabic], whose adventures closely resemble those attributed to Habibi in *al-Fajr*.

59. Kleber and Brom, *Coping with Trauma: Theory, Prevention and Treatment*, 158–61, 170–1.

victim. According to Habibi, on one occasion he managed to remove a soldier who tried to force him out of his house in Haifa.[60]

It seems that Habibi had a developed mechanism of self-criticism. He believed that the *Nakba* was not some kind of natural disaster but an event shaped by human causes, and that the search for a remedy for the Palestinian plight necessitated a critical and unsparing analysis of past and present behavior.[61] His optimistic worldview was also significant. He always searched for the good in people and sought to instill in his readers the same optimistic belief in human nature.[62]

This is not to claim that Habibi was utterly free from the trauma's burden. Rather, he managed to gain a critical acclaim on it. In *Saraya, the Ogre's Daughter* he admits his inability to organize his memories into a linear narrative with a clear beginning and ending. Instead, he lets his thoughts and memories flow freely to coalesce into a past he has ownership of.[63] Habibi's writings lend support to the claim that despite the trauma's resistance to understanding, trauma victims might still eventually distill meaning from the sensations, images, and memory fragments that make up the experience, and even convey it to others.[64]

Just a Bad Dream?

For many Palestinians the *Nakba* was an occurrence too traumatic to absorb, and thus the new reality to which it gave rise remained on the divide between reality and fantasy. The pre-*Nakba* past invaded the present, confining reality to a mirror image of a nostalgic past—harmony and innocence as opposed to rift, humiliation, and confusion.[65] Habibi expresses this conception of the present in *Saraya, the Ogre's Daughter*. The story abounds with descriptions of the present as mirror images of the past, arousing emotions only in relation to that past. Its conception as desolateness is manifested in the words of a song the narrator recites to himself: "Where is the tumult of her people, the bustle of her markets?"[66]

60. Habibi, *The Ogre's Lamp*, 40–1.

61. Habibi, "Emile Habibi's Complete Notes," 13–14.

62. Emile Habibi, "The Self and Society," *al-Jadid* 11–12 (1996): 21–5 [Arabic].

63. Shimon Ballas, "Emile Habibi: Between Memory and Political Committedness," *Al-Karmil* 18–19 (1997–98): 71 [Arabic].

64. Jane Robinett, "The Narrative Shape of Traumatic Experience," *Literature and Medicine* 26.2 (2007): 290–2; Kaplan and Wang, "From Traumatic Paralysis to the Force Field of Modernity," 12.

65. Ghanim, *Reinventing the Nation*, 56.

66. Habibi, *Saraya, the Ogre's Daughter*, 76. Naomi Shemer, the acclaimed Israeli song writer, used similar descriptions in her "Jerusalem of Gold."

Habibi often ridicules the present and conveys a feeling of a world turned upside down.[67] This description expresses his refusal to accept this abnormal reality as a *fait accompli,* though he feared that such a method of resistance would contribute to the normalization of the abnormal post-*Nakba* reality and push people to seek metaphysical explanations for the incomprehensible.[68]

Bewilderment in the face of the post-*Nakba* reality is aptly described in *The Pessoptimist.* One night, Sa'id awakens to find himself sitting on a dull-edged khazooq,[69] his feet dangling over an abyss, unable to move for fear of falling. The puzzled Sa'id asks himself how he got to that situation. He tries to convince himself that it is against the laws of nature and reason that one minute he is in bed and the next he is on a khazooq, and that therefore it must be a dream, despite its duration. But what if it is not? He might fall to his death. Sa'id then weighs his options: he cannot descend, since the shaft is too slippery. He cannot climb up like a magician but can only stay put until the end of the dream, which could not be much longer. Eventually he concludes that the situation's incompatibility with the laws of nature is not a sufficient proof that he is dreaming. Thus he remains stranded on top of the khazooq.[70]

Habibi realized that for the Palestinians in Israel to work through their traumas, they must acknowledge the traumatic depth of past and present experiences and, no less important, receive outside recognition of it. Self-denial of trauma keeps it in the divide between reality and fantasy while external denial haunts the victim's inner world.[71] Habibi emphasized the cost of suppressing past traumas and sought to confront the Palestinians in particular, and the Arabs in general, with these realities.

Habibi drew a connection between the Palestinians' inability to extricate themselves from their present plight and their suppression of the trauma they suffered from the *Nakba.* Suppressed memories act as open wounds, unconsciously permeating the present. In *Ikhtayya,* Habibi tells the story of 'Abd al-Karim, who leaves his meaningless life in the US and returns to Haifa to seek Ikhtayya.[72] After arriving in Haifa he realizes that not only had Ikhtayya been haunting him from the inside (even though he tried to suppress her memory) but

---

67. Habibi, *Luka Son of Luka,* 61.

68. Habibi, *The Secret Life of Sa'id,* 10.

69. An Ottoman pike used for executions by impaling through the anus.

70. Habibi, *The Pessoptimist,* 163–6.

71. Antonius C. G. M. Robben, "How Traumatized Societies Remember: The Aftermath of Argentina's Dirty War," *Cultural Critique* 59 (2005): 138.

72. 'Ikhtayya' signifies the collective past, involving love and longing, but also shame and guilt.

that in reality he had unconsciously been chasing her. He fears accepting this realization, knowing that it will necessitate coping with unbearable memories.[73]

Habibi maintained that in order to change the present the Palestinians must accept their traumatic loss as a memory belonging to the past. Only from this new perspective could they learn from their experience and apply their lessons in the struggle for change. For instance Sa'id, the "pessoptimist," mentions that he became able to deal with the memory of his Tanturian wife, Baqiyya, after coming to terms with the fact that both she and (her original village) Tantura are gone.[74] In the story "al-Nuriyya," the magical figure Zanuba returns to an Arab neighborhood in Haifa. She refuses to cooperate with the elders' attempt to embellish the past and asks that her memory be passed on to the next generation.[75] She declares that only when the children will look to the future instead of dwelling on the past, she will return to what she truly is—a past that is a source of knowledge for building a better future.[76]

A major impediment to "working through" was Palestinians' persistent disregard for their brothers' realities of life inside Israel. Up until 1967 the Palestinian citizens of Israel were virtually absent from the Palestinian national discourse that was shaped by refugees in the Arab states. While some considered Israeli Arab citizens as collaborators with the state, others ignored their cultural or even social existence.[77] This perception changed drastically following bloody events in the Galilee on 30 March 1976, "Day of the Land," after which Israel's Arab citizens were increasingly brought into the national liberation discourse. However, even though awareness of the realities of those who remained in Israel grew deeper after the 1967 war, unwillingness to acknowledge the changes that had occurred in the homeland and with its Arab dwellers persisted until after the Oslo agreements. The Palestinian vision of a victorious return to an unchanged homeland necessitated retaining an image of an uncontaminated homeland, excluding from it the Palestinians who remained in Israel. A modified image of the homeland germinated following Oslo, when it became apparent that a collective return is impossible in the foreseeable future.[78]

By sticking to a static image of the homeland, foreign Arabs and displaced Palestinians alike negated the post-traumatic reality of the Palestinian citizens of Israel. Habibi therefore worked to convey the unpleasant reality of Palestinian-Israeli life and the pain of being ignored. In the play *The Pedlar Woman*, Hind, a resident of Haifa's Arab neighborhood of Wadi Nisnass, laments that the refugees

73. Emile Habibi, *Ikhtayya* (Haifa, 2006 [1985], 108–11 [Arabic].

74. Habibi, *The Secret Life of Sa'id*, 117.

75. "Zanuba" symbolizes the collective memory.

76. Emile Habibi, *The Hexad of the Six Days* (Haifa, 2006 [1968]), 119 [Arabic].

77. Ghanim, *Reinventing the Nation*, 61; Shilo, *Israeli Arabs in the Eyes of the Arab States*, 38.

78. Tamari, "Bourgeois Nostalgia and the Abandoned City," 174–6.

who returned to visit their houses after 1967 saw only the houses and failed to see or even listen to the Palestinians who stayed behind.[79] In another scene, one of the visitors is surprised to hear about the harsh realities of Palestinian life in Haifa. When a girl tells him that her father is a drug addict who only comes home to beat his wife and steal her gold, he coldly suggests that she find a husband and leave the house.[80]

In *The Pessoptimist*, Habibi presents another major impediment to "working through": the Palestinians' tendency to seek refuge from reality in the transcendent, which is manifested in the relationship between Sa'id and his extraterrestrial friends. The night after his return from Lebanon, Sa'id encounters a majestic man from outer space whom he expects to be his savior. Sa'id beseeches the man to deliver him from this harsh life, but the latter refuses and criticizes the Palestinians' unwillingness to truly take their destiny into their own hands.[81] Sa'id explains the encounter with the man (who eventually acquiesces to Sa'id's appeal) as inevitable since he had sought and awaited it all his life to be delivered from his worldly troubles.[82]

Sa'id proclaims that he had been chosen by the alien for his extraordinariness—his life was saved thanks to a donkey—a beast symbolizes imbecility—when he was fired at on his journey back from Lebanon, but no less because he represents all the Palestinians in Israel.[83] Throughout the story donkeys continue to serve Habibi to demythologize the persistence of Palestinian existence in Israel. For instance, Sa'id arrives from Lebanon and enters the military commander's office riding a donkey, eager to fulfill his father's last request that his son serve the Jewish state.[84] Despite what he believed, Sa'id remained in Israel not by a miracle but due to his willingness to collaborate with authorities and later endure punishment after leaving their service.[85] Indeed, contrary to the heroic Palestinian presented in Palestinian poems from the '50s and '60s,[86] Habibi's protagonists are ordinary people with obvious weaknesses and faults. Hence for him remaining in the homeland was neither a conscious decision nor a miracle but a natural act of resistance.[87]

---

79. Emile Habibi, *The Pedlar Woman* (2006 [1992]), 12–14, 26 [Arabic].

80. Ibid., 29–30. On the social atmosphere after the war and the deteriorating state of the city, see Habibi, *The Pessoptimist*, 26, 67.

81. Ibid., 57.

82. Ibid., 10–12.

83. Ibid., 13–14.

84. Ibid., 16–18.

85. Ibid., 170.

86. Ghanim, *Reinventing the Nation*, 80–2.

87. Habibi, *Luka Son of Luka*, 100. According to Ghanim, *Reinventing the Nation*, 167, Habibi sought to engender an alternative to the collective Arab memory, according to which the

Habibi's call to face reality and strive for change was not detached from sensibility to the difficulties involved. The necessity of constantly struggling to remain in their homeland and change their harsh realities compelled the Arabs in Israel to remain in an arduous state of constant arousal. In *Luka Son of Luka* the clown expresses this sentiment with bitterness, not on account of the efforts required but toward a situation forced upon them, and the lack of recognition for the difficulties involved in it—a recognition of human weaknesses.[88] Habibi shows understanding toward his protagonists, who suppressed their painful memories and ran away from the past. He does not rebuke them but tries to understand the reasons for their behavior and shows their process of dealing with the past.[89]

Reconceptualizing the Self and its Relation to the World

Another central issue in Habibi's works was the impact of the *Nakba* and of remaining in Israel on the individual and collective identity of Palestinian-Israeli citizens. The recovery process, which Habib sought to instigate, was based on the assertion that the *Nakba* had changed the collective identity of Palestinians, contrary to the prevalent assumption throughout the '50s and the '60s among poets of his generation. The latter depicted the Palestinian identity as essentialist and a-historical in order to secure national unity and defy Israel's dismissal of such identity.[90] Only in the aftermath of the 1967 war did Palestinian intellectuals start asking questions about the specific making of the identity of the Palestinian citizens of Israel. This change did not lead to definite answers but only to a more ambivalent stand about this group identity: Palestinian, Arab, and Israeli, who remained disintegrated.[91] Against this backdrop, Habibi stands out among Palestinian writers as one who acknowledged the complex realities created by the *Nakba* for the Palestinians in Israel and sought to enable them to understand and deal with the roots of their ambivalence. The recovery process he sought to instigate involved reaffirming the convergence of individual and collective identity, dealing with emotions emanating from the traumatic experiences, and rebuilding schemas that are not based on them.

The reaffirmation of consistent identity was crucial in light of the violent jolt the Palestinians suffered in the *Nakba*, and what they perceived as a continuous

---

Palestinians who remained in Israel were traitors. He argued that the Palestinians struggled to maintain their existence, just like the refugees were struggling to return.

88. *Habibi, Luka Son of Luka,* 29, 31.

89. Habibi, *Ikhtayya,* 109; *The Hexad of the Six Days,* 26–35.

90. Ghanim, *Reinventing the Nation,* 75.

91. Ibid., 104.

Israeli policy of detaching Palestinians from their collective past.[92] Habibi illustrates the impact of the *Nakba* on identity through stories of people who believed that in order to survive they must dissociate themselves from their past. For instance, in *At Last the Almond Blossoms* Habibi tells the story of a teacher who, after the *Nakba*, lost touch with his friends from the West Bank, believing they had forgotten him. He also severed his relations with his childhood friend, a political dissident, so that he might keep his job under the Israeli military administration. Dissociation from the collective past led not only to seclusion and low self-esteem but also to dissociation from his individual past. During a trip to the West Bank (after the 1967 war), the scents and sights along the road between Ramallah and Nablus conjured up a childhood memory, evoking powerful emotions inside of the teacher. However, he experienced it as if it had happened to someone else: he recalls a beautiful love story that had occurred to a friend of his at a spot on that road. He sets out to shed light on the story through his old friends and the reader eventually discovers that it was actually the teacher, the boy from the love story, but he had completely dissociated himself from it.[93]

According to Habibi, the rift between the memory of the past and identity persists primarily due to feelings of guilt that weigh on traumatic memories and drive people to suppress them, a mechanism he calls "merciful forgetting."[94] Habibi thus sought to promote awareness of feelings that inhibit memory in order to address them. As the reader encounters public displays of such feelings, he realizes that they are not uncommon and that he ought not to be ashamed of them and conceal them from himself and his surroundings. Coping with these feelings turns them into something that connects him to others who share similar traumatic experiences. In "Ikhtayya" Habibi expresses the guilt and shame Palestinians felt for failing to prevent traumatic events of the *Nakba*.[95] In other works, he expresses the guilt that Palestinian-Israelis felt for remaining in the homeland under Israeli rule instead of accepting exile or death in the battlefield.[96] Instead of these feelings he sought to engender ones of pride for remaining in the homeland as an act of resistance. The ambivalence toward the Palestinians outside of Israel is expressed in a somewhat less explicit manner. In "'Um al-Rubabikiyya" Hind voices her pain and anger at the visiting refugees who ignored her presence

92. Ibid., 60–1; Sa'di, "Catastrophe, Memory and Identity," 184; Habibi, *Luka Son of Luka*, 61–4.

93. Habibi, *The Hexad of the Six Days*, 25–39. For a similar theme, see his *The Pessoptimist* and *Ikhtayya*.

94. Habibi, *Ikhtayya*, 14, 126; Habibi, *The Hexad of the Six Days*, 31.

95. Habibi, *Ikhtayya*, 123, 126, 133, 148.

96. Habibi, *Luka Son of Luka*, 178; Habibi, *The Hexad of the Six Days*, 25.

and the sacrifices she had made to stay in the homeland.[97] Nevertheless, she remains loving and loyal to them.[98]

The story "The Crab's Elegy" well illustrates the use of projection: it tells of a man who lost faith in the world, became secluded, and developed an addiction to alcohol, following the *Nakba*. This loss of faith meant he saw only vague threatening shadows around him with no possible change in reality, pushing him to seek recourse in alcohol.[99] The story of Sa'id's disappearance is a good example of dissociation: unable to deal with reality, Sa'id imagines joining his extraterrestrial friends to watch the earth from above, thus dissociating himself from his "experiencing self."[100]

For many years after 1948 Israeli Arab citizens were broadly accused by other Arabs of collaboration with Israel, selling their land to the Jews, failing to fight for their own homeland, and betraying the Arab armies. This perception derived from three main logics:

A. Given that so many Palestinians fled the country in panic over Jewish atrocities, those that stayed were suspect. In *The Pedlar Woman* Hind was said to have abandoned her family in favor of staying, or been left behind by them, due to her questionable character, or because of certain immoral acts.[101]

B. While many villages were destroyed others managed to remain intact, suggesting they had connections with Jews. In *The Pessoptimist*, Habibi exempts the village Furaidis of such blame ascribing its escape from the fate of other villages to the intervention of its Jewish patrons of neighboring Zikhron Yaakov to ensure a continued supply of Arab labor force in their vineyards.[102]

C. The return of over 20,000 Arab refugees to Israel's territory in the first few years after 1948, clandestinely or through legal procedures of family unification, was often brokered by Arab figures collaborating with the Israeli administration and seeking to widen their influence by helping members of their community.[103]

97. Habibi, *The Pedlar Woman*, 53.

98. Ibid., 31–2. See also Habibi, *The Hexad of the Six Days*, 134–50; Habibi, *Luka Son of Luka*, 29.

99. Habibi, *The Hexad of the Six Days*, 153–62.

100. Habibi, *The Secret Life of Sa'id*, 10.

101. Habibi, *The Pedlar Woman*, 15–16.

102. Habibi, *The Secret Life of Sa'id*, 110–12.

103. According to official data, 20,500 refugees clandestinely returned up until October 1953 and received citizenship, on top of 3,000 refugees who were allowed to return on humanitarian grounds. Hillel Cohen, *Army of Shadows, Palestinian Collaboration with Zionism, 1917–1948* (Jerusalem, 2006), 42, 70, 119–20 [Hebrew]. Habibi raises this issue in his short play "The Way of the World" in Habibi, *The Hexad of the Six Days*, 142–3.

Habibi daringly tackled this issue of accusation in his first novel, *The Pessoptimist*. Sa'id, Habibi's anti-hero, works for the security services for twenty years, yet Habibi does not condemn him or present him as a one-dimensional character. Instead, he chooses to examine the human weaknesses at the root of Sa'id's actions. Sa'id determinedly worked against the communists, believing he might thus get back his first wife, Yu'ad, and prevent the deportation of his second, Baqiyya.[104] On various occasions Sa'id challenged the totality of the military administration and disobeyed his supervisors.[105] Following the disappearance of his wife Baqiya and his son, Wala', Habibi shifts Sa'id's image: was he, like Jaroslav Hašek's Brave Soldier Svejk, only pretending to be naive? Was this Sa'id's way of resisting oppression without arousing suspicion?[106] Later on Sa'id decides to leave the service of the state and rejects the pressures exerted on him to stay.[107] Sa'id thus seems to be mainly a victim of himself and of the circumstances and, as Habibi repeatedly stated, "The victim is not to blame!."[108]

Typical of trauma survivors, many Palestinians carried a sense of guilt for remaining in the homeland. Accusations from other Palestinians thus fueled these feelings. In *Luka Son of Luka* Budur expresses this feeling with harsh words: "They cheapened their lives to such a degree, that to continue living started to feel as a betrayal."[109] Habibi challenged the concept that the only legitimate options Palestinians had were death in the battlefield or exile, regarding it as a romantic way of thinking, inconsistent with the complicated reality.[110] He seemed to believe that to stay behind was in many ways the tougher of options: They remained, isolated and deprived of social support networks, alienated from their surroundings, under military administration, and forced to face the harsh unromantic reality.[111]

On the one hand, Habibi maintained that Palestinian-Israelis do not have to justify staying in their homeland, and on the other hand he defended their decision, employing the same discourse of national duty upheld by the Palestinian national movement outside of Israel. He qualified it as a social responsibility that was bequeathed to them,[112] that is, to act as guardians of what was left of the

104. Habibi, *The Secret Life of Sa'id*, 91–2.

105. Ibid., 76–7, 89.

106. Ibid., 170.

107. Ibid., 188.

108. For example, Habibi, *Luka Son of Luka*, 20.

109. Ibid., 178.

110. Habibi, *The Hexad of the Six Days*, 25–8.

111. For a similar view see Nabih Qasim, *Palestinian Short Stories Dealing with the June War* (Shafa 'Amr, 1989), 10 [Arabic].

112. Habibi, *Luka Son of Luka*, 178.

homeland.[113] Hind, in *The Pedlar Woman,* did not simply wait passively for the return of the refugees but directed her entire existence after the *Nakba* to the moment of return.[114] She dedicated her life for the absentees by preserving the memory of the pre-*Nakba* Palestinian existence, collecting personal belongings, such as love letters and songs, and keeping the memory of the past alive in her everyday thoughts. Hind persisted even though her selfhood was ignored: representing those who remained in the homeland, she was regarded by other Arabs only as a place—a mosque, a church, or a cemetery.[115]

Habibi's apologetic portrayal of the Palestinians who remained in Israel is somewhat contradictory, though entirely reasonable. These Palestinians were human beings caught in terrible conditions and thus forced to make individual compromises to survive and stay put. At the same time they constituted "a barrier" against Israel's efforts to erase the Arab character of the land—an objectification that defined them as guardians of the land and doing a great service to the Palestinian cause. Habibi seemed to comply with this contradiction for the purpose of highlighting the suffering of the Arab citizens of Israel as meaningful and as one that should be considered within the context of the historical Palestinian national struggle. The urge to emphasize the role of the Palestinians in Israel in this national struggle was necessary in view of their perception among the other Palestinians and Arabs alike as bystanders in the conflict.[116]

In *Ikhtayya* we realize the deeper meaning of the duty to remain in the homeland. This work maintains that the essence of the homeland is not the land and the houses that remained or were destroyed but its people, without whom it would perish. Hence we cannot truly know the homeland without acknowledging the human weaknesses of its people.[117] Especially after traumatic events it is very important to prevent the sense of helplessness from being fixated in self-perceptions, because unless the victim regains confidence in his agency he might become trapped in perpetual victimhood.[118] To this purpose Habibi called on Palestinians not to accept the role of victims as a given destiny and provided examples of possible avenues of resistance and change. The change he wished to effect was first and

113. Ibid., 18–19.

114. Habibi, *The Pedlar Woman,* 10.

115. Ibid., 53. For another reference to self-sacrifice see: Habibi, *Saraya, the Ogre's Daughter,* 189.

116. On the efforts to change this perception see Shilo, *Israeli Arabs in the Eyes of the Arab States,* 60, 76–8; Kanafani, *The Palestinian Resistance Literature,* 13.

117. Habibi, *Ikhtayya,* 161.

118. On collective victimhood see Daniel Bar-Tal, Lily Chernyak-Hai, Noa Schori, and Ayelet Gundar, "A Sense of Self-Perceived Collective Victimhood in Intractable Conflicts," *International Review of the Red Cross* 91(2009): 229–58.

foremost internal: rejecting the sense of victim, leaving outer change vaguely aspired as a possible result of the inner change. On top of the helplessness they experienced during the *Nakba*, Israel's Palestinian citizens lived for almost twenty years under a military administration, whose suffocating totality greatly contributed to the fixation of that sense.[119]

In *The Pessoptimist* Sa'id recounts the sense of helplessness during those twenty years in which he felt he was drowning, unable to breathe or to communicate with others. He tried to cry out to them but all he could produce was the meow of a cat. At first he felt very frustrated about that but after two decades he started to believe in reincarnation and accepted his situation. Later on he sought relief through his extraterrestrial friend,[120] illustrating the sense of a silent victim who loses faith in his ability to communicate his distress and change his situation.

Habibi saw the 1967 war, which reconnected Palestinians from Israel with those of the newly occupied West Bank and Gaza Strip as a relief of the former's isolation imposed by Israel, although it further aggravated their sense of helplessness due to the Arabs' military defeat.[121] Habibi likened them to imprisoned people who one day woke to find that the rest of their family, from whom they were separated for twenty years, were thrown into the same prison.[122] What was particularly hard to grasp was the swiftness of the change that further diminished their sense of security.[123] In *The Pessoptimist* Habibi notes that following the war the number of fishermen increased, as if "they hoped to find in the sea something stronger than our state."[124]

Habibi considered determinism to be one of the greatest impediments to overcoming victimhood, since it frustrates the possibility of envisioning an alternative situation in which the Palestinians are no longer compelled or willing to be victims. In *The Pessoptimist,* Sa'id compares the Palestinians to Voltaire's naive hero, Candide. Like Candide, they believed that all is for the better and accepted all that befell them as predestined.[125] For years Sa'id held these beliefs, but during his stay in prison he discovered a different side of himself—a higher and nobler one, truer to his self. Suddenly his horizons expanded and he started to realize that his life could be different.[126] He came to forgive himself for his past mistakes, and

119. Rabinowitz and Abu Baker, *The Stand Tall Generation*, 31–6; Ghanim, *Reinventing the Nation*, 35–6, 68.

120. Habibi, *The Secret Life of Sa'id*, 107–8.

121. Habibi, *The Hexad of the Six Days*.

122. Ibid., 9.

123. Ibid., 187.

124. Habibi, *The Secret Life of Sa'id*, 98.

125. Ibid., 105.

126. Ibid., 185–7.

stopped working as a collaborator though he was still lacking the will to strive for a deeper change, seeking redemption through his extraterrestrial friends.[127]

Facing this hopeless situation, Habibi reminds his readers of an Arab cultural asset—"the vivid oriental imagination." Like *Scheherazade,* who managed to save her life by inventing stories, the Palestinians employed their vivid imagination to survive in Israel: since they could not be themselves in public, imagination was crucial to save their sense of selfhood.[128] Habibi, who lets his own imagination run wild in his works, draws a link between a vivid imagination and mastery over one's surroundings: "The land was our land, and the imagination was our imagination, to run wild with it however we pleased. . . . This was before the advent of the white man, and the extraction of the black gold."[129] Hence his generous use of imagination is not only a literary tool, but also a subversive act: by mixing reality and fantasy Habibi challenges the repressive reality.

In addition to his effort to ensure the role of the Arabs in Israel in the Palestinian collective memory, Habibi also made efforts to help his fellow Palestinians regain confidence in their agency as a significant element in the struggle over the memory of the *Nakba* and other traumas.[130] In his writing, he sought to stop the victimization of Palestinians in attempts to silence them and deny their traumas: "The dead shall not be killed a second time."[131] Essential to the *Nakba* was the continued Israeli attempts to erase the land's Arab history, through effacing remnants of Palestinian villages and the renaming of places.[132] Habibi thus set out to preserve through his works the memory of the places that were lost in the *Nakba.* Although Palestinians could not prevent those acts, Habibi was able to use words to create an alternative consciousness that rejected the one the victors tried to shape. He mocked the Israeli policy of arbitrary use of power to change reality that further highlighted the Israelis' foreignness to the land. Habibi references examples of Israelis changing the original Arab name of streets, such as Salah al-Din, in the Arab neighborhood Khalisa in Haifa to ha-Gibborim (the heroes), commemorating "those who drove the Arab residents of

127. Ibid., 187–8, 222.

128. Ibid., 138–40.

129. Habibi, *Luka Son of Luka,* 62.

130. On the intra-societal conflict over collective memory, see Robben, "How Traumatized Societies Remember."

131. Habibi, *Luka Son of Luka,* 74. See also his efforts to shape the memory of the Kfar Qassim massacre in 1956, *Kfar Qassim: The Massacre and the Politics* (Beirut, 1977) [Arabic]; *Luka Son of Luka,* 37–48. On mourning as a form of resistance, see Rebecca Saunders and Aghaie, Karman, "Introduction: Mourning and Memory," *Comparative Studies of South Asia, Africa and the Middle East* 25.1 (2005): 23.

132. Sa'di, "Catastrophe, Memory and Identity," 184.

Wadi Rushmiyya out of their houses and shacks."[133] In *The Pessoptimist,* Habibi takes much care to remind us of the names of many of the destroyed or erased Galilee villages. Whereas Sa'id was passive during the war,[134] and did not even realize the magnitude of the disaster that befell his people, he was still able to play an active role as an agent of memory: He registered what was lost and what remained after the *Nakba*.[135]

A complementary part of Habibi's efforts to help the Palestinians regain confidence in their agency, was the representation of reality as generally positive and open to change. He created this image by underlining the humanity of his characters, Israelis as well as the Palestinians, thus giving hope for cooperation and coexistence. The Israeli characters in his works are usually positive ones: simple people who show human empathy with the plight of the Palestinian characters. In *Saraya, the Ogre's Daughter* Habibi mentions two Jewish families who help hide refugees that clandestinely returned to Haifa.[136] His book on the Kfar Qasim massacre notes in several places Israeli anger toward the perpetrators of the massacre.[137] Even the representatives of state oppression are capable of acts of empathy. For instance, in *The Way of the World,* the policeman, who was thought to have come to the family to arrest the returning brother Hassan, actually comes to inform them of his arrest so they might go and bail him out.[138] Even though Habibi ridicules those state agents who play negative roles, he still portrays them as human and not omnipotent. Sa'id refuses to be impressed by his security service operator,[139] whom he describes as "the big man of the small stature."[140]

Habibi, however, does not clearly define the change he seeks to achieve. He believes it shall become possible only after individuals, as well as society, undergo an inner change.[141] Habibi's optimistic character shows not in promises of a complete shift from the traumatic present, but in his belief that the Palestinians can go through a process of inner change.

133. Habibi, *Ikhtayya*, 33–7.

134. See the chapter "How Sa'id participated in the war for the first time," in *The Pessoptimist*, 22–5.

135. For example ibid., 31–3.

136. Habibi, *Saraya, the Ogre's Daughter*, 211–12.

137. Habibi, *Luka Son of Luka*, 50–1, 66.

138. *Habibi, The Hexad of the Six Days*, 145–6. See also ibid., 103–5.

139. Habibi, *The Pessoptimist*, 72–5.

140. Ibid., 169.

141. Ibid., 220; Habibi, *Ikhtayya*, 159–60.

Conclusion

Massive traumatic events often call for social and psychological reconstruction or at least leaving the painful past behind for the sake of returning to normalcy, and the 1948 disaster of the Palestinians is no exception. La Capra points to the example of the Israeli society which sought to execute a "great leap": from the Holocaust victim to the new Israeli, without stopping to really deal with the traumatic past. But the attempt to simply transcend victimhood is not only impossible, but also harmful to individual survivors and to society as a whole.[142] Criticizing de Gaulle's calls to return to normal after the Nazi occupation, Marguerite Duras contends that people's hope for a better future can rise only from dealing with its grief over what was lost.[143] Otherwise, what basis is there for change?

Following the *Nakba*, Palestinian writers sought to utilize their skills to promote social and political change, but by making their oeuvre subservient to political goals they substantially limited the literature's potential role in dealing with the trauma. In the discourse of national liberation there is usually little place for human weakness that is the core of trauma and for the multitude of experiences and points of view that characterize collective trauma.

In contrast, Habibi maintained that the Palestinians will not be able to extricate themselves from their plight without working through their traumas. Having experienced the collective trauma and worked through it himself, Habibi was able to turn his personal experience into collective knowledge, so as to help others extricate themselves from the haunting past while acknowledging the unique circumstances of Palestinian Israelis.

This chapter has addressed three components of the process Habibi tried to instigate. The first was encouraging acknowledgment of the trauma and its aftermath. He showed that avoiding that prevents the trauma from becoming part of the past, thus rendering it a resource with which to change the present. The second component was demythologizing the allegations about the Palestinians remaining in Israel. He confronted the Palestinians and the Arabs with the harsh realities of those who stayed in the homeland, and with the pain they felt for being ignored and demeaned by their fellow countrymen. The third element was addressing the identity crisis of Palestinian Israeli citizens following the *Nakba* by explaining the root causes of that crisis, thus providing a basis for a reconstructed collective identity.

Habibi skillfully employed literature to deal with the individual and collective facets of trauma. His protagonists are individuals in crisis situations, representing

142. La Capra, *Writing History, Writing Trauma*, 157.

143. Marguerite Duras, *Wartime Diaries and Other Texts*, ed. Sophie Bogaert and Oliver Corpet (Paris, 2006), 223–4 [French].

human experiences of loss and vulnerability, which he placed in the social, political, and cultural historical context in an attempt to stimulate empathy and even appreciation toward the Palestinian Israelis.

Habibi's efforts, however, are not without weaknesses. Foremost of which, he does not attempt to explain the *Nakba*, only the difficulties in dealing with its consequences. By explaining the trauma, he might have been able to point out avenues for change but, like many other Palestinian intellectuals, Habibi describes the event in terms of overwhelming natural forces beyond man's capability to resist, implying no responsibility whatsoever for the disastrous event that befell the Arabs of Palestine in 1948. Another shortcoming is that in his search for meaning of their suffering, Habibi objectifies Palestinian Israelis as "Sites of Memory," serving a greater national cause of defying the Israeli policy of effacing the Palestinian presence in the land and efforts of silencing and forgetting the Palestinian past. One might argue that it is a reasonable price to pay for a much-needed sense of meaning, but the answer would probably vary between individuals and cultures.

ASSAF PELED holds a graduate degree in international relations from the Hebrew University of Jerusalem.

7 Wa-Ma Nasayna (We Have Not Forgotten)

Palestinian Collective Memory and the Print Work of Abed Abdi

Tal Ben-Zvi

Introduction

Palestinian art created within Israel's 1948 borders possesses unique characteristics deriving from its being part of the visual culture of the Palestinian minority in Israel. In this artistic-national construct, artist, graphic designer, and printmaker Abed Abdi played a leading role as a consequence of his work over the decade between 1972 and 1982 as graphics editor of the publications of the Communist Party and its successor, the Democratic Front for Peace and Equality, the Arabic language journal *Al-Ittihad,* and the *Al-Jadid* literary journal. Additionally, many of his works were also published in the Communist Party's Hebrew language paper, *Zo Haderekh* (*This Is the Way*), and in a variety of election and other posters for the Communist Party and the Democratic Front. The fact that Abdi often reused images he created in various contexts also reinforced the iconic status of many of his works.

The chapter focuses on the significant role in shaping the visual culture and collective memory of the Palestinian minority in Israel. "The art of print" is a term I employ to define the presentational space and practice of works of art printed in relatively large editions in the press, books, booklets, posters, and postcards. Although these works are often accompanied by political, journalistic, literary, and poetic texts, they are not illustrations *per se* but rather visual texts that are often of equal status to verbal ones. By means of this space and practice, the reproduced works gradually establish the visual culture of their target audience. Hence, they are an autonomous alternative presentational space and practice of works of art that played a most important role in shaping the national culture of all sections of the Palestinian people.

The War of 1948 (2016): 171–193, DOI: 10.2979/warof1948.0.0.09

The Trailblazer: Abed Abdi

Biographical Milestones

Abed Abdi was born in 1942 in the church quarter of downtown Haifa. In April 1948, he, his mother, his brothers and sisters were uprooted from their home, while his father remained in Haifa. From Haifa the mother and her children traveled to Acre from where, two weeks later, they sailed on a decrepit boat to Lebanon. In Lebanon they were first housed in the "quarantine" transit camp in Beirut port, and later moved to the Miya Miya refugee camp near Sidon, from where they continued to Damascus. After three years of wandering between refugee camps, the mother and her children were allowed back into Israel as part of the family reunification program.

In his youth Abdi joined the Communist Youth Alliance in Haifa, where he also began his artistic journey. In this environment he was first exposed to Social Realism and Israeli artists who adopted this style and who, at the time, were close to the Israeli socialist-communist Left. In 1962 Abdi was accepted for membership in the Haifa Association of Painters and Sculptors, becoming its first Arab member, and also held his first exhibition in Tel-Aviv. In 1964 he was sent by the Haifa branch of the Israel Communist Party to study graphic design, mural art, environmental sculpture and art in Dresden in the German Democratic Republic (GDR). Abdi lived in Germany between 1964 and 1971 where he completed a master's degree in arts. At the Dresden Academy of Fine Arts graphics and printing department he met the woman who was to become his teacher and most important source of inspiration, the Jewish artist Lea Grundig, who had gained a reputation for her protest works against fascism and Nazism. During those years Abdi was also influenced by German artists such as Gerhard Kattner and Gerhard Holbeck.

He returned to Haifa in 1971, and in November 1972 the city awarded Abdi the Herman Struck Prize;[1] to mark the occasion he held an exhibition of his works at the city's Beit Hagefen Gallery. In 1973 the works shown in this exhibition were printed and published in a portfolio, and in the following years some of them were also published on occasion in *Al-Ittihad*, *Al-Jadid*, and in poster form. In the 1970s and '80s he also made illustrations for the texts of Palestinian and Israeli writers and poets. In 1978, two years after the bloody events of Land Day (30 March 1976) in Sakhnin, together with Gershon Knispel he created and erected the monument commemorating those who were killed on Land Day. Later, Abdi also created monuments in Shfaram, Kafr Kana, and Kafr Manda.

---

1. A. Niv (the pseudonym of poet Moshe Barzilai), *Zo Haderekh*, 11 July 1973, 7, noted that the Hebrew dailies ignored Abdi's being awarded the prize: "The first Arab artist to win the prize in his homeland, the Herman Struck Prize," 7.

Over the years Abdi worked as an art teacher in Kfar Yasif, and since 1985 has served as an art lecturer at the Arab College of Education in Haifa. He served as the graphic editor of *Al-Ittihad* and *Al-Jadid* (1972–82); many of his illustrations appeared in those papers, in journals and books, and also in numerous political posters including those marking Land Day, posters marking the Kfar Kassem massacre of 1956, and Israel Communist Party election posters.

Dresden, the Formative Period: Artistic-Ideological Influences

Clearly identifiable in Abdi's works from his Dresden years are traces of a consistent artistic and subject matter trend that focused on figures of refugees and were done in a Social Realism style using artistic graphic means such as drawings, stone prints, and etchings accompanied by political and literary texts dealing with justice and morality. To a great extent this trend was influenced by the sociopolitical worldview adopted by Abdi in his youth when he joined the Communist Party, but it was also mediated by the artists of the Social Realism school in Israeli art. These trends, however, matured in Dresden, inspired by the works of two women artists: the printmaker, painter, and sculptress Käthe Kollwitz and painter and print artist Lea Grundig.

Käthe Kollwitz (1867–1945) devoted her work to creating empathic descriptions of universal suffering resulting from a life experience of distress, exploitation, and discrimination, and from revolutionary or traumatic historical events; she had firsthand knowledge of a life of suffering, poverty, and hunger: after her marriage to Dr. Karl Kollwitz (1891) the couple moved to a poor neighborhood in Berlin and it was this environment that provided her with the materials that fortified her political consciousness and nourished her work until her death.[2] Her most famous works include the "Weavers' Revolt" cycle (1893–97), which is based on a play by Gerhardt Hauptmann that describes the Silesian weavers' revolt in 1844; the "Peasant War" cycle (1901–08) that is dedicated to the peasants' revolt in southern Germany in the second half of the sixteenth century; the "Grieving Parents" memorial (1914–32); and the numerous leaflets she designed for *Internationale Arbeitshilfe* (IAH) from 1920 onward. In the Weimar Republic Kollwitz enjoyed canonical status and her works were studied and disseminated throughout Germany. Following the Nazis' rise to power, Kollwitz was forced to resign from the Academy of Fine Arts, her works were declared "decadent art" and were removed from public exhibitions. She spent most of the war years in Berlin but in 1943 was evacuated to Dresden where she died on April 22, 1945, two weeks before Nazi Germany's surrender.

2. See Martha Kearns, *Käthe Kollwitz: Woman and Artist* (New York, 1976), 69.

Abed Abdi was well acquainted with Kollwitz's work before he left for Germany. In the 1950s they had been printed in Israel in art journals such as *Mifgash*, and communist newspapers like *Kol Ha'am*, *Zo Haderekh*, and *Al-Ittihad*. Abdi's friends and colleagues, such as Ruth Schloss, Yohanan Simon, Moshe Gat, and Gershon Knispel, all diligently studied Kollwitz's work.[3] Her drawings, prints, and etchings influenced generations of socio-politically conscious artists sensitive to human suffering both inside and outside Germany.

Whereas Abdi became acquainted with Kollwitz's work mainly through reproductions, the influence of Lea Grundig on his work was more direct. Grundig had known Käthe Kollwitz, and in many respects continued her tradition into the 1960s. But in addition to underscoring the suffering of the working class, Grundig's work was marked by the horrors of WWII, and the iconography she created focuses on issues such as refugeeism, expulsion, survivors, and so forth, issues that in the twentieth century had become identified with that war. The profound influence of Grundig's works is clearly evident in Abdi's development as an artist during his studies and in the iconographic shaping of refugeeism in general, and the *Nakba* iconography in particular, in his work.

Lea Grundig (née Langer) was born in Dresden in 1906 and died during a trip to the Mediterranean countries in 1977. She studied with Otto Dix at the Dresden Academy of Fine Arts, married the painter Hans Grundig, and the two became active members of the German Communist Party (KPD) in Dresden. Following the Nazis' rise to power, Lea and Hans Grundig were persecuted, detained for questioning, and were even arrested on several occasions. In 1939, a short time before her husband was sent to a concentration camp, Lea finally left Germany and reached Palestine in 1940. In 1944 she exhibited her "Valley of the Dead" cycle (1943) that directly addressed the events of the Holocaust: refugeeism, expulsion, freight wagons, executions, concentration camps, and so forth. The Israeli artistic establishment was unsympathetic toward "Valley of the Dead" and Lea, who was in Palestine during WWII, had difficulty in understanding how the country's Jewish artists could ignore the Holocaust.[4]

Following her husband's liberation from the camps, in 1947 Lea joined him in Soviet-occupied Dresden, which in 1949 became part of GDR, where she became an important and respected artist and lecturer at the Dresden Academy of Fine Arts, whereas in Israel she was almost completely forgotten.

The encounter between Abed Abdi, a 22-year-old Palestinian recently arrived from Israel, and Lea Grundig, his teacher at the print and etching department at

3. Gila Balas, "The Artists and Their Works," in *Social Realism in the 1950s* (Haifa Museum of Art, 1998), 15–32.

4. Ziva Amishai-Maisels, *Depiction and Interpretation: The Influence of the Holocaust on the Visual Arts* (Oxford, 1993), 382.

the Dresden Academy, was of great significance for him.[5] Their relationship went far beyond the usual student-teacher format; Grundig opened her home to him and was his social and cultural mentor for most of the time he spent in the GDR.

It is important to emphasize that this somewhat surprising encounter between a young Arab victim of the *Nakba* and the Jewish Holocaust survivor Lea Grundig was marked by their political and experiential common denominator, their commitment to social and political justice, their protest against war and the heavy toll it exacts from humankind. It was not therefore, influence derived from a Jewish cultural or historical context, but rather one of a communist cultural and philosophical context. It was actually their communist, cosmopolitical, and a-national identity that enabled their encounter and friendship, and their great mutual admiration.

Palestinian Art in the Diaspora, the West Bank and Gaza Strip

One of the most prominent characteristics seen in a perfunctory review of the various branches of Palestinian art is the important role played by printing as a vehicle for disseminating the messages that this art seeks to advance. In the context of the art of print, clearly evident is the influence of Ismail Shammout (1930–2006), one of the first Palestinian artists. After his expulsion from Lod in 1948, Shammout reached a Gaza refugee camp after a long and arduous journey through Jordan, and in 1956 moved on to Beirut. He left Beirut for Kuwait after the 1982 Israeli invasion of Lebanon, spent several years in Germany, and died in Amman in 2006. Shammout's life embodies the ordeal of the Palestinian odyssey since he defined himself first as a Palestinian and a political man, and only second as an artist.[6]

Shammout took upon himself the mission of a witness whose role it was to tell the world and its future generations the story of his people through art. He served as the first head of the PLO's Art Education Department immediately after the organization was founded in 1964, and his book *Art in Palestine* (1989) was the first publication on Palestinian art and its history. For these and other reasons the role he played was of particular importance for both the establishment of the field of Palestinian art and the formulation of modes of representation of the *Nakba*, which were also disseminated in the works of other artists in the Palestinian diaspora, the West Bank, and the Gaza Strip from the 1950s to Shammout's death

5. The relationship with Lea Grundig was founded on the sensitivity she displayed toward war and injustice, and inter alia due to her belonging to the Jewish minority that had suffered so greatly during the Nazi era. Interview with Abed Abdi, 19 March 2007.

6. Paula Stern, "Portrait of the Artist (Palestinian) as a Political Man," http://www.aliciapatterson.org/APF0001970/Stern/Stern11/Stern11.html.

in 2006. Furthermore, many of his works were reproduced and widely disseminated in posters, postcards, and calendars. Shammout's influence on Abdi's work is of particular importance in all matters regarding the image of Palestinian refugees.

Abdi attests to the mutual influence and reciprocal artistic relations in the 1970s and '80s with Palestinian artists of his own generation from the West Bank and the Gaza Strip who acquired their education at art schools in the Arab world (mainly in Cairo, Alexandria, and Baghdad), among whom are Nabil Anani (b. 1943, Latroun), Taysir Barakat (b. 1959, in a Gaza refugee camp), Ibrahim Saba (b. 1941, Ramla), Issam Bader (b. 1948, Hebron), Vera Tamari (b. 1945, Jerusalem), Tahani Skeik (b. 1955, Gaza), Taleb Dweik (b. 1952, Jerusalem), Kamal Moghanni (b. 1944, Gaza), and Fathi Ghanem (b. 1947, Gaza). The most notable is Suleiman Mansour (b. 1947, Bir Zeit) who, in contrast with the abovementioned group, studied at the Bezalel Academy of Art and Design in Jerusalem for one year (1969–70).

Abdi also became very familiar with the work of artists active in the Palestinian diaspora who engaged in the pure symbolism of "Palestinian suffering." Among the notable refugee camp artists are Naji al-Ali (b. 1936 in the Galilee and grew up in a Lebanese refugee camp) who worked in Lebanon, Kuwait, and London;[7] Ibrahim Hazima (b. 1933 in Acre and grew up in Ladhiqiya, Syria) who won an art scholarship in East Germany and later continued to work in Europe; Tamam al-Akhal (b. 1935, Jaffa) who studied art in Alexandria and Cairo, married Ismail Shammout and worked in Beirut from where she moved to Jordan; and Kamal Boullata (b. 1942, Jerusalem) who studied art in Rome and Washington and on completing his studies in 1968 remained in the US, where he wrote the history of Palestinian art in a large number of books, catalogues, and articles.[8]

In the context of Palestinian art in Israel it is notable that as a result of the *Nakba* and life under military government, Palestinian artists became active within Israel's borders only at a relatively late stage, some 25 years after Israel's establishment. The military government period (1948–66) on the majority of Arab residential areas by virtue of British Mandate emergency laws restricted the freedom of expression, movement, and organization of the Arab citizens.

7. Naji al-Ali worked as an illustrator for newspapers in Lebanon and the Gulf States (1963–87). In 1987, when walking to his newspaper's London office, he was wounded in a drive-by shooting and died a month later. The Intifada in the West Bank broke out that same month.

8. See Kamal Boullata, *Palestinian Art, 1850–2005* (London, 2009); Kamal Boullata, "Palestinian Expression Inside a Cultural Ghetto," *Middle East Report* 159 (1989): 24–8; and Kamal Boullata, "Art," in *Encyclopedia of the Palestinians,* ed. Philip Mattar (New York, 2000), 81–90.

It also caused harsh isolation of artists who remained within Israel's borders. It was therefore only after the ending of the military government in 1966 that young Palestinians began to study art in Israel and abroad. After Abdi's return to Israel, in the 1970s and '80s, the artists Asad Azi (b. 1955, Shafa 'Amr), Ibrahim Nubani (b. 1961, Acre), Asim Abu-Shakra (b. 1961, Umm al-Fahm), and Osama Said (b. 1957, Nahaf) went to study art, and their work reflects the unique culture of the Palestinian minority in Israel.[9]

Social Realism in Israel

Before his departure for Germany and on his return Abdi worked together with others identified as "Social Realism" artists in Israel who in the 1950s and 1960s came together in "Red" Haifa, the ethnically mixed city with its large workers population.[10] They engaged in every facet of Israeli reality out of a profound identification with its deprived and discriminated against sections. They sought to create art with social messages that would be understood by and be accessible to "the masses," and thus they created artistic prints that were both affordable and which conveyed their message. Gershon Knispel was the driving force behind the Haifa Social Realism artists' circle, whose ranks included Alex Levi and Shmuel Hilsberg, and maintained contact with artists who created in this style and resided in other locations in Israel, such as Avraham Ofek, Ruth Schluss, Shimon Zabar, and Naftali Bezem.

Commitment to this global idea and worldview is also clearly evident in Abdi's words at a panel discussion[11] held in 1973 by the Haifa Association of Painters and Sculptors at Chagall House, under the title "Artists in the Wake of Events":

> In the same way that an artist lives the events of the past, present and future, he also lives the conflict between Man and the forces of evil and destruction. And when society and humankind are in crisis, the artist is required to express himself harmoniously by means of the artistic vehicle at his disposal . . . and so . . . the role of the artist in his work, thoughts and worldview is to reinforce the perpetual connection between himself and the society in which he lives. I was brought up according to this approach and thus I understand the connection between my artistic work and the role defined by Kokoschka, who sought to remove the mask for all those who want to see reality as it is. The role of fine art is to show them the truth.[12]

9. Tal Ben-Zvi, Hanna Farah, eds. *Men in the Sun* (Herzliya Museum of Contemporary Art, 2008).

10. Balas, "The Artists and Their Works," 8.

11. In addition to Abdi, also participating in this panel were the artists Avshalom Okashi and Gershon Knispel, art critic Zvi Raphael, and architect Haim Tibon.

12. A. Niv, *Zo Haderekh*, 13 February 1974.

Speaking about his art and the 1973 War, Abdi said:

> Out of my worldview and my loathing of war, and also out of my profound
> concern for the future of relations between the two peoples, Arab and Jewish, I have
> shown my two works here in the exhibition [entitled "Echoes of the Times" in which
> artists from Haifa and the north of Israel participated]. When the cannons
> thundered on the Golan [Heights] and the banks of the [Suez] Canal, and when
> the future of the region was at risk, I recalled the words of Pablo Picasso and in my
> work I said "no to war" in accordance with my artistic beliefs; art must be com-
> mitted and play a role.[13]

In this way, as an artist he expressed his commitment to Palestinian society in
Israel, and the unique role played by art in raising the social and political consciousness.

The Refugee Print Portfolio

In the GDR Abdi created a most impressive corpus of illustrations, lithographs,
and etchings mainly dedicated to either the *Nakba* or the Palestinian refugees. A
group of his refugee paintings created in Germany (1968–71), published in 1973 as
a set of 12 black and white prints entitled "Abed Abdi—Paintings," offers a glimpse
of central motifs that would later recur in many of his works. In these and other
works, clearly evident is the mark left by his childhood experiences when he
moved between refugee camps, and from the period following his family's reunification in Haifa. To depict the refugees Abdi adopted a Social Realism approach
of the kind to which he was exposed prior to his departure for Germany, and
which he refined while he was there.

All the figures in the print portfolio are of refugees. In the pen and ink
drawing, "The Messiah Rises" (no. 1), no. 10 in the portfolio, the figure of a
barefooted, elderly, tall, bearded man is seen walking alone, behind him tumble-
down huts or houses with sloping roofs, and around his head are allusive rays. Not
included in the portfolio, "Refugee in a Tent" (no. 2) again emphasizes the loneliness of the refugee. The etching presents a close-up of a bearded, wrinkled face, a
sad mouth and eyes, and a kind of headdress that seems like a tent. In contrast
with the loneliness of the elderly refugee in the two previous works, Abdi places
him in a social context in print no. 4 of the portfolio, the lithograph "Revelation of
the New Messiah" (no. 3). Here he depicts a human wave on whose crest is a man
borne on the shoulders of the people. The figures of the anonymous refugees are
drawn in filament-like lines that create a single body-mass-wave. United in one
fate, barefoot, they are shrouded in long robes. The man borne on their shoulders
seems to emerge from within them and his long arms are spread wide in either a

---

13. Ibid.

blessing or an attempt to maintain his balance. The entire mass of figures is surrounded by a void, similar to the figures in other works in the portfolio (and similar to many of Kollwitz's works). The religious context of a redeeming messiah is somewhat surprising in the work of a communist, Social Realism artist. This messiah is a man of the people, a man who has nothing, the chosen one who comes from the people, spreads his arms/protection over them, the man who is to lead them to a better future. Compared with Ismail Shammout's famous 1953 painting "Where To?," in which the frightened refugee looks forward along the road he treads in a barren geographical expanse, the refugee messiah in Abdi's work is looking with pride at the observer from the height of his elevated position. Compared with another of Shammout's works, the 1954 "We Shall Return," Abdi's proud refugee figure, drawn in bold black lines, conveys resolve, not helplessness or fear.

However, Abdi too addressed the helplessness of the Palestinians and emphasizes it in print no. 8, the charcoal drawing "Refugees in the Desert" (no. 4). In this drawing the refugees are seen from afar as a human swarm, similar to the way in which Grundig presented her refugees, but with Abdi they do not fill the entire "frame" and it is impossible to discern their expressions. In his expressive drawing the hundreds of unidentifiable refugees create a meandering road that vanishes into the hills close to the horizon. High above the refugees stands the burning sun that is drawn in several bold lines in a completely cloudless sky.

In the context of landlessness and loss of familial identity, the feminine presence is particularly emphasized. In print no. 2, a pen and ink drawing of dense lines, "Women" (no. 5), two women are seen, their heads covered, curled up in their long dresses/cloaks, as they sit withdrawn into themselves facing one another. The face of the woman sitting on the right of the drawing looks directly at the observer with a sad and worried expression. Except for a low horizon and the same burning sun, here too the background is devoid of character and the women appear to be floating in the space of the paper. Another picture of a woman refugee appears in print no. 1 of the portfolio, the pen and ink drawing "Weeping Woman" (no. 6), in which a close-up of her tears can be seen in her eyes in a composition reminiscent of Käthe Kollwitz's "The Widow" (1922–23).

The sense of tragedy and loneliness is expressed differently in print no. 8, the pen and ink drawing "Sleeping in the Desert" (no. 7), in which two figures, a child and his mother, are seen sleeping alone on the ground under the sky. The figures are covered with a sheet whose folds resemble a sharp and desolate landscape reminiscent of the landscapes in the portfolio. The real landscape in the drawing is summarized in a few broken lines marking the horizon, and several electric poles and wires. Mother and child are extremely and dramatically foreshortened. Despite the change of orientation from the heads downward and not from the legs, this foreshortening calls to mind the work of one of the first artists to employ this technique, the Italian Renaissance artist Andrea Mantegna, "The Lamentation over the Dead Christ" (circa 1480). To intensify the dramatic effect Abdi exposed one of the mother's feet, which peeps from under the sheet, and this touching exposure of part of her body underscores the harsh conditions of sleeping on the ground.

The last two Abdi prints in the portfolio are landscapes painted in Germany that are characterized by a return to lengthened black lines and an atmosphere of expressive tempest. In print no. 11 (no. 8), the pen and ink drawing "The Dam," waves are seen breaking against a high rampart with towering turrets, the silhouettes of minuscule figures on a high dam, and a black sun drawn in dark circular lines like a coil of wire. In print no. 12 (no. 9), the pen and ink drawing "Wild Landscape," what appear to be rocks or tree stumps are seen, a kind of path wending its way through a black and depressing landscape, clouds drawn in expressive black lines, and a black sun. It is a landscape of consciousness, a black landscape of scorched earth. In the absence of people and signs of life, it seems that this earth represents a post-traumatic experience or a landscape in the aftermath of a terrible catastrophe, after the *Nakba*. It is another means of concretizing the atmosphere of the tragedy, the storm, and the struggle that imbues all the works in the portfolio.

In a critique of the print portfolio in *Zo Haderekh*, A. Niv (poet Moshe Barzilai's pseudonym) noted the connection between Abdi's works and those of Käthe Kollwitz, and that the works in the album speak in "a clear language of non-acceptance of Palestinian fate. . . . The album is a single totality despite the differences between its subjects. For the subject is but one: identification with the fate of the refugees, non-acceptance of this fate, and an expression of hope and emotional turmoil."[14]

The prints in the portfolio were also reproduced in the *Mifgash* journal and *Zo Haderekh*, together with cultural articles and Hebrew poetry and literary texts ("Sleeping in the Desert," for example, was reproduced in *Zo Haderekh* on 15 November 1972, and print no. 1 of the portfolio, the pen and ink drawing "Weeping Woman," was reproduced in the same paper on 11 July 1973). The presence of these drawings and prints in the bi-national cultural system of the Israel Communist Party was of great significance, and thanks to it they were preserved in the memory of the readers of these journals as the ultimate representation of the *Nakba*.

"Mandelbaum Gate" and "The Pessoptimist" by Emile Habibi

From time to time during his years in Germany, Abdi visited his hometown, Haifa. It was on these visits that he became acquainted with several notable

---

14. A. Niv, *Zo Haderekh*.

Palestinian writers and poets. During these years and later, many of his drawings illustrated the publications of writers such as Emile Habibi, Anton Shammas, Taha Muhammad Ali, Salman Natour, and Samih al-Qasim. In this context Abdi's figures on white paper draw their local, concrete force from the textual literary space. From this standpoint his work is marked by the tremendous textual influence of Arabic literature, poetry, and spoken language on Palestinian art in general, by means of what Kamal Boullata terms "the hidden connotations of words."[15]

In his relationships with writers and poets, of particular note is the relationship Abdi formed with Emile Habibi,[16] who like him was a native of Haifa. The fruitful collaboration between them was given expression, inter alia, in a 1968 illustration by Abdi for Habibi's story "Mandelbaum Gate"[17] (no. 10) prior to his return to Israel. The Mandelbaum Gate—the only crossing point between the two parts of pre-1967 Jerusalem, was opened for diplomats and UN personnel and, once a year, at Christmas, for Christian pilgrims. The gate symbolized both the division of Jerusalem and that of the Palestinian people following the *Nakba*.[18]

In his illustration "Mandelbaum Gate" Abdi depicts the parting of a wrinkled woman leaning on a cane, and a girl-child with unkempt hair standing behind her with head bowed by the barbwire fence. The girl's heavy shadow follows the woman, takes her right hand, and returns like an echo on the shape of the cane she is leaning on, held in her left hand. The figures are standing in a setting in which only the vital details are drawn in an empty space—barbwire fences and two tall posts with an allusive barrier between them. Abdi turns our gaze toward the no-man's-land at Mandelbaum Gate. Balas describes Habibi's writing as "consciousness of the torn homeland" and the no-man's-land as symbolizing a dual schism of "those forced to live outside their land hoping to return to it, and those living detached from the majority of their people and hoping to be reunified with them."[19]

Following Abdi's return to Israel, he created illustrations for the original Arabic edition of Emile Habibi's *The Pessoptimist: The Secret Life of Saeed Abu el-Nahs al-Motashel* published in 1977.[20] The one that opens the book (no. 11) is a

15. Kamal Boullata, "Israeli and Palestinian Artists: Facing the Forest," *Kav* 10 (1990):171 [Hebrew].

16. Emile Habibi (1921–1996), author, publicist, and one of the founders of the Israeli Communist Party, which he represented in several Knessets. He was also editor of *Al-Ittihad* for 45 years.

17. Abdi's illustration appears in Emile Habibi, *The Six-Day Sextet* (Haifa, 1970) [Arabic].

18. Shimon Balas, *Arabic Literature in the Shadow of War* (Tel-Aviv, 1978), 33–5 [Hebrew].

19. Ibid.

20. Abdi's drawings appear in Emile Habibi, *The Secret Life of Sa'id, the Ill-fated Pessoptimist* (Jerusalem, 1974) [Arabic] but not in the Hebrew translation.

close-up of a man's face partly concealed by his hand that is seemingly signaling the observer-reader to halt—"No further." The hand does not enable identification of the face, but seemingly invites the observer to read the man's future in its lines. In this way Abdi depicts Habibi, a product of Israeli reality and the complex identity of the Palestinian minority living in it, which conducts a complex dialogue with its environment as it holds its cards close to its chest.

In illustration (no. 12) on the book's frontispiece, a gaunt, bearded old man is seen whose face is furrowed and whose eyes are sunken. He is wearing a jalabiya whose stripes/folds are heavily marked. His big left hand rests on his chest and his right hand hangs at his side. Within the background scribbles that partly appear to be an abstract representation of Arabic script, planted beside his head is a barred aperture alluding to a prison or solitary confinement cell. The story describes, inter alia, the imprisonment of Saeed Abu el-Nahs al-Motashel in an Israeli jail and his ironic/cynical responses to the Israeli interrogator's questions, whereas Abdi's illustration conveys sorrow and exhaustion and is devoid of any form of irony.

An oppressive and melancholy atmosphere also pervades the drawing (no. 13) that appears in the chapter entitled "More than Death Is Hard on Life, this Story Is Hard to Believe." The partly covered lower torso of a corpse is seen lying on a wooden surface with its feet visible. Behind the improvised stretcher stand grieving women dressed in the hijab, and in front of it stands a man with his back to the observer, and who is turning his face away from the body at his feet.[21] A tear can be seen in the corner of the man's eye.

In a scene from Habibi's book, Walaa's parents, Saeed (the narrator) and Baqiyya, are making their way to Tantura to save their son, and their story is related in the following chapters until the son and mother mysteriously vanish into the sea. Habibi's ironic and allegorical text ridicules the efforts of the Israeli security forces as they chase shadows. However, this gloomy drawing of Abdi's chooses to ignore the text's irony and instead depicts the parents' terrible grief for their dead son.

The tension between the text's ironic tone and the dark, expressive drawings is present in each collaboration between Abdi and Habibi. Abdi translates Habibi's multifaceted irony into simple and accessible language, and focuses on the tragedy of the Palestinian people. The "consciousness of the torn homeland" described by Habibi ably qualifies the entire gamut of Abdi's work, which is populated by Palestinian villagers and city dwellers together with refugees and displaced

---

21. A similar image of a corpse recurs in Abdi's work and Käthe Kollwitz's influence in it can be seen as attested by her last print in the "Weavers Revolt" cycle (1897) (no. 26), depicting two men bearing a corpse into a room of a hut in which the bodies of two workers are already laid out.

persons. Yet this "consciousness" also aspires to universal justice and equality, and is expressed in a universal artistic language that crosses national borders and identities.

Stories of the *Nakba*: "Wa-Ma Nasayna"[22]

The epitome of explicit reference to the *Nakba* in Abed Abdi's work is a series of his illustrations for the collection of short stories by Salman Natour, *We Have Not Forgotten*. The stories were first published in 1980–82 in *Al-Jadid*, and later as part of a trilogy by the author.[23] In the magazine, the title of each story appears within or next to an illustration by Abdi. The names of the stories are: *So We Don't Forget, So We Shall Struggle, Introduction by Dr. Emil Tuma; A Beating Town in the Heart; "Discothèque" in the Mosque of Ein Hod; Om Al-Zinat is Looking for the Shoshari; "Hadatha" Who Listens, Who Knows?; Hosha and Al-Kasayer; Standing at the Hawthorn in Jalama; A Night at Illut; "Like this Cactus" in Eilabun; Death Road from al-Birwa to Majd al-Kurum; Trap in Khobbeizeh; The Swamp . . . in Marj Ibn Amer; What is Left of Haifa; The Notebook; Being Small at Al-Ain . . . Growing Up in Lod; From the Well to the Mosque of Ramla; Three Faces of a City Called Jaffa.* These names reflect a remapping of Mandatory Palestine, the lost Palestine, resembling that which was carried out by Palestinian historians.[24]

Unlike the format of the short stories published in *Al-Jadid*, in which a different illustration by Abdi accompanied each story, only two were chosen for Salman Natour's book, which reflects the space of Palestinian memory, comprising a combination of abstract and concrete elements. The cover of the book features detail from an illustration originally made for the story "Being Small at Al-Ain . . . Growing Up in Lod (no. 14)."[25] The original illustration depicts three refugee women—one of whom is sitting and tenderly embracing or protecting a baby, and behind her two monumental figures completely covered in their heavy robes, against a backdrop of a round sun and a strip of obscure buildings. In the detail featured on the cover of the book the image has been cut and all that remains are a section of the seated figure and a section of the figure standing to the left, her head bowed toward the figure sitting at her feet. *We Have Not Forgotten*, states the title, and the original version of the illustration, and especially

22. A previous version of the following appeared in the exhibition catalogue, "Abed Abdi: 'Wa Ma Nasina,'" of which I was curator in 2008 at Abed Abdi's studio in Haifa; see http://wa-ma-nasina.com/index.html.

23. Salman Natour, *Memory* (Bethlehem, 2007) [Hebrew].

24. Mustafa Murad al-Dabbagh, *Our Country, Palestine* (Beirut, 1965) [Arabic]; Walid Khalidi, *All That Remains: The Palestinian Villages Occupied and Depopulated by Israel in 1948* (Washington, 1992).

25. Salman Natour, "Being Small at Al-Ain . . . Growing Up in Lod," *Al-Jadid*, October 1981 [Arabic].

the detail, indicates an abstract consciousness of memory that is not located in a concrete geographic space.

The second illustration was originally published as part of the story *What Is Left of Haifa*" (no. 15),[26] and it is a detailed illustration of the city of Haifa. This story relates to a specific place and time, Haifa and 22 April 1948, the date of the Jewish conquest of the city followed by mass Arab exodus, and thus both the story and the illustration are anchored in time and place as a biographical, personal, and collective milestone in the history of the Palestinian residents of Haifa.

This illustration is reproduced and recurs beside the title of every short story in this book and thus becomes a kind of "logo," linking Abdi's personal biography as a native of Haifa with a symbolic sequence of wandering: from Haifa to Lod, from Haifa to Ramla, from Haifa to Jaffa, etc. A space of geographic memory, place names, details of streets, businesses, and the names of people along the continuum of the *Nakba*.

This illustration is "The Father Illustration," one that largely contains the essence of the *Nakba* iconography developed by Abdi over the years. It is designed as a triptych: in the left-hand section a large number of figures are sketched as black patches, becoming a human swarm that seeks to leave from the Haifa Port in haste and congestion; in the central part there is the figure of the father, Qassem Abdi, with a simple worker's hat on his head, and behind him the churches' neighborhood, with its churches, mosque, and clock tower, as well as the family home. In the right-hand section there is a graphic sketch of the ruins of the Old City of Haifa.

Natour relates in his story:

> The wrinkled sheikh walks hand in hand with the years of this century . . . When the *Nakba* is mentioned he says: "I was 48" and adds, "I witnessed it on the day their cannons were on the tower, and they dropped a yellow sulfur bomb on the Jarini mosque clock, and the clock fell, and I said: the clock has fallen and the homeland will follow." Haifa was not erased from the face of the homeland . . . but all its characteristics have changed. . . . The people of the Old City of Haifa were mostly stonecutters and fishermen. . . . They quarried the stones in Wadi Rushmia and sold them, and later, when the British came and extended the harbor, people started to work there as well. . . . Rifa't was a skilled fisherman like no other, he had a black donkey which he used to ride and look out to sea, and see where the fish gather, then he would cast his net, and not miss even a single fish. Time passed, and the sea began to bring people and take people away. And Abu Zeid's boats took the Arabs away . . . Where to? To Acre Port . . . Where to? To Beirut Port . . . Where To? To hell . . ." (Natour, 1982)[27]

26. Salman Natour, *What Is Left of Haifa*, *Al-Jadid* October 1980.

27. *What Is Left of Haifa* was published in Hebrew and English in *Remembering Haifa* (Zochrot, 2004).

To a certain extent Salman Natour's story about Haifa is based on the stories of Abdi's family. Thus, for instance, Rif'at the fisherman is Abdi's great-uncle. The detailed story of the family appears in the book written by Deeb Abdi (Abed Abdi's brother), *Thoughts of Time*, which was published posthumously in 1993. In the book, short stories he had written and which had been published over the years in *Al-Ittihad* were collected, including the story of the family's grandfather and his departure from Haifa in April 1948. The cover illustration (no. 16) is also related to the departure from Haifa.[28] The images in this illustration are arranged in a composition of a cross, so that the horizontal line is formed from the houses of Haifa, sketched in black and outlined by the waterline of Haifa Port, while the vertical line is formed of a fishing boat, with heavily outlined figures on it in black lines. The three figures in the foreground are in detail: the figure of a woman holding a kind of package close to her body, the figure of an older man, and beside him, the figure of a young child holding on to him. Deeb Abdi relates:

> This is what our leaving Haifa for Acre on board British boats was like. . . . In April, the sea was stormy, which is unusual at that time of the year, and the high tide almost took us to the deep waters, deeper and deeper to the bottom of the sea. My grandfather Abed el-Rahim was standing upright as if he were challenging the waves and other things; he was looking back at Haifa, as if they were saying goodbye to each other. For the first time he was leaving Haifa, and she was leaving him, and she faded away bit by bit, and my grandfather Abed el-Rahim watched the length of the shore from Haifa to Acre, the wheels of a horse-drawn wagon bogging down in the moist sand. A short journey, then we go back. That is what my grandfather Abed el-Rahim said when I was still a little boy, hardly eight, and I was afraid of the dark, of the sea. For the first time in my life I was sailing to an unknown world—unknown. From the big mill they were shooting bullets like heavy rain, and my grandmother Fatma el-Qala'awi hid us in her lap, continuously reciting the Throne Verse from the Qur'an and we did not dare raise our heads. So we remained where we were until we were far from the shore and reached the deep sea, and approached Acre. We stayed in Acre for a couple of weeks, its walls were suffocated by refugees, and the refugees were suffocated by crowds of immigrants who had escaped by land and sea to its walls. A short time afterwards, Acre fell, and people left it by land and sea. We went on board at night and sailed deep into a world foreign to Haifa and Acre. It was the beginning of a journey . . . and another journey . . . and another.[29]

The narrator, a child who is afraid of the dark and the sea, is waiting for a savior to save him from his misery. The expectation of a savior to rescue him from drowning is familiar to Abdi from his mother's stories about El-Khader. This character appears in Salman Natour's story *What Is Left of Haifa* in which a group of people

---

28. In 1996 Abdi returned to this illustration and created "Leaving Haifa" in which he used his father as an updated model. His father passed away a year later.

29. Deeb Abdi, *Thoughts of Time* (Haifa, 1991). First published in *Al-Ittihad*, 27 April.

is visiting Elijah's (El-Khader's) cave. They drink and eat, and when they go into the sea somewhat tipsy they begin to drown. "The old people began to pray: Please, Khader, save us, Khader," writes Natour, and suddenly they saw a man in a boat in the sea, but he disappeared like a grain of salt. And of course nobody drowned.

This savior-messiah figure of El-Khader, as the Prophet Elijah, as Mar Giryis, recurs in many of Abdi's illustrations, two of which appear in the 1973 print portfolio. Six years later, in an illustration from 1979 (no. 17) the savior reappears as a manneristic figure, the folds of whose garment is reminiscent of those of the saints in Byzantine icons. It flies with arms outstretched over a village, but all it can offer the refugees is consolation, not real protection and rescue; it is a mythological, religious, and community figure detached from its land and the source of its power.

In contrast, the old and wrinkled sheikh, the narrator of all Natour's *We Have Not Forgotten* stories, who also appears in the majority of the illustrations that accompanied these stories in *Al-Jadid*, represents a man of flesh and blood. However, there is a tension between the text, in which the sheikh is the narrator who remembers in detail all the events of the *Nakba* (names of people, dates, and places), and the universality of the illustration, as it is manifested in the archetypical face of the old man and the faces of the other figures in the illustration series.

Thus, for example, the illustration that accompanies the story *From the Well to the Mosque of Ramla*[30] (no. 18) incorporates heavy religious allusions with real suffering. The old man with his deeply furrowed face appears here as if crucified in sacrifice or as protecting the figures of the wailing women standing behind him with a dead, shrouded body lying beside them on wooden boards. Here, Natour's narrator relates the story of the bomb that exploded in the middle of Ramla's Wednesday market in March 1948, killing many. He describes the ensuing chaos and the numerous bodies lying among the market stalls and crates of fruit and vegetables. The incorporation of the religious image into the scene of mourning against the background of a few buildings and the schematic depiction of a mosque's minaret charges the event with timeless and placeless symbolism. Despite the highlighted word "Ramla" in stylistic script that appears within the background architecture, the body lying with its face hidden is simultaneously a specific and universal victim.

In other illustrations, the dialectical tension between detailed text and symbolic illustration recurs. An example of this is the illustration that accompanies the story *Like this Cactus in Eilabun*[31] (no. 19). It depicts a corpse lying on the ground at the foot of a bare tree, and the figure of a woman who is touching the body's face

---

30. Salman Natour, "From the Well to the Mosque of Ramla," *Al-Jadid* November 1981.

31. Salman Natour, "Like this Cactus in Eilabun," *Al-Jadid* March 1981.

with a hesitant hand. Behind them, several women are sitting covering their faces in shock. The figures are situated in a desolate space, far from the village that is seen on the horizon, and far from any source of help. The story opens with a long scene in which Natour describes the dirt road leading to Eilabun, the surrounding fields and mountains, and the tension between a young Palestinian woman and her children and an Israeli soldier who is with them on a truck traveling from Eilabun to Tiberias. Later, the narrator relates the story of the massacre in Eilabun, the death of Azar, a poor man, the children's favorite, who was killed while leaning against the church door, and the death of Sam'an al-Shufani, the janitor of the Maronite church, whose body lay on the ground for three days.

In *Trap in Khobbeizeh*[32] the wrinkled old sheikh tells the story of a shepherd trapped in a minefield near Khobbeizeh in Wadi 'Ara, the total destruction of the village, its inhabitants' struggle to return to their lands after they were declared a closed military zone, and the trial of one of the villagers for trespassing. He goes on to describe the massacre in Khobbeizeh in which 25 men were taken from the village, forced to kneel beside a cactus hedge, and were shot to death in full view of the women and children. The narrator dwells on the story of one of the victims, the only son of Abu Daoud Abu Siakh, who begged the soldiers to let him take his son's place. The soldiers denied his request and shot his son. The father loses his mind, and for years afterward sees his dead son's face among the village children.

The three figures accompanying the story do not describe the killing and horror, but the stunned expression of the villagers watching the atrocity. On the story's frontispiece (no. 20) a group of grieving women with their heads covered is seen, one of whom is bending her head to a small child clinging to her waist. In this work Abdi returns to the circle motif, which here is seen as if through a magnifying glass or as a close-up of the faces of the weeping, wailing women. Seen in the narrow and elongated illustration that appears with the story, are upright, grave-faced men with big, wide eyes and big, emphasized hands (no. 21). The third illustration (no. 22), a lateral woodcut printed on the lower part of the two columns of p. 25, presents grief-stricken figures standing behind barbwire and wooden fence posts.

Conclusion

In 2008 Abed Abdi became the first Arab artist living in Israel to win the Minister of Science, Culture and Sport Award, together with six other artists, all of whom were Jews and younger than him. In other words, he was the first Arab artist to gain recognition by mainstream Israeli culture. Replying to a question from an interviewer regarding the excitement generated by the event in the Israeli media,

---

32. Salman Natour, "Trap in Khobbeizeh," *Al-Jadid* June 1981.

Abdi said, "If I really am the first Arab artist, it is neither a compliment to me nor to 60 years of the State of Israel."[33] It seems that thus Abdi faithfully summed up the attitude of both the state and the Israeli art establishment toward Palestinian art inside the Green Line. Abdi, the prolific and groundbreaking artist in so many respects in the sphere of Palestinian art, was forced to wait until he was sixty-six to gain this recognition.

This important artist, whose great work was compared by the award's panel of judges to that of Nahum Gutman, has devoted himself for close to 50 years to a wide range of artistic endeavor in varied fields: painting, murals, illustration, prints, sculpture, graphic design, and monument design. I focused on one expression of his multifaceted work—"the art of print" based on the degree of exposure to the broad Palestinian public and its role as a "memorial site" and a sort of "Palestinian museum," and of course, their contribution to the development of the *Nakba* theme, depictions of refugees, and the struggle for the land in the national collective memory of the Arab minority living in Israel.

TAL BEN-ZVI is Vice President of Bezalel Academy of Arts and Design, Jerusalem. Her recent publications include "Landscape Representations in Palestinian Art and Israeli Art Discourse: The Case of Asim Abu Shaqra," *Journal of Levantine Studies*; "The Photographic Memory of Asad Azi" in *Narratives of Dissent: War in Contemporary Israeli Arts and Culture*; and *Men in the Sun* (with Hanna Farah-Kufer).

33. See Anat Zohar, "It Doesn't Compliment Me or the State," http://bidur.nana10.co.il/Article/?ArticleID=600807.

Fig. 1. Abed Abdi, pen and ink drawing, no. 10 in the portfolio, *The Messiah Rises,* 1973

Fig. 2. Abed Abdi, *Refugee in a Tent,* 1973

Fig. 3. Abed Abdi, print no. 4, lithograph, *Revelation of the New Messiah,* 1973

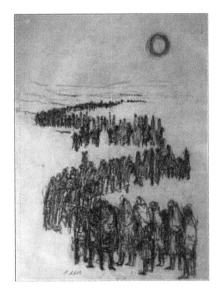

Fig. 4. Abed Abdi, print no 8, charcoal drawing, *Refugees in the Desert,* 1973

Fig. 5. Abed Abdi, print no. 2, pen and ink drawing, *Women,* 1973

Fig. 6. Abed Abdi, print no. 1, *Weeping Woman,* 1973

Fig. 7. Abed Abdi, print no. 6, pen and ink drawing, *Sleeping in the Desert,* 1973

Fig. 8. Abed Abdi, print no. 11, pen and ink drawing, *The Dam,* 1973

Fig. 9. Abed Abdi, print no. 12, pen and ink drawing, *Wild Landscape,* 1973

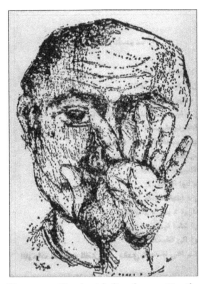

Fig. 11. Abed Abdi, from Emile Habibi, *The Pessoptimist: The Secret Life of Saeed Abu el-Nahs al-Motashel,* 1977 [frontispiece]

Fig. 10. Abed Abdi, from Emile Habibi, *Mandelbaum Gate,* 1968

Fig. 12. Abed Abdi, from Emile Habibi, *The Pessoptimist: The Secret Life of Saeed Abu el-Nahs al-Motashel,* 1977 [page facing the frontispiece]

Fig. 13. *The Pessoptimist: The Secret Life of Saeed Abu el-Nahs al-Motashel,* 1977 *The Pessoptimist:* Abed Abdi, from Emile Habibi, 1977 [p. 193]

Fig. 15. Abed Abdi, from Salman
Natour, *Wa Ma Nasina, What Is Left
of Haifa*, Al-Ja did, December 1980

Fig. 14. Abed Abdi, from Salman
Natour, *Wa Ma Nasina* cover illustra-
tion [from the story *Being Small at Al-
Ain . . . Growing Up in Lod*]

Fig. 17. Abed Abdi, *Untitled*, 1979

Fig. 16. Abed Abdi, from Deeb
Abdi, *Thoughts of Time*, 1993
[cover illustration]

Fig. 18. Abed Abdi, from Salman Natour, *Wa Ma Nasina, From the Well to the Mosque of Ramla,* Al-Jadid, November 1981

Fig. 19. Abed Abdi, from Salman Natour, *Wa Ma Nasina, Like This Cactus in Eilabun,* Al-Jadid, March 1981

Fig. 20. Abed Abdi, from Salman Natour, *Wa Ma Nasina, Trap in Khobbeizeh,* Al-Jadid, June 1981

Fig. 21. Abed Abdi, from Salman Natour, *Wa Ma Nasina, Trap in Khobbeizeh,* Al-Jadid, June 1981

Fig. 22. Abed Abdi, from Salman Natour, *Wa Ma Nasina, Trap in Khobbeizeh,* Al-Jadid, June 1981

8 The Palestinian Exile—Drama Shapes Memory

Mustafa Kabha

"The true picture of the past flits by. The past can be seized only as an image, which flashes up at the instant when it can be recognized and is never seen again. . . . For every image of the past that is not recognized by the present as one of its own concerns threatens to disappear irretrievably."[1]

Introduction

The chapter attempts to link memory to history through the genre of "historical drama," where the collective memory of a people is presented through the story of certain groups of this people at a defined point in time.

The question "What is memory to history?" has occupied and continues to occupy many historians. In the opinion of Pierre Nora, history is a problematic and incomplete reconstruction of what is no more, while memory is always relevant. Memory is life, borne constantly by living groups, and is therefore constantly developing, open to a dialectic of remembrance and forgetting, sensitive to all uses and manipulations, knowing lengthy periods of latency and sudden bursts of liveliness.[2]

In a time when the visual media is a growing presence and the digital revolution is increasingly dominant, the debate on the issue of shaping memory and on agents and manners of presentation has become an important field in its own right, capable of illuminating extensive subjects such as history, photography, architecture, cinema, mass media, and discourse on social networks, as well as society and culture.

Establishing the identity of the individual and the collective and the ability to preserve the contents of acts, events, photographs, and issues from the past, is one relevant field influenced by the enormous revolution in the digital technology. How is the past organized, and how is it represented in present-oriented discourse? The concepts of "memory" and "collective memory"[3] are obscure concepts, and they

---

1. Walter Benjamin, *Illuminations* (New York, 1968), 255.

2. Pierre Nora, "Between History and Memory: Les Lieux de Memoire," *Representations* 26 (1989): 8–9.

3. See Noa Gedi and Yigal Elam, "Collective Memory—What is It?," *History and Memory* 8 (1996): 36.

The War of 1948 (2016): 194–202, DOI: 10.2979/warof1948.0.0.10

are very hard to delimit. Hence, every discussion of them might arouse objection. Anita Shapira contends that "The mere attempt to define collective memory raises questions of trustworthiness, of definition, and of delimitation."[4]

The attempt to reconstruct the historical facts is nearly impossible. Walter Benjamin went even further in his description of the inability to reconstruct authenticity and said: "The whole sphere of authenticity is outside technical . . . reproducibility."[5] Hence, in discussing the drama series *al-Taghriba al-Filastiniyya* I am well aware of the difficulty of reconstructing authentic events within the time frame covered by the series, but I would not go as far as Benjamin and reject the producer's capacity to try and investigate past events.

The television series, created in the early twenty-first century, is part of a wave of similar series that may be called "historical dramas" that attempt to shape pan-Arab "collective memory" while utilizing the high viewing rates of Arabic satellite TV channels, which potentially reach nearly 300 million Arabic speakers.

In the three recent decades, the number of drama series attempting to reconstruct crucial historical periods in the history of the region or biographies of people who played important roles in shaping the form and essence of local processes, particularly in the modern era, has been gradually increasing. This began in Egypt with a series on the Revolt of 1919 and the period between the world wars, and later continued with series on figures who constitute cultural and political symbols, such as Sa'ad Zaghlul,[6] Gamal 'Abd al-Nasser,[7] and Umm Kulthum.[8]

If in Egypt the emphasis was local, emphasizing in particular modern Egyptian nationalism, in Syria the emphasis is more classical, emphasizing the pan-Arab national dimension, and even referring to pre-Islamic periods such as the Kingdom of Tadmur (Palmyra)[9] or the mythological cultural hero from the Jahili (pre-Islamic) era, al-Zeer Salem.[10]

4. Anita Shapira, "The Holocaust: Private Memory and Public Memory," *Zmanim* 57 (1996): 4–13 [Hebrew].

5. Benjamin, *Illuminations*, 3.

6. Sa'ad Zaghlul (1876–1927), founder and head of the al-Wafd Party and leader of the Egyptian popular revolt against the British in 1919. Prime Minister of Egypt (1922–1927).

7. Gamal 'Abd al-Nasser (1918–70), leader of the July 1952 "Free Officers" revolution and president of Egypt (1954–70).

8. Umm Kulthum Ibrahim al-Biltagi (1903–75), better known as Umm Kulthum, famous Egyptian singer and one of the greatest symbols of Arab culture.

9. An ancient Semitic city in the Syrian desert and capital of the short-lived autonomous Palmyra Kingdom, which reached its zenith in the mid-260s CE. It was destroyed by the Roman Empire in 273 CE.

10. Al-Zeer Salem Abu Layla al-Muhalhal: Arab poet of the Jahliyya era whose heroic character served as the basis of many tales.

The decision evident in the Syrian drama to stress the pan-Arab national dimension appears to have chosen opportune timing, with the growing spread and influence of Arab satellite channels, which stress pan-Arab themes across borders and audiences. This managed to erode, maybe for the first time, the status of the dominant Egyptian drama, considered for decades the heart of television productions in the Arab world, and led to a rise in the status of dramas from the periphery, such as Syria, Jordan, Lebanon, North Africa, and the Persian Gulf.

The competition between the different centers of production grew with the rise in rating of Arab satellite channels, particularly during Ramadan, considered the month with the highest rating. One of the recurrent topics in recent years is the Palestinian issue and the Arab-Israeli conflict.[11]

One series that sought to present the Palestinian subject and its various dimensions was *al-Taghriba al-Filastiniyya* (The Palestinian Exile). This series begins its historical review in 1933 (the year in which the struggle for the land became a public matter, as evident in the contentious case of Wadi al-Hawarith lands[12]) and ends in 1968 (a year marked by the growing influence of Palestinian armed organizations, the employment of guerilla warfare, and the popular war of liberation[13]), with a special emphasis on the Arab Revolt of 1936–39 and the War of 1948.

The series describes the ordeals of a rural Palestinian family from a village in the district of Haifa during the British Mandate, followed by the years of exile and the villagers' life as refugees. It is based on the premise that this family represents a wide segment of the Palestinian people, a living symbol of the struggle against the Zionist enterprise and the leadership of this struggle, as well as the fundamental processes that affected the internal structure of Palestinian society and the interrelations between its various components.

The Series: General Description

The series was produced and funded in Syria in the summer of 2004. Most of it was filmed in various sites in Syria, for example the villages of Safita and 'Imar al-Hesin and the cities of Tadmur and Aleppo. It was written by Dr. Walid Sayf, a

---

11. On rating percentages of Arab satellite channels and their effect on public opinion in the Arab world see Zeyad al-Hedaithy, "The relations between the Arab satellite TV and their audiences" (PhD diss., Griffith University, 2011).

12. An extensive area extending over some 30,000 dunums in the region between Hadera—Tulkarm—Netanya. See Raya Adler (Cohen): "The tenants of Wadi Hawarith: Another view of the land question in Palestine," *International Journal of Middle East Studies* 20:2 (1988): 197–220.

13. On this transition see: Mustafa Kabha, *The Palestinian People Seeking Sovereignty and State* (Boulder, CO, 2014), 221–37.

lecturer of communication at the Jordan University of Amman, born in the town of Tulkarm. Dr. Sayf has written many scripts for films and dramas based on historical stories. The director of the series is Hatem 'Ali, a refugee from a village in the Golan that was destroyed following the 1967 War. The actors are Syrians, Jordanians, and Palestinians living in Syria, Jordan, and Lebanon.

Outline of the Series

The series is about a rural family, the Shaykh Yunis family that originally lived in a village on the southern slopes of Mount Carmel in the district of Haifa. The family consisted of two parents, four sons, and a daughter. The family was not among the village's most important or largest and had little property and land. The father did odd jobs together with the eldest son, Ahmad, and with the little money they managed to save they bought a small plot of land and began to cultivate it, thus gaining some economic independence, to the chagrin of the village leaders.[14]

The slight improvement in the family's status led to constant clashes with local representatives of the upper class: the Mukhtar and the affluent landowner Abu 'Ayid, who owned most of the property in the village. This conflict had many twists and turns, reflected in the high points of the series, and was also evident in exile, when the former social status of the two sides lost its relevance, leaving only their hard feelings toward each other.

The fortunes of each of the family members (the four sons and the daughter) relates the story of the Palestinian people and their exile. Ahmad, the eldest son, is a very central figure in the story. He was the first to try and confront the social divisions in the village and to rebel against the control of the ruling class. His efforts paid off, but at a heavy price. The first time he refused the local leaders his father and he were punished with a reprimand at the Mukhtar's house as well as a public beating.[15] This did not prevent him from trying yet again to erode the status of the local tyrants.

Ahmad developed his social consciousness when he travelled to Haifa in search of work in 1934 due to the acute economic crisis in rural areas in those years. In the city of Haifa he noticed the social contrast between the working class (consisting mostly of villagers who settled mainly in the shantytowns around the Port of Haifa) and the urban class. He also became aware of new dimensions of the national conflict between the Palestinian National Movement and the Zionist Movement, in addition to the struggle for national liberation from Britain, the mandatory power . . . His emerging national activity greatly enhanced his political and social awareness, and when returning to the village at the time of the Great

---

14. The drama series *Al-Taghriba al-Filastiniyya*, henceforth *Al-Taghriba*, chapters 1–2.

15. *Al-Taghriba*, chapter 6.

Strike and the Revolt of 1936–1939,[16] this helped him upgrade his status and become an alternative leader to the traditional leadership he had confronted before leaving for Haifa. Immediately after his return, Ahmad organized an armed band (*fasil*) consisting of men from his and an adjacent village. He began to arm and train them, and was assisted by an urban intellectual whom he had met in Haifa, and who served as a guide and counselor on all matters of national consciousness.[17]

In time, Ahmad became the acknowledged leader of the village, and all problems, demands, and complaints were referred to him. Even the traditional leaders of the village recognized his rising status, as evident from two incidents. The first was during the olive harvest in the autumn of 1937. In this year Abu 'Ayid, owner of the village's olive press, sent his men to the home of Ahmad Shaykh Yunis to collect the olive sacks and then to deliver the jugs of olive oil. In years past Ahmad and his father had to fight for their turn at the olive press, and when they complained about the long wait they were driven out in disgrace. However, the highest point was when Ahmad Shaykh Yunis was appointed the presiding judge of the revolt's court in his region, and when a complaint against Abu 'Ayid was brought before him, he then called for the defendant and made sure that his assistants explained to him the new order.[18]

After the revolt ended, Ahmad became a wanted man, living in the hills, with the old leadership trying unsuccessfully to reinstate their previous domination and status. Marriage ties, formed between the two families during the revolt (unheard of in previous years), did nothing to reduce the tension or dissipate the hard feelings.

A "honeymoon" period was evident during the War of 1948. Ahmad Shaykh Yunis reassumed his command of the youth, who banded together to defend the village from assaults by the Jewish militias. One of these was 'Ayid, son of Abu 'Ayid, who after a disagreement with his father managed to convince him of the need to join the national struggle under the leadership of Ahmad Shaykh Yunis and to obey his instructions.

In this context, the series relates the Palestinian story—the village was attacked and it was clear that the Jewish forces had more military means at their disposal—tanks, etc., compared to the more outdated means on the Palestinian side. However, the Palestinians did not run away, rather stood their ground as

---

16. See Mustafa Kabha and Nimer Sirhan, *Lexicon of the Leaders, Rebels and Volunteers in the 1936–1939 Revolt* (*Dar al-Huda*, 2009) [Arabic]; Yehoshua Porath, *The Palestinian Arab National Movement: From Riots to Rebellion, 1929–1939* (London, 1977).

17. *Al-Taghriba*, chapter 8.

18. Ibid.

long as possible. The residents eventually left in convoys of people of all ages with few belongings, leaving behind the ruins and smoke of the bombed village.[19]

In exile the two figures were in a similar situation: In a revealing scene, Ahmad Shaykh Yunis and Abu 'Ayid stand beside the line for soup, organized by the United Nations Relief and Works Agency for Palestine Refugees officials, refusing to stand in line and assume the status of "destitute refugees." When queuing for a refugee certificate, Ahmad Shaykh Yunis reminds the UNRWA official of his past and his position during the revolt, and when this makes no impression on the man Ahmad, enraged, beats the official, saying "I am Abu Salah, I am Abu Salah," his *nom de guerre* as a band leader during the revolt. Abu 'Ayid, in contrast, is delighted when one of his former neighbors appeals to him as *ma'dhun*, one authorized to award the wedding signature. This gives him, in the midst of the torments of exile, a moment of satisfaction reminiscent of the period before the exile.[20]

The second son, Mas'ud, symbolizes the average young Palestinian born in the early 1920s, who received very basic schooling at the *Kuttab* (the traditional schoolroom at the *Shaykh*'s house) and then joined his father and older brother in the fields and housework. Mas'ud had a well-developed economic and business sense. This sense was particularly evident when choosing a wife: During the revolt, when his family's status was upgraded thanks to his older brother's place in the revolt, he sought to take advantage of this situation and begged his father to ask for the hand of Abu 'Ayid's daughter in marriage. During the exile, Mas'ud was the first of all the brothers to come to terms with the situation and to try and break out of the refugee camp, leaving for the nearby city of Tulkarm.[21] When this city did not live up to his hopes, he emigrated to Kuwait, where he became a well-known businessman.[22]

The third son, Hasan, symbolizes the "Palestinian Shahid." He received basic schooling and relinquished his right to further studies outside the village to his younger brother, 'Ali, because the family was unable to pay for two students. He joined his brother Ahmad in the revolt and became one of his aides. He rebelled against the social strictures by falling in love with a girl with a lower social status

---

19. Ibid., chapter 17.

20. Ibid., chapters 19–20.

21. Ibid., chapters 18–19.

22. The reconstruction of the tiring route taken by Mas'ud with a group of young Palestinians was copied by the screenwriter almost in full from Ghasan Kanfani's book, *Rijal fi al-Shams* [Men in the Sun], where he tells the story of young Palestinians seeking to make a living in Iraq and the Gulf States, where many found their death when smuggled in tankards in the sweltering heat. For an English translation see Kanafani, *Men in the Sun and Other Palestinian Stories* (Boulder, CO, 1997).

(as a foreigner who was not originally from the village) and asking for her hand in marriage despite the protests of his parents. His brother Ahmad helped convince their parents, and when he began visiting his fiancé, who lived alone with her mother, her relatives from the nearby village became incensed and killed her before Hasan's unbelieving eyes.[23] During the 1948 War Hasan served as the right hand of his brother Ahmad in the defense of the village. After the village was occupied and its inhabitants left under pressure from artillery bombing by the attacking forces, he insisted on visiting his fiancé's grave and died there.[24]

The fourth son, 'Ali, symbolizes the generation of new rural students who left their villages to study in the city and there encountered the national activities and the struggle against the Jewish Settlement and the Mandate government. He serves as a narrator for considerable parts of the series and constitutes, in fact, a type of spokesperson for the screenwriter Walid Sayf, for conveying ideas and intentional comments to the viewers. 'Ali studied in Haifa, Acre, and at the Arab College in Jerusalem. At the college he was awarded a scholarship to the American University of Beirut. During his studies in Beirut the *Nakbah* occurred and the family became refugees living in the Tulkarm refugee camp. Later 'Ali became an important academic, married a woman from a higher class (who refused to live with him in the refugee camp), and lived the dilemma of the class struggle until the end of his life.

Khadra, the family's only daughter, did not receive any formal education. She fell in love with one of the rebels who joined her brother Ahmad and married him. Her husband 'Abed died in battle against the British and left her with a tiny baby.[25] After the revolt she married another man who was the complete opposite of 'Abed, a greedy opportunist who was not even averse to trading the rifle of her former husband, which she had saved as a memento of him from the defense of the village in 1948. While in exile her family fell apart (as did many other Palestinian families): She and her husband settled in Umm al-Fahm (an Arab village passed to Israeli control in May 1949) and the son moved with his grandparents to the refugee camp in Tulkarm. From 1948 to 1967 the son dreamt of meeting his mother, an encounter that took place after the 1967 War. The lost son (played by the film director himself) reclaimed the rifle that had belonged to his father (who had fought in the 1936–39 revolt) from the arms dealer who had bought it from his mother's husband, took it with him to the refugee camp, hid it there, and in the final chapter of the series (chronologically in the spring of 1968)

23. *Al-Taghriba*, chapter 12.

24. *Al-Taghriba*, chapter 17.

25. *Al-Taghriba*, chapter 9.

he took the rifle from its hiding place and joined one of the armed Palestinian resistance organizations, thereby attaining closure.[26]

Analysis

With regard to the relationship between the events presented in the series and the historical events, the screenwriter tried to follow the historical narrative based on written sources. In these cases accuracy was maintained and almost no significant deviations were recorded on the macro level. The names of historical persons were used, for example Haj Amin al-Husseini,[27] 'Iz al-Din al-Qassam,[28] and 'Abd al-Rahim al-Haj Muhamad.[29] In contrast, the producer obscured the names of people whose Palestinian national role was doubtful (such as the participants in establishing The Peace Bands (*fasa'il al-salam*)[30] who collaborated with the British Mandate in repressing the revolt identified with the Arab Palestinian national leadership. Despite the attempt to avoid historical mistakes, there are some conspicuous errors, for example placing the refugees of Wadi al-Hawarith in 1935 on the Haifa beach.[31]

Nonetheless, the series is a first attempt by a Palestinian screenwriter to critically discuss internal Palestinian matters, inner conflicts, and disagreements with no bias and touching on topics previously considered taboos with which Palestinian historians and writers found it hard to deal. For example, the topic of selling lands or the help provided by Palestinians to the Zionist institutions in purchasing lands. Furthermore, the courageous treatment of the final stage of the 1936–39 revolt, which developed into the equivalent of a civil war after establishment of what was known as The Peace Bands, with the encouragement of the British authorities.

It is worthy of note that the scriptwriter emphasizes the rehabilitation process of Palestinian Arabs who became citizens of Israel. For many years they were accused of collaboration with Israel and even disloyalty to the Palestinian cause. These accusations were voiced by wide parts of the Arab world, and members of

26. On the separation of Khadra and her son as a result of the *Nakbah* of 1948 and the renewed encounter in 1967 see *Al-Taghriba*, chapters 30–32.

27. Haj Amin al-Husseini (1898–1974) was the undisputed leader of the Palestinians from the early 1920s until 1948.

28. 'Iz al-Din al-Qassam (1881–1935) was a Syrian cleric who came to Palestine in the early 1920s, was killed in a battle with the British in November 1935, and became a symbol of the Palestinian armed struggle.

29. 'Abd al-Rahim al-Haj Muhamad (1900–39) was the general leader of the Palestinian revolt in 1936–39. He was killed in a clash with the British in March 1939.

30. See Kabha and Sirhan, *Lexicon of the Leaders, Rebels and Volunteers*, 30–1.

31. *Al-Taghriba*, chapter 3.

this group were called Jews' Arabs (*'Arab al-Yahud*) or Arabs' Jews (*Yahud al-'Arab*).[32] In this series the writer, Walid Sayf, made an effort to correct this impression through a dialogue between Rushdi, the son separated from his mother, and a young boy from Taybeh who transported him secretly from the Tulkarm refugee camp to Umm al-Fahem, the village where his mother went to live after *al-Nakbah*. In their conversation, the son speaks in favor of the Palestinians living in Israel and their survival and efforts to hold on to the land.[33]

Conclusion

Al-Taghribah al-Filastiniyya is an important step in the continued efforts of Palestinian creators to outline and shape the collective memory of the Palestinian people, particularly in the formative era, beginning with the amplified struggle for the land and homeland in the early 1930s and ending in the emergence of the armed resistance organizations and the Palestinian attempt to take control of their fate. The main unique element of this series is the interesting innovative endeavor to turn the critical view inwards, observing the internal struggles and rifts within Palestinian society, in addition to revealing other odd factors, which brought upon the Palestinians the great disaster of the *Nakbah*. Such a perspective has been missing in Palestinian descriptions of the pre-1948 *Nakba*, which largely ignored the struggle within and emphasized the ideal Palestinian life (the "lost paradise").[34]

As a step in shaping collective memory through historical drama, *al-Taghriba al-Filastiniyya* has earned a significant place in shaping Palestinian national identity in which trauma, exile, resistance, and the quest for statehood are primary elements.

MUSTAFA KABHA is Professor in the Department of History, Philosophy and Judaic Studies at the Open University of Israel. His recent publications include *The Palestinian People: Seeking Sovereignty and State*; *The Palestinian Arab In/Outsiders: Media and Conflict in Israel* (with Dan Caspi); and *Writing up The Storm—The Palestinian Press Shaping Public Opinion*.

32. Eliya Zureik, "Prospects of the Palestinians in Israel," *Journal of Palestine Studies*, 22:2 (1993): 90–109.

33. *Al-Taghriba*, chapter 31.

34. An exception in this context is Issa Khalaf, *Politics in Palestine, Arab Factionalism and Social Disintegration 1939–1948* (Albany, NY, 1991).

Epilogue

Reflections on Post-Oslo Israeli and Palestinian History and Memory of 1948

Avraham Sela and Neil Caplan

THE CHAPTERS IN this volume have discussed various Israeli and Palestinian approaches to, and perceptions of, 1948 commonly represented in historiography, literature, films, and other public realms of culture and knowledge. In presenting their case studies, the authors have made valuable contributions to a field increasingly marked by perceptive interpretations of the nature and fluctuating trends among Israelis and Palestinians as they remember and narrate their respective histories.

These in-depth studies underline the rigid nature of collective memory and identity, especially in intractable ethno-national conflicts such as the Israeli-Palestinian one. At the same time, however, they also demonstrate the dynamic nature and fluctuating selection of means and strategies of commemoration, forgetfulness or suppression of memory, and a seemingly unending reproduction of new interpretations of the past reflecting changing political conditions, especially with regard to relations with the "other."

While there are many commonalities and parallels between Israeli-Jewish and Palestinian perceptions of their shared history of what happened in the 1948 War, there are also asymmetries and gaps between them, as well as multiple versions on each side of the divide. This diversity presents itself not only through different individual, local, and communal experiences that find their way into unifying frameworks of "collective memory" and "canonical narratives" but also in what is supposed to be critical and impartial historical research.

A primary common feature of both parties in relation to their shared history, with 1948 as its pivotal event, is the unending quest for *legitimacy*. History and legitimacy are tightly intertwined elements for peoples living in protracted conflict. This connection is common to all actors in the Arab-Israeli conflict, but particularly the Israeli and Palestinian political communities situated at the core of this conflict.

In this epilogue we highlight the main shifts and continuities underpinning Israeli and Palestinian perceptions of "self" and "other," of history and memory, especially in the context of efforts to resolve this century-long conflict.

The War of 1948 (2016): 203–222, DOI: 10.2979/warof1948.0.0.11

In particular, we examine the manifestations of the parties' historical narratives in historians' dialogues and indirect intellectual debates, and reflect on their significance for the Israeli-Palestinian peace process.

An Unconsummated Quest for Legitimacy

Despite the time that has elapsed since the formative events of 1948, the past stubbornly preserves its immediacy and continuous relevance and refuses to become a closed chapter of "history," especially for the Palestinians. Any discussion about that past thus transforms quickly into a debate about legitimacy in the present. A major reason for this grip of the past over the present is the unfulfilled quest of both Israelis and Palestinians for legitimacy, in one or more of the following three senses: (a) each party's sense of its own legitimacy as a national community entitled to its own sovereign state; (b) each party's willingness to grant legitimacy to at least part of the competing national narrative of the other; and (c) the international community's extension of legitimacy to the competing rights and claims of Israelis and Palestinians.

Regardless of their lopsided post-1948 victor-vanquished relationship and the diametrical asymmetry between them in terms of national resources and international status, Israelis and Palestinians have adopted similar ways of coping with their distinctive collective memories. Both are engaged, to this day, in a quest for legitimacy through the propagation of mutually exclusive narratives of 1948. Directed inward and outward, continuous efforts on both sides evoke a past that cannot remain in the past; both draw on and contribute afresh to refurbishing a collective memory that refuses to disappear and become history. Given the festering grievances flowing from their unresolved conflict, Israelis and Palestinians compete for legitimacy by, among other things, clinging to conflicting versions of 1948 that are designed to reinforce their contemporary claims to sovereign—and in extreme cases, exclusive—national existence on the same land. As in other cases of protracted conflict, Israelis and Palestinians alike have been selective in their preoccupations with commemoration. Alongside glorification of heroes and vilification of enemies, both societies have engaged in systematic forgetfulness, repression, and silence about one's historical miscalculations and unflattering chapters of their past.

Within this context, the Palestinian refugee problem and the circumstances of its birth remain the single most prominent issue, a living monument to the yawning abyss between Israelis and Palestinians, both in the realm of academic historiography and in the sphere of popular collective memory. In Pierre Nora's terms, it is a tangible "lieu de mémoire" that refuses to disappear from the reality of life of Israelis and Palestinians alike, like a black hole that swallows every attempt to bypass it.

Despite the expanding fields and perspectives of historical research and increased resources available to academic historians, the latter have been overtaken by powerful popular avenues of memory construction, such as the press, literature, poetry, film, television, the Internet and, more recently, social networks. The resultant proliferation of historical narratives has contributed to a communal "politics of identity," which has tended to displace critically examined historical accounts of events. The result, mainly on the Israeli side of the divide, is a growing gap between academic ("ivory tower") research and collective memory. Against this backdrop, Israeli and Palestinian historiography and discourses of memory have developed at different paces and in different directions.

Narratives of Victimhood: The Holocaust—Nakba Nexus

One effective strategy utilized by both parties has been to adopt the self-image of the victim of evil and injustice, as a means of self-justification of past and present policies while projecting moral blame onto the "other." Indeed, nothing represents this embrace of victimhood more than the fixation in both Israeli-Jewish and Palestinian consciousness and discourse than the terms *sho'a* and *nakba*, respectively; both connote a catastrophe, though of different characteristics and unequal dimensions. Nonetheless, as of the late 1990s these two events came to be increasingly discussed as closely interconnected, both historically and morally.

Every people "remembers" its past but Jews are also religiously obligated to remember their roots as a people.[1] Israeli Jews are often viewed as a post-traumatic society whose collective memory has been infused by repeated cycles of destruction, persecution, and inherent existential threat, from time immemorial long before the Holocaust. The unprecedented cataclysmic nature of this chapter in Jewish history and its proximity to the 1948 War, however, provided a national narrative centered on the ultimate historic necessity and justification for a sovereign Jewish state, which faced an intransigent and hostile Arab world openly committed to its annihilation. Zionist and Israeli institutions thus took advantage of the collaboration of the Mufti Haj Amin al-Husseini with Nazi Germany during World War II to portray him as a partner in the Jewish genocide in an effort to delegitimize Palestinian national claims.[2] The participation of Germans in the Arab irregular and regular armies in the 1948 War served as further evidence of the continued Arab-Nazi collaboration against the Jews.

1. Yosef Haim Yerushalmi, *Zachor: Jewish History and Jewish Memory* (Seattle, 1996), 27.

2. This claim, dating back to the Anglo-American Committee of Inquiry in 1946, has been echoed in a recent speech by PM Benjamin Netanyahu, accusing the Mufti of no less than *initiating* the idea of mass extermination of the Jews, an egregious claim from which the PM later retreated. See Jeffrey Herf, "Netanyahu, Husseini, and the Historians," *The Times of Israel*, 22 October 2015. http://www.meforum.org/5576/husseini-hitler. For a convincing critique of this claim, see Gilbert Achcar, *The Arabs and the Holocaust: The Arab-Israeli War of Narratives* (New York, 2010), 145–73.

The challenges facing Israel's quest for legitimacy have grown significantly since 1967, especially in view of the continued occupation of the West Bank and (until 2005) the Gaza Strip and growing international support for Palestinian self-determination and statehood over these territories and East Jerusalem. Hence, while the mainstream Zionist historiography still perceives the conquest of territory in 1948 as the result of a necessary life-or-death defensive war of a beleaguered people, over recent decades this school has come to realize that the quest for Jewish national existence collided with the collective rights of another people and the latter's refusal to accept the Jewish people's right to national existence in its historical homeland. This dissonance among Israeli Jews has invigorated mechanisms of suppression of inconvenient chapters of the past—primarily Israeli responsibility for the Palestinian refugee problem—an existential necessity in strengthening self-righteousness, banishing self-doubt, and overcoming the traumatic prospect of unending conflict, both inwardly and outwardly.

The emergence of Israeli "new history" and "critical sociology" in the late 1980s[3] unleashed a flood of critical reexaminations of Israel's collective narratives and founding myths. Some of the proponents of this current readily applied the term "colonial/ist" to the Zionist project and the nature of Arab-Zionist relations during the pre-1948 decades, thereby challenging the two main self-justifications upon which the legitimacy of the Jewish state had been based: namely, the Jews' Biblical ties to the Land of Israel and, more recently, the historical "necessity" and rebirth (*tekuma*) of a Jewish nation-state in the wake of the Holocaust (*sho'a*).[4]

As pointed out in the introductory chapter, haunted by the dread of the mass return of Palestinians to their original homes, popular Israeli attitudes to the refugee problem have been marked by "blaming the victims"—accusing them of being responsible for their own misery, interpreting the phenomenon of Palestinian refugees as the result of Arab hostility, disorganization, and demoralization, and as a tragic result of war that *they* initiated, rather than exclusively as the result of deliberate expulsion by Israeli forces.[5]

By contrast, academic research in Israel on 1948 tends to look for immediate causal explanations at the local and regional levels, presenting the results of the

3. This reflected a generational shift as well as social and political transformation from a collectivist to increasingly individualistic society. See Gershon Shafir and Yoav Peled, eds., *The New Israel: Peacemaking and Liberalization* (Boulder, CO, 2000); Yael Yishai, *Between Mobilization and Conciliation: Civil Society in Israel* (Tel-Aviv, 2004) [Hebrew].

4. On this current see Laurence Silberstein, *The Postzionism Debates: Knowledge and Power in Contemporary Israel* (New York, 1999); Anita Shapira and Derek J. Penslar, eds., *Israeli Historical Revisionism: from Left to Right* (Portland, OR, 2003).

5. This is well demonstrated by Amal Jamal and Samah Bsoul, *The Palestinian Nakba in the Israeli Public Sphere: On the Forms of Denial and Responsibility* (Nazareth, 2014) [Arabic].

war as contingent on the flow of battle and the voluntary/involuntary movements of threatened populations—rather than on any masterplan or evil intentions that would raise questions about Israel's legitimacy.[6] This approach is well-represented in the vast majority of critical works produced during the last two decades on 1948 by Israeli historians, some of which represent a counter historical discourse or different methodological approach to those of the so-called New History.[7]

The ongoing critical research into 1948 by Israeli scholars has by no means been matched by their Palestinian counterparts, who have largely and increasingly given priority to "memory" over critical history. In contrast to the Israeli tendency to employ memory and history for bolstering its political achievements while retaining the self-image of "a lamb among wolves," the Palestinians have constructed their collective identity and historical memory in relation to their unsuccessful struggle against the Zionist enterprise under the British Mandate, culminating in their dispossession and dispersion during the 1948 War—the *nakba*.

The impact of massive Palestinian dislocation and losses on shaping Palestinian identity was amplified by the attitude of rejection and alienation manifested by the host Arab states and societies during and after 1948. This collective sense of victimization as Palestinians was further intensified by a cynicism bred of the constant gap between indignation and repeated calls for justice, on the one hand, and the absence of effective solidarity needed to alleviate the real deprivations and suffering they experienced on a daily basis, on the other. Articulations of such perspectives are especially present in Palestinian poetry, literature, and film.[8]

6. A case in point is Alon Kadish and Avraham Sela, "Myths and Historiography of the 1948 Palestine War Revisited: The Case of Lydda," *The Middle East Journal* 59.4 (2005): 617–34. For a similar approach to the expulsion of the Arab Palestinian population from Lydda, see also Martin Kramer, "What Happened at Lydda?" *Mosaic*, July 2014. Accessed 5 July 2014, http://mosaicmagazine.com/essay/2014/07/what-happened-at-lydda/.

7. Most comprehensive of them are Yoav Gelber, *Palestine 1948: War, Escape and the Emergence of the Palestinian Refugee Problem* (Brighton, 2001); David Tal, *War in Palestine 1948: Strategy and Diplomacy* (London, 2004); Alon Kadish, ed., *The War of Independence 1948–1949: A New Approach* (Efal, 2004) [Hebrew]; Benny Morris, *1948: A History of the First Arab-Israeli War* (New Haven, 2008). See also Alon Kadish, ed., *1948 and After: Studies of the Jerusalem School on War, Military and Society* (Ben Shemen, 2015) [Hebrew].

8. For a discussion of these perspectives based on Palestinian writings and statements, see A. L. Tibawi, "Visions of the Return, The Palestine Refugees in Arabic Poetry and Art," *The Middle East Journal* 17.5 (1963): 507–26; Yehoshafat Harkabi, *The Palestinians from Hibernation to Awakening* (Jerusalem, 1979), 24–42 [Hebrew]; Fawaz Turki, *The Disinherited: Journal of a Palestinian Exile* (New York, 1972); Fawaz Turki, *Poems from Exile* (Washington, D.C., 1975); Elias Khouri, *Gate of the Sun* (Beirut, 1998) [Arabic]; Muhammad Bakri, *1948* (Israel, 1998) (documentary).

The foundation of the State of Israel through war with its catastrophic consequences for the Arabs of Palestine in fact confirmed the latter's worst fears well before 1948 over the linkage between the Holocaust and the solution of the Jewish problem at their expense, adding further weight to the sense of being victims of a Zionist conspiracy abetted by the international powers. Hence the relatively rare acknowledgement by Arabs and Muslims of the tragedy of the European Jews, even their condemnations of Holocaust denial, have often been joined within the Palestinian "war of narratives" against Zionism and the very legitimacy of the State of Israel, with a repeated equation of Zionism with the Nazi practices.[9]

The disaster that befell the Palestinians in 1948, at a time when this society was in its early stages of consolidation as a political community, became the hallmark of their history, portrayed as an unending chain of traumas, massacres, and abuse of their basic rights as individuals and a people, whether by Israel, Arab states, or international powers. Indeed, one observer considers the image of being victims of evil "others" as being so powerful and ingrained in the Palestinian identity and political discourse that for them "giving up the victimhood narrative seems incompatible with survival itself."[10]

Although preceded by the Lebanese thinker Hazim Sahghiyya,[11] it was Edward Said's 1998 public call for mutual acknowledgement of Israelis and Palestinians of the other's past trauma and suffering that left its problematic watermark on the intellectual discourse of the Israeli-Palestinian conflict.[12] Said later asserted that Israelis should issue an apology for "the wrong done by their government against a relatively innocent people."[13] Whereas Said stressed the incomparability of the annihilation of millions of Jews to the dispossession by Israel of the Palestinians from their land, he still remained faithful to the mainstream Arab denial of the historical and cultural attachment of the Jewish people

9. Edward Said, "The Challenge of Israel: Fifty Years On," *al-Ahram Weekly*, 15–21 January 1998; Meir Litvak and Esther Webman, *From Empathy to Denial: Arab Responses to the Holocaust* (New York, 2009); Achcar, *The Arabs and the Holocaust;* Neil Caplan, "War of Narratives" (review article), *Middle East Journal* 65.2 (2011): 327–31.

10. Trudy Govier, *Forgiveness and Revenge* (London & New York, 2002), 148, quoted in Yehudit Auerbach, "The Reconciliation Pyramid: A Narrative-Based Framework for Analyzing Identity Conflicts," *Political Psychology* 30.2 (2009): 291–318, esp. 311.

11. Hazim Saghiyyah, *In Defense of Peace* (Beirut, 1997), 63–4 [Arabic].

12. Said, "The Challenge of Israel." For an Israeli response to Saghiyyah's and Said's calls, see Amnon Rubinstein, "The Holocaust Memory and Peace," *Ha'aretz*, 12 March 1998. For a non-Israeli response, see Mohammed Dajani Daoudi and Robert Satloff, "Why Palestinians Should Learn about the Holocaust," *International Herald Tribune*, 30 March 2011.

13. Edward Said, *The End of the Peace Process: Oslo and After* (New York, 2000), 9. See the comment on Said's statement in Zohar Kampf and Nava Löwenheim, "Rituals of Apology in the Global Arena," *Security Dialogue* 43.1 (2012): 54.

to the Land of Israel and the nature of Zionism as a legitimate national liberation movement. He argued that there could be no symmetry between the Israeli and Palestinian narratives of victimhood: while Zionism is colonialist and racist by nature and anti-humanist in practice, Palestinian counter-violence justly aims to attain liberation from the yoke of colonialism.

This asymmetry clearly defined the Palestinians as the ultimate victim of Nazism, Zionism, and Western civilization together, warning of "the danger of using an historical trauma remembered too vividly as a screen to obscure or justify what these former victims are doing, which is nothing less than creating victims of their own."[14] Indeed, even though Said holds that the Palestinians are "relatively innocent people," he still believes that an apology ought to come only from the Israeli offender. Hence, for the sake of justice the Palestinians must extract from Israel a clear recognition of its wrong doings to the Palestinians and the Arabs as a whole.[15]

The *sho'a-nakba* linkage was elaborated during the post–Cold War "age of apology" in intra-societal and international conflicts, buttressed by expanding scholarship on the significance of historical narratives in conflict resolution. More directly, it was significantly affected by the Oslo Accords and their collapse, the continued Israeli occupation of the West Bank and Gaza Strip, the Palestinian uprisings, and Israel's military responses. Above all, it drew on the Arab-Muslim discourse which had increasingly been portraying the Israelis as "Nazis" and the Palestinians as their victims. According to this victim-victimizer relationship, the Jewish victims of the Nazis became Nazis themselves, committing crimes against humanity by inflicting disasters, massacres, and terror on the helpless Palestinians.[16]

The Palestinian Quest for A National Historical Narrative

Palestinian collective perceptions of the past did not evolve in tandem with changes on the Israeli side of the barricade but remained, by and large, static and unchanged. From the outset, the collective Palestinian narrative was built on foundations of the claim of ancient origins in, exclusive ownership of, and indigenous rights to, Palestine. After 1948, this narrative came to focus on the loss of homes and homeland, exile and statelessness, and the unrequited grievances against colonialism and Zionism.

---

14. Edward Said, "Methods of Forgetting," *al-Ahram Weekly*, 22–28 October, 1998.

15. Said, "The Challenges of Israel" and *The End of the Peace Process*, 9.

16. Meir Litvak and Esther Webman, "Perceptions of the Holocaust in Palestinian Public Discourse," *Israel Studies* 8.3 (2003): 123–40; Jawad Al-Hamad, *The Palestinian People Victim of the Zionist Terror and Massacres* (Amman, 1995), 7–10 [Arabic]; Neil Caplan, "Victimhood in Israeli and Palestinian National Narratives," *Bustan: The Middle East Book Review* 3 (2012): 7–8.

The intensity, frequency of violent clashes, and longevity that characterize the Arab-Jewish conflict in Palestine have left their undeniable imprint on the crystallization of the ethnic identity of both communities.[17] This impact has not, however, been equally shared between the two parties. Notwithstanding claims by Palestinian and foreign scholars of the existence of ancient attributes of Arab-Palestinian identity,[18] the conflict became the paramount single contributor in defining their identity as a twentieth-century national community. This is clearly seen in the abundant national anniversaries and commemoration days in the Palestinian calendar, most of which are directly connected to their conflict with the Jews and Zionism.

The writing of modern history in the Arab-Muslim world is broadly perceived by Western and Arab scholars "less as a genuine inquiry than as a psychological defense," lacking a professional tradition and methodology, suffering from low self-image and rarely confronting present issues with self-critical insights taken from the Arab or Muslim past.[19] The apologetic nature of twentieth century Arab-Muslim historiography is all the more understandable in view of the huge gap between the memory of a glorious distant past and a bitter sense of more recent social and political decline represented, among other events, by the 1948 Arab debacle over Palestine. Indeed, despite significant efforts made by Palestinian official institutions and academic associations since the mid-1960s, and numerous valuable sociological and historical studies of pre- and post-1948 Palestinian society and politics,[20] Arab and Palestinian narratives of the 1948

17. James D. Fearon and David D. Latin, "Violence and the Social Construction of Ethnic Identity," *International Organization* 54.4 (2000): 845–77.

18. Rashid Khalidi, *Palestinian Identity: The Construction of Modern National Consciousness* (New York, 1997); Baruch Kimmerling and Joel S. Migdal, *Palestinians: The Making of a People* (New York, 1993); Neil Caplan. *The Israel-Palestine Conflict: Contested Histories* (Oxford, 2010), 41–3, 52–3.

19. Quoted from Wilfred C. Smith, *Islam in Modern History* (New York, 1957), 124, and more generally, 120–4. For similar approaches, see G. V. von Grunebaum, "Self-Image and Approach to History," in *Historians of the Middle East*, ed. Bernard Lewis and Peter Malcolm Holt (Oxford, 1962), 457–83; Albert H. Hourani, "The Present State of Islamic and Arab Middle East Historiography," in his *Europe and the Middle East* (London, 1980), 161–96; Yehoshafat Harkabi, *Arab Attitudes to Israel* (London, 1972), 362; Emanuel Sivan, "Modern Arab Historiography of the Crusades," *Asian and African Studies* 8.2 (1972): 142–3; Elie Kedourie, *Arab Political Memoirs* (London, 1974), 177–8. For a critique of Arab historiography by a Kuwaiti-based Syrian historian, see Mustafa Shakir, "The Crisis of Arab Historiography," *The Jerusalem Quarterly* 46 (1988): 65–70.

20. For example: Issa Khalaf, *Politics in Palestine: Arab Factionalism and social Disintegration 1939–1948* (Albany, NY, 1991); Yezid Sayigh, *Armed Struggle and the Search for State: The Palestinian National Movement 1949–1993* (Oxford, 1997); Amira Habibi, *The Second Exodus: An Analytical Field Study of the 1967 Exodus* (Beirut, 1970); Basim Sirhan, *Transformations of the*

War are still dominated by memory, both written and oral, rather than based on documentation and other primary sources assembled and accessible in archives—still not released for research by Arab governments.[21] The limited freedom of expression in the Arab world and self-imposed conformity with collective Arab national and Islamic values further stifle the development of a critical Arab and Palestinian historiography.

In general, Arab and Palestinian historiography of the 1948 War is indeed apologetic and defensive, employed as a means to settle historical accounts with political rivals by projecting blame for the defeat onto them and refuting counter allegations made by fellow Arabs and Palestinians and Israelis alike. Within this context, Palestinians are often held responsible for their own catastrophe. Indeed, beginning with the memoirs and polemical publications of the Mandate's Arab Palestinian leadership led by al-Haj Amin al-Husseini and his followers up to the present, Palestinian historical narratives have been markedly imbued with an effort to refute such allegations.[22]

Being blamed for their disaster by Israeli official accounts and professional historians[23] was particularly disturbing due to its legal and moral implications for the Palestinian refugees, challenging their claim for justice and return to their homes. Especially since the early 1990s, Palestinian scholars and commentators have made a discernible effort to revise their counter arguments about the mass exodus of their people from their homes and reframe their history as victims of overwhelming international and regional powers.

It was thus no surprise that as of the late 1980s Walid Khalidi, the pre-eminent Palestinian historian of 1948 who dedicated much of his efforts to disproving the official Israeli argument that the Arab exodus was voluntary, republished his articles from the late 1950s and early 1960s, consistently claiming that the Palestinians were deliberately expelled by the Zionists.[24] As of the late

Palestinian Family in Exile: A Sociological-Comparative Study (Beirut, 2005) [both in Arabic]; Mustafa Kabha, *The Press in the Eye of the Storm - Palestinian Newspapers as a Catalyst for Formulating Public Opinion, 1929-1939* (Jerusalem, 2004) [Hebrew].

21. Avraham Sela, "Arab Historiography of the 1948 War," in *New Perspectives on Israeli History*, ed. Lawrence Silverstein (New York, 1991), 140–6, 151 (footnote 71).

22. For Palestinian responses to those allegations, see chapter 1 in this volume (notes 21–23).

23. Yoav Gelber, *Palestine 1948: War, Escape and the Emergence of the Palestinian Refugee Problem* (Brighton, 2001); Tom Segev, *One Palestine, Complete: Jews and Arabs under the Mandate* (New York, 2000). These accusations are also echoed forcefully in the work of Efraim Karsh, inter alia in his *Palestine Betrayed* (New Haven, 2010).

24. For Khalidi's early responses on this matter, see his articles "Why did the Palestinians Leave?" *Middle East Forum* 35.7 (1959): 21–4; "The Fall of Haifa," ibid., 35.12 (1959): 22–32. For his republished versions, see "Plan Dalet Revisited: A Masterplan for the Conquest of Palestine," *Journal of Palestine Studies* 18.1 (1988); "Why Did the Palestinians Leave, Revisited," *Journal of*

1980s Israeli "New Historians"—especially Benny Morris—seemed to validate many of the arguments made by Khalidi concerning the expulsion of Palestinians from their homeland, despite their insufficient corroboration of this dominant Palestinian position.[25]

While some Palestinian historians and writers lament that history has overlooked their people, or that the Palestinians have overlooked history,[26] others would agree with Rashid Khalidi's statement that "There is no established, authoritative Palestinian master narrative,"[27] especially not of the 1948 War. In effect, Palestinians do have a unifying standard narrative—though not a critical history—shaped by their struggle against the Zionist enterprise and the British Mandate but especially fashioned by the disasters that befell them in 1948 and after.

Rashid Khalidi and other historians provide a number of explanations for this state of Palestinian historiography: a) The dispersed and fragmented community living in temporality, in which the future is uncertain and the past is conceptualized in dichotomous terms of *either* a pre-1948 utopia *or* the trauma of the *nakba*; b) Divided identity—Arab and Palestinian; c) destruction, loss, or appropriation by Israel of official documents and libraries during the war; d) fears lest a critical review of the 1948 events might weaken their still-unsatisfied national claims, and e) a psychological barrier of guilt and remorse over the mass exodus and bitter defeat, hence describing it in metaphysical terms almost as the result of supernatural forces.[28] In the words of one Palestinian scholar, their collective

---

Palestine Studies 34.2 (2005): 42–54; "The Fall of Haifa Revisited," 37.3 (2008): 30–58. For a similar argument, see Edward Said, *The End of the Peace Process: Oslo and After* (New York, 2000), 9; Nur Masalha, *Expulsion of the Palestinians: The Concept of "Transfer" in Zionist Political Thought 1882–1948* (Washington, D.C., 1992). The only Israeli historian who entirely identifies with the Palestinian argument regarding the deliberate expulsion of the Palestinians is Ilan Pappe. See his *The Ethnic Cleansing of Palestine* (Oxford, 2007), especially Ch. 5, 86–126.

25. Nur-eldeen Masalha, "On Recent Hebrew and Israeli Sources for the Palestinian Exodus 1947–49," *Journal of Palestine Studies* 18.1 (1988): 121–37; Mustafa Kabha, "A Palestinian Look at the New Historians and Post-Zionism in Israel," in *Making Israel*, ed. Benny Morris (Ann Arbor, MI, 2007), 299–318.

26. Quoted in Nurit Gertz and George Khleifi, *Palestinian Cinema: Landscape, Trauma, and Memory* (Bloomington, IN, 2008), 1.

27. "Although," he adds, "there is a Palestinian nationalist narrative that includes its share of myth." Khalidi, *The Iron Cage: The Story of the Palestinian Struggle for Statehood* (Boston, 2006), 33–4.

28. Rashid Khalidi, "The Creation of History," (Review article) *Journal of Palestine Studies*,1.4 (1972): 125; Rashid Khalidi, "The Palestinians and 1948: The Underlying Causes of Failure," in *The War for Palestine: Rewriting the History of 1948*, ed. Eugene Rogan and Avi Shlaim (Cambridge, 2001), 12–36; Saleh Abdel Jawad, "The Arab and Palestinian Narratives of the 1948 War," in *Israeli and Palestinian Narratives of Conflict, History's Double Helix*, ed. Robert I. Rotberg (Bloomington, IN, 2006), 72–114; Mustafa Kabha, *Toward Shaping a Historical Narrative of the Nakba: Problems and Challenges* (Haifa, 2006), 1–3 [Arabic]; Gertz and

narrative has been markedly "emotional and weeping," focused primarily on the memory of individual suffering and victimization. As a result, the sense of time is lost in an ongoing state of trauma ("traumatic structure") that yearns for a return to a "paradise lost."[29]

Palestinian historians often assert the need to write their own historical narrative, not the least in order to counter the dominant Zionist narrative of the Palestine conflict. Aware of the scarcity of documented history, Palestinian historians strongly emphasize the use of oral history as a legitimate and reliable source.[30] Among other things, this trend has resulted in a growing interest in popular history, especially the need to accentuate and commemorate the heroes of the Palestinian struggle for national liberation during the Mandate years, especially those who fought and died in the 1936–39 Arab revolt and the 1948 War.[31]

Yet, although they encounter a real problem of scarce archival sources,[32] most Palestinian historians of the 1948 War show little interest in using Israeli,

---

Khleifi, *Palestinian Cinema*, 1–10; Jamil Hilal, "Reflections on Contemporary Palestinian History," in *Across the Wall: Narratives of Israeli-Palestinian History*, ed. Ilan Pappé and Jamil Hila (London, 2010), 177–215; Issam Nassar, "Palestinian Nationalism: The Difficulties of Narrating an Ambivalent Identity," ibid. 217–34.

Khalid A. Sulaiman, *Palestine and Modern Arab Poetry* (London, 1984), 118–27. For elaboration of this perception, see chapter 1 in this volume.

29. Kabha, *Toward Shaping a Historical Narrative of the Nakba*, 2. See also Khalid A. Sulaiman, *Palestine and Modern Arab Poetry* (London, 1984), 118–27; Gertz and Khleifi, *Palestinian Cinema: Landscape*, 1–10.

30. Saleh Abdel Jawad, "The Arab and Palestinian Narratives of the 1948 War," in *Israeli and Palestinian Narratives*, ed. Rotberg, 72–114; and Salih 'Abd al-Jawad, "Why We Cannot Write Our History without Employing the Oral Sources. The 1948 War—A Case Study," in *Toward Shaping a Historical Narrative of the Nakba*, ed. Kabha, 25–55 [Arabic]. On the growth and usability of Palestinian oral history, see Sherna B. Gluck, "Oral History and the Nakba," *Oral History Review* 35.1 (2008): 68–80, and Ahmad H. Sa'di and Lila Abu-Lughod, eds., *Nakba: Palestine 1948, and the Claims of Memory* (New York, 2007), 5–13.

31. This is specifically reiterated by Mustafa Kabha and Nimer Sirhan, *Register of the Commanders, Rebels and the Volunteers in the 1936-1939 Revolt* (Dar al-Huda, 2009), 16–7 [Arabic]. For an early commemoration and mythologization of a Palestinian national hero, see Nabil Khalid al-Agha, *The Question of Palestine in the Biography of a Hero: The Live Martyr 'Abd al-Qadir al-Hussayni* (Acre, 1982). For more recent publications commemorating those heroes, see Muhammad A. Abu Gharbiyya, *Palestine, Heroisms and Struggle* (Amman, 1991); Haroon Hashim Rashid, *Abu Jilda and al-'Armit, O How Many Hats [heads] They Broke* (Amman, 2007); Nazih Abu Nidal, ed., *Memoirs of Abu Ibrahim al-Kabir (Khalil Muhammad 'Isa 'Ajak): The Qassami Commander of 1936-39 Revolt* (Ramallah, 2010). [all in Arabic]

32. On the asymmetries between Israeli and Arab archives and archives-based historical writing, see Khalidi, *Iron Cage*, 34–7; Adel Yahya's remarks, in *Shared Histories: A Palestinian-Israeli Dialogue*, ed. Paul Scham, Walid Salem, and Benjamin Pogrund (Walnut

British, and other official archives, preferring instead to draw on Palestinian sources—mostly oral testimonies and semi-academic studies—or selected Israeli studies[33] Indeed, although Israeli archives are accessible to all researchers, in practice only a handful of Palestinian historians—mostly Israeli citizens—have effectively used them, underlining the language and other barriers related to access to primary and secondary Hebrew sources.[34] Similarly, most Israeli historians of 1948 are incapable of accessing available Arabic sources, and are forced to treat the "Arab side" primarily through the lens and perspectives of Jewish/Israeli and British intelligence files.

The language gap is doubly more debilitating given that, on both sides of the divide, most publications see the light only in their authors' original language with only a minute proportion being translated Hebrew-to-Arabic and Arabic-to-Hebrew or into English. Included in this category are many recent academic works, written as doctoral dissertations and master's theses (most of which remain unpublished but are available at university libraries), memoirs, and novels on the 1948 War, published only in Hebrew or Arabic. This huge body of research remains out of reach to most Israeli, Palestinian, and international scholars lacking adequate language skills, rendering much of the existing research in English on memory and historiography of 1948 incomplete at best.

These language barriers encountered by researchers on both sides of the divide serve to reinforce the existing gap between Israeli and Palestinian scholarly accounts of the 1948 War, which, combined with the parties' different approaches and methodologies, ensures that no common ground for a thorough academic exchange can be expected anytime soon. In fact, with both Israelis and Palestinians still locked in their quests for legitimacy, perceiving their respective historical narratives as crucial assets in their continuous conflict, the historians'

Creek, CA, 2005), 232–5. Both Khalidi and Yahya accuse Israel of seizing and controlling several Palestinian archives.

33. Especially Benny Morris' studies on the origins of the Palestinian Refugee Problem. See for example: Salih 'Abd al-Jawad, "Preface," in *Al-Duwayma Village*, ed. Ahmad al-'Adarbah, 7, see also 212 and 223 in this book [Arabic]. On the need to cease drawing on studies of Israeli scholars such as Morris, see Saqr Abu Fakhr, "Abu Jildah and 'Armit," *al-'Arabi al-Jadid*, 16 September 2015. Accessed 11 October 2015, https://www.alaraby.co.uk/opinion/153fbf29-8cfe-45df-9b17-e57c47dd21e5. [both in Arabic]

34. See for example the works of Mustafa Abbasi, "The End of Arab Tiberias: The Arabs of Tiberias and the Battle for the City in 1948," *Journal of Palestine Studies* 37.3 (2008): 6–29; "The Fall of Acre in the 1948 Palestine War," ibid., 39:4 (2010): 6–27; and "The Conquest of Nazareth: The Arab City That Survived the War," *Iyunim Bitkumat Israel* 20 (2010): 101–21 [Hebrew]; *Nur Masalha, Expulsion of the Palestinians: The Concept of "Transfer" in Zionist Political Thought 1882–1948* (Washington, D.C., 1992).

debates conducted during the euphoric years of the Oslo Accords and after resembled a dialogue of the deaf.[35]

From Theory to Practice: Memory, Narratives, and Conflict Resolution

In the last two decades, largely due to the widespread impact of constructivist theories on conflict resolution studies, scholarly interest in 1948 experienced a discernible shift from the historical to the psychological, from the rational to the cultural and symbolic, and from impartial critique of deeds and misdeeds to empathy with the alleged victim and calls for the mutual acknowledgement of each other's narrative as an essential step toward ending protracted conflicts.

These new emphases directly enhanced discussion of historical narratives that, in turn, accounted for three major developments affecting Israeli-Palestinian conflict resolution:

First, while prior to the mid-1990s "positivist" historians dominated the field of study of the 1948 War in its military and diplomatic aspects, since then the focus has shifted increasingly to theoretical socio-psychological and ethical aspects of conflict resolution. The literature on 1948 thus came to focus largely on contrasting national narratives and to assume an increasingly *theoretical and prescriptive* approach, one aimed at promoting resolution of the conflict.

The promoters of this trend have been mainly social psychologists and political scientists, writing primarily about memory and narratives of the 1948 War rather than the war itself. Indeed, many of these scholars are engaged in "cultural studies" and have neither studied the history of the Palestine conflict before, during, or after 1948, nor have they found such expertise necessary for writing about it. The proliferation of this literature in some of the best international forums and adoption by peace studies programs notwithstanding, they have hardly ever been put to an empirical test, and when tested, only some of their findings proved convincing or "promising."[36]

The new trend stemmed from, and drew on, the rise and collapse of the Israeli-Palestinian Oslo Accords initiated in 1993. This coincided with new academic approaches to conflict resolution: studies focusing on cognitive aspects of memory and historical narratives as core problems, especially in protracted

---

35. For a discussion of the 1998 dialogue in Paris, see Bruce Maddy-Weitzman, *Palestinian and Israeli Intellectuals in the Shadow of Oslo and Intifadat al-Aqsa* (Tel-Aviv, 2002). For the June 2002 dialogue in Nicosia, see Scham, Salem, and Pogrund, *Shared Histories*.

36. A case in point is Auerbach, "The Reconciliation Pyramid," empirically tested by Auerbach herself. See her "Bridging the Gaps of Narratives in the Israeli-Palestinian Conflict: Castles in Spain or an Attainable Vision?," in *The Nakba in Israel's National Memory*, ed. Amal Jamal and Ephraim Lavie (Tel-Aviv, 2015), 143–59 [Hebrew].

ethno-national ones such as the Israeli-Palestinian case.[37] Whether through "problem solving" workshops or intensive Israeli-Palestinian dialogues, scholars sought to not only better understand the nature, hierarchies, and role of narratives in shaping collective identities and perpetuating conflict but also to change perceptions of "self" and "other" as a means to bridge gaps and reduce longstanding mutual hostility. Especially since the late 1990s, students of conflict resolution brought to center stage the unresolved problem of the Palestinian refugees in the context of historical and moral responsibility, victimhood and guilt, acknowledgement of each other's historical narrative and past wrongs, and the role of apology as a transitional healing mechanism toward reconciliation.

Inspired by these approaches, Israeli and Palestinian scholars have developed a "dual narrative" educational approach aimed at bringing about a pluralist discourse between disputed communities with different historical narratives, which culminated in the writing of a book designed to be incorporated into Israeli and Palestinian school curricula.[38] The book, however, was disqualified by both Israel's Ministry of Education and the Palestinian Authority.[39]

Some Israeli and Palestinian scholars have examined the textbooks employed by the parties' respective school systems in an effort to analyze their role in constructing identity and perceptions of self and the other, and identifying elements of mutual recognition and denial. This interest was not only academically motivated, textbooks were conceived as important indicators of the views and values societies want to instill in their youth. At one point it also turned into a political tool in Israeli-Palestinian mutual recriminations concerning guilt and

37. For examples of this literature, see Herbert C. Kelman, "Social-Psychological Dimensions of International Conflict," in *Peacemaking in International Conflict: Methods & Techniques*, ed. I. William Zartman and J. Lewis Rasmussen (Washington, D.C., 1997), 191–237; Nadim Rouhana and Daniel Bar-Tal, "Psychological Dynamics of Intractable Ethno-national Conflicts: The Israeli-Palestinian Case," *American Psychologist* 53 (1998): 761–70; Neelke Doorn, "Forgiveness and Reconciliation in Transitional Justice Practices," *Ethical Perspectives* 15.3 (2008): 381–98; Daniel Bar-Tal, Lily Chernyak-Hai, Noa Schori, and Ayelet Gundar, "A Sense of Self-Perceived Collective Victimhood in Intractable Conflicts," *International Review of the Red Cross* 91.874 (2009): 229–58; Auerbach, "The Reconciliation Pyramid"; Zohar Kampf and Nava Lowenheim, "Rituals of Apology in the Global Arena," *Security Dialogue* 43.1 (2012): 43–60; Caplan, "Victimhood," 1–19; Yaacov Bar-Siman-Tov, *Justice and Peace in the Israeli-Palestinian Conflict*, ed. Arie M. Kacowicz (New York, 2014).

38. Sami Adwan, Dan Bar-On, 'Adnan Musallim, and Eyal Naveh, *Learning the Other's Narrative* (Beit Jala, 2003); Sami Adawan and Dan Bar-On, "Shared History Project: A Prime Example of Peace Building under Fire," *International Journal of Politics Culture and Society* 17.3 (2004): 513–22; Sami Adwan, Dan Bar-On, and Eyal Naveh, *Side by Side: Parallel Histories of Israel-Palestine* (New York, 2012).

39. Nathan J. Brown, *Palestinian Politics after the Oslo Accords: Resuming Arab Palestine* (Berkeley, 2003), Ch. 6.

blame for the failed Oslo Accords and the deterioration of their relations into unprecedented violence that erupted in late 2000.[40] More recently, Israeli and Palestinian historians and social scientists have resumed their efforts at presenting side by side Israeli and Palestinian historical narratives about the 1948 War and beyond in an effort to lay the foundations for a dialogue, which has so far shown little follow up.[41]

The Oslo Accords of September 1993 triggered a flurry of dialogue opportunities on many levels.[42] Among Israelis, it paved the road for changes in their approaches to the Palestinian refugee problem. Most conspicuously, Prime Minister Ehud Barak went as far as expressing his sorrow about the Palestinian tragedy that resulted from the 1948 War, though he was unequivocal in his refusal to accept responsibility or guilt for the past.[43] During the years of the Oslo Accords, Israeli intellectuals on the center-left of the political spectrum were increasingly open to empathizing with the Palestinians' plight; some even came to admit the occurrence of unjustified expulsions or atrocities in the past.

This empathetic trend, however, had its limitations and, much like the deadlocked Israeli-Palestinian negotiations, did not completely do away with the traditional narrative of 1948 as a Jewish war of defense, if not of survival, against Arab aggression from both within and without. Indeed, even at its zenith, the adoption of post-Zionist perspectives was a short-lived episode represented by a decreasing minority of Israeli leftists. Even among the Israeli Left, where there is some recognition of a moral debt to the Palestinians because of the suffering inflicted on them by Israel, there is a deeply ingrained resistance to the Palestinian demand for official Israeli recognition of full and exclusive responsibility for the creation of

---

40. Ruth Firer and Sami Adwan, *The Israeli Palestinian Conflict and Civic Textbooks of both Nations* (Hanover, Germany, 2004); Elie Podeh, "History and Memory in the Israeli-Educational System: The Portrayal of the Arab-Israeli Conflict in History Textbooks (1948–2000)," *History & Memory* 12.1 (2000): 65–100; Goetz Nordbruch, *Narrating Palestinian Nationalism: An Inquiry into the new Palestinian Textbooks* (2001) http://www.us-israel.org/jsource/Peace/paltext.html. For a critique of Israel's complaints, see Elisa Morena, *"Israel or Palestine: Who Teaches What History?—A Textbook Case"* (Ramallah, 2001); Nathan Brown, *Democracy, History, and the Contest over the Palestinian Curriculum* (Jerusalem, 2001), 1–27.

41. Pappé and Hilal *Across the Wall: Narratives of Israeli-Palestinian History* (London, 2010); Motti Golani and Adel Manna, *Two Sides of the Coin: Independence and Nakba, 1948: Two Narratives of the 1948 War and its Outcomes* (Dordrecht, 2011); Adwan, Bar-On, and Naveh, *Side by Side*.

42. See, e.g., Mohammed Abu-Nimer, *Dialogue, Conflict Resolution, and Change: Arab-Jewish Encounters in Israel* (New York, 1999).

43. For a detailed analysis of this statement see Zohar Kampf, "From 'There Are No Palestinian People' to 'Sorry for Their Suffering': Israeli Discourse of Recognition of the Palestinians," *Journal of Language and Politics* 11.3 (2012): 427–47. See also Michal Ben-Josef Hirsch, "From Taboo to the Negotiable: The Israeli New Historians and the Changing Representation of the Palestinian Refugee Problem," *Perspectives on Politics* 5.2 (2007): 241–58.

the Palestinian refugee problem. Such resistance is fueled, in large part, by fears of Jewish Israel being over-run by hundreds of thousands of Palestinians exercising their claimed "right of return" to their pre-1948 homes.

From a Palestinian viewpoint, Israeli "new history" is only a validation of the Palestinian narrative since 1948, according to which Israel's very existence is immoral and illegitimate because it came into being through aggression and injustice. Accordingly, Palestinian historians would have "nothing to confess to the priest of history," in the words of poet Zakaria Mohammed, but rather to maintain their resistance to the other's fabricated and flawed narrative.[44] The Palestinians, in this narrative, are only the victims of history, carrying no essential responsibility for their fate; the new Israeli historiography represents only a first step toward acceptance of the Palestinian version of the *nakba* narrative.

Second, Arab and Palestinian calls for Israeli and Palestinian mutual acknowledgment of each other's historical trauma have scored a growing international acceptance of the historical and moral connection between the Jewish Holocaust (*sho'a*) and the Palestinian catastrophe (*nakba*).[45] Perceiving them as closely linked collective historical traumas—though not of equal nature, scope, and gravity—scholars (especially of peace studies and conflict resolution) have fully or prudently adopted the assumption that these two traumatic events must be mutually acknowledged by Israelis and Palestinians as a necessary prerequisite for healing their traumatic wounds.

The perception of the Holocaust and the *nakba* as psychologically and morally interconnected was first initiated by Arab and Palestinian intellectuals in the late 1990s and soon became a prevalent assumption, including among some Israeli leftist scholars though it remained unheeded or utterly rejected by the Israeli public.[46] In recent years Israeli scholars, both Jewish and Arab-Palestinian, have openly debated the pros and cons of discussing the Holocaust and *nakba* together, albeit repeatedly stressing their awareness of the essential differences between these two historical cases. Sponsored by mainstream Israeli research institutions, the initiators of these debates have essentially aimed at developing empathy to each other's suffering, creating "a common civil sphere" and "fraternity of victims" instead of competing for the status of the ultimate victim—all of this hopefully enabling the two societies to attain reconciliation.[47]

---

44. Caplan, *The Israel-Palestine Conflict*, 242–4. For a similar approach see Khalidi, "The Palestinians and 1948," 17; Kabha, "A Palestinian Look," 299–318.

45. This is best illustrated by Gilbert Achcar's book, *The Arabs and the Holocaust*.

46. See for example Baruch Kimmerling, "al-Nakba," *Theory & Criticism* 12–13 (1999): 33–3 [Hebrew]. For a mainstream response to Said's call, see Rubinstein, "The Holocaust Memory and Peace."

47. Yair Oron, *The Holocaust, the Rebirth and the Nakba* (Tel-Aviv, 2013); Bashir Bashir and Amos Goldberg, eds., *The Holocaust and the Nakba: Memory, National Identity and Jewish-Arab*

Third, by the late 1990s, the Palestinians succeeded in inculcating their reductive concept of 1948, focusing on their disaster in this war—expulsion, refugee life, and unjust treatment by the international community—as the ultimate and exclusive meaning of that war. While the term *nakba* had long been in use regarding the Palestine cause, in recent decades it has fully become a "founding myth," saturated with historical and ethical connotations.[48]

The growing familiarity with this term in academic and public discourses can be seen in its common and frequent use with its exclusive focus on the injustice done to the Palestinians and the unresolved refugee problem. The breakthrough made by this term into the public consciousness and discourse of Israeli and international audiences was indeed striking, significantly because of its close connection to the Israeli-Palestinian Oslo Accords and their collapse.

Reducing the 1948 War to the exclusive connotation of a Palestinian *nakba* is no less than a distortion of the historical significance of this complex war. It brushes aside the pan-Arab involvement of states and non-state political, social, and military actors in the "Palestine Question" before, during, and after the war. It ignores the increased inter-Arab competition and selfish interests that sought to fill the vacuum as the British abdicated their authority over Mandatory Palestine. Furthermore, it overlooks the war's length of more than a year during which the balance of capabilities, real or perceived, fluctuated between Jews and Palestinian Arabs—before April 1948—and between Israel and the Arab states following the latter's invasion of Palestine on May 15, 1948. This conflict was also greatly affected by the Powers' competing interests in the Middle East and the outside efforts to contain the conflict by diplomacy and by arms embargo, aiming eventually to put an end to this conflict and resolve the Palestinian refugee problem.

Sadly, the 1948 War ended in disaster for the Palestinians, but the Palestinian Arabs were never entirely passive or sheer victims as portrayed in the *nakba* narrative. Nonetheless, the *nakba* has become the alternative name for the 1948 War, with its complex historical context replaced by the unique Palestinian disaster as the only issue that mattered about this war. It is noteworthy that in contrast to this reductionist and idealized usage of the *nakba*, Palestinian accounts of the war often commemorate their hero warriors and sacrifices made

---

Partnership (Jerusalem, 2015), especially the editors' article "Reflections on Memory, Trauma and Nationalism in Israel/Palestine," 19–51 [all in Hebrew]. For an opposing view see Elhanan Yakira, *Post-Holocaust, Post-Zionism: Three Essays on Denial, Forgetting and the Delegitimation of Israel* (Cambridge, 2007).

48. Esther Webman, "The Evolution of a Founding Myth: The Nakba and its Fluctuating Meaning," in *Palestinian Collective Memory and National Identity*, ed. Meir Litvak (New York, 2009), 27–45; Achcar, *The Arabs and the Holocaust*; Anaheed Al-Hardan, "Al-Nakbah in Arab Thought: The Transformation of a Concept," *Comparative Studies of South Asia, Africa and the Middle East* 35.3 (2015): 622–38.

throughout the war and point to the disastrous impact of local and foreign military forces on the exodus of Palestinian Arabs from their towns, and the disarray among Palestinian and Arab leaders.

The collapse of the Oslo peace process went hand in hand with official and public efforts to reclaim the Palestinian repressed memory of 1948 by systematically documenting, recording, and publicizing testimonies and academic writings that highlighted the painful memory of Palestinian refugeehood and displacement in 1948 and ever since. Jewish-Israeli responses to this tendency were fierce, taking the form of refutation and sometimes even utter denial of the *nakba*. Palestinian efforts to frame public discourse on their conflict with Israel in terms of the latter's historical responsibility for the Palestinian disaster of 1948 and the consecutive misfortunes that befell the Palestinians since then have been largely successful, and are accompanied by calls for Israel's admission of responsibility for this generations-long suffering, and for restitution in some form. In response, the more Israel loses international legitimacy, primarily due to its continued occupation and settlement of the Palestinian territories and repeated cycles of violence with their Palestinian population, the more intense become Israeli reminders of the horrors of the Holocaust and fears of current threats to Israel's existence.

The Israeli-Palestinian experience confirms that memory and historical narratives are products of political and social realities, and not vice versa. Efforts at acknowledging the other's narrative or rewriting one's historical memory have little or no bearing on the politics of protracted conflicts that have become deeply underpinned by history, symbolic values, and taboos.

A Final Note

Owing to the asymmetry of power between Israel and the Palestinian community, the still-unattained Palestinian national rights and Palestinian engagement in constructing a collective, mobilizing narrative to legitimize their efforts at nation building, there has been little or no Palestinian movement toward narrowing the gap with the Israeli narrative about guilt and responsibility for wrongs of the past. The weaker Palestinian side is still encumbered by taboos; not everything is discussable or negotiable.

Compared to the relatively secure Israeli-Jewish identity, the Palestinian national project is still fragile and vulnerable—which may explain the rigid and mythical nature of its official narrative.[49] Notwithstanding some beginnings of critical approaches to the Palestinian narrative made, however hesitantly or

---

49. Nancy Partner, "The Linguistic Turn along Post-Postmodern Borders: Israeli/Palestinian Narrative Conflict," *New Literary History* 39.4 (2008): 823–45.

inconclusively, by Palestinian scholars since the late 1990s,[50] the dominant approach among intellectuals and commentators has remained largely unchanged.

Efforts by both Israeli and Palestinian social scientists to address the parties' narratives of conflict, in hopes of bringing about mutual acquaintance if not acknowledgement of each other's canonical memory of their shared history, have not been very successful, revealing instead the rigidity of such versions of history and the difficulties of revising them. Sadly, the noble efforts—initiated and encouraged by well-meaning international agencies and dedicated scholars—to bring Israeli and Palestinian colleagues together to conduct direct dialogues over the past decades have had little impact on closing the gaps between the parties' mainstream perceptions and grievances.

In fact, rather than bridging the gaps, most of these meetings have only highlighted the abyss between the two parties' basic assumptions and conclusions.[51] It is thus likely that, in the absence of tangible progress in Israeli-Palestinian relations toward a settlement (however imperfect), the enduring and worsening conflict would continue to frustrate the academic, theoretical, and prescriptive work on narratives that aim to help resolve it.

AVRAHAM SELA is Professor Emeritus of International Relations and a senior research fellow at the Truman Institute of the Hebrew University of Jerusalem. Among his publications are "Arab and Jewish Civilians in the 1948 Palestine War" in *Caught in Crossfire: Civilians in Conflict in the Middle East*; *The Palestinian Hamas: Vision, Violence and Coexistence* (with Shaul Mishal); and "Myths and Historiography of the 1948 Palestine War Revisited: The Case of Lydda," *Middle East Journal* (with Alon Kadish).

NEIL CAPLAN is Affiliate Faculty in the Department of History at Concordia University and Scholar-in-Residence at Vanier College, Montreal. His publications include *The Israel-Palestine Conflict: Contested Histories*; *Negotiating Arab-Israeli Peace: Patterns, Problems, Possibilities* (with Laura Zittrain Eisenberg) (IUP, 2010); and "Why Was Moshe Sharett Sacked?: Examining the Premature End of a Political Career, 1956," *Middle East Journal*.

50. This is one of the themes covered in a special issue of the *Palestine-Israel Journal* 9.4 (2002), entitled *Narratives of 1948;* see especially 3–4, 7–14, 39–49, 58–66. See also discussions of Phillip Mattar's unpublished manuscript and Rashid Khalidi's *The Iron Cage*, in Caplan, *The Israel-Palestine Conflict*, 237–41.

51. In addition to Maddy-Weitzman, *Palestinian and Israeli Intellectuals*, and Scham, Salem, and Pogrund, *Shared Histories*, see also Rotberg, *Israeli and Palestinian Narratives of Conflict*. Such has also been the experience of both authors of this article when participating individually in various efforts at dialogue and the joint study of historical narratives between 2000 and 2010.

Index

Printed and bound by CPI Group (UK) Ltd, Croydon, CR0 4YY

13/04/2025

14656546-0001